WALLACE
LEGEND OF BRAVEHEART
Book 6

Wolf and the Wildcat

Seoras Wallace

1st Edition

Published in 2021 by Wolf and Wildcat Publishing

Copyright © Seoras Wallace 2021

Seoras Wallace has asserted his right to be identified as the author of this Work in accordance with the Copyright, Designs and Patents Act 1988

ISBN Paperback: 978-1-8383470-2-4
Ebook: 978-1-8383470-3-1

All rights reserved. No part of this publication may be reproduced, stored in a retrieval system, or transmitted in any form or by any means, electronic, mechanical, photocopying, recording or otherwise, without the prior permission of the copyright owner.

All characters and events in this publication, other than those clearly in the public domain, are fictitious and any resemblance to real persons, living or dead, is purely coincidental.

A CIP catalogue copy of this book can be found in the British Library.

Published with the help of Indie Authors World
www.indieauthorsworld.com

www.facebook.com/InDiScotland

Wolf & Wildcat publishing
Associate: Jade Macfarlane
+44(0)7766 584 360
www.wolfandwildcat.com
www.facebook.com/Wallace.Legend
Clan Wallace PO Box 1305 Glasgow G51 4UB Scotland

Dedicate to the memory of a great clansman…
RIP
Tam White 'MacGregor'
- A Wallace -

Dedicate to the memory of a great clansman…
RIP
John MacPhee
- A Wallace -

Acknowledgements

Big thank you for the writing support from
my hard working family and friends

About the Author:
Seoras Wallace

After a career in the film industry spanning over thirty years, in such films as Highlander, Gladiator, Rob Roy, Braveheart, Saving Private Ryan and many more. In 1997 following a serious horse riding accident, Seoras turned his valuable experience to becoming an author, and parallel to his professional life. Seoras has also served as acting chief executive of the Wallace Clan Trust for Scotland.

"An experience like no other," said Seoras, "One of the constants in my vocation has been the revelation of private or secretive documents and accounts from many unusual sources that gave me a wholly different perspective of William Wallace, that shaped him as a man who became a nations Iconic patriot and world hero in the eyes and hearts of many. At first I used to think that the information I witnessed was too incredible to be true, but when certain parts of that narrative repeated from different sources, another story from the academic norm began to emerge. Growing up in a remote west coast village, that was extremely patriotic and nationalist, I was taught from the clan elders at an early age the family legend of Wallace, but that too did not match the publicly available narrative. On my many travels around the world, especially after the release and success of the film Braveheart, people would often say upon hearing my account, "You should write a book about the Wallace." "I have always replied that no one would ever believe it, but following my accident, I decided to leave the family legacy as a fact based fictional narrative for my family and future generations, almost as a historical bloodline diary. The epic account I have written about the Life and Legend of William Wallace has been an inspiration and brought to me a newfound love for the man, the people and the country he fought for. Many who have been test reading the epic series as it developed, have a constant response that stands out more than any other comment, "Seoras, I've researched what you've written, and it's true…" My reply has always been… "Naw… it's just fiction!"

Chambers of Crosshouse

The stout claustrophobic walls of Crosshouse tower enclosure, do nothing to ease the tumultuous thoughts rampaging through the mind of Lord Ranald Crauford. The chaotic and distracting noises of children screaming, laughing and playing somewhere in the distance, and the nearby sounds of his clan labouring at their chores, cannot break his distress and feelings of desolation since news reached him, that English "Peacekeepers" had cruelly executed his beloved daughter Margret. The guilt he feels near overwhelms his every waking moment, for he personally advised her to seek safety and shelter with their Wallace relations up in their Perthshire fortalice of Kilspindie. Also, news that wee Maw too had died as a result of English brutality, is tearing at every fibre of his heart and being. For just a brief moment, Ranald smiles feebly while trying to imagine the stoic resilience of wee Maw's predictably brave but ultimately futile fight for life. His attempt to avoid visualising her struggle during her last moments, only serves to bring the darkness flooding back, leaving him bereft and totally distraught.

For Ranald, there is no escaping the raging emotions eating at his soul like a voracious cancer, his state of mind is descending into crazed confusion, akin to demented insanity. Even closing his eyes in an effort to hide away his thoughts, denies him an escape from his imagination, for he sees how his beautiful daughter Margret must have suffered such fearful and unspeakable terror when English soldiers ravished her, then finally dropped the hangman's noose around her neck, the constant thoughts of this living nightmare cause him to become nauseas. In despair, he buries his face in his hands, but still he sees his beloved Margret in his mind's eye, he senses how she must have felt… how he wasn't there to save her. Ranald sobs quietly as his mind continues to race, constantly tormented, thinking of how gentle Margret must have suffered, how she must have cried out for her father to come and save her as the hangman gleefully commenced his cruel and hideous duties of slow, deliberate strangulation. Ranald suddenly feels faint and weak, he staggers a little then reaches out to place a hand against the roughcast tower wall to steady himself, then cautiously, he lowers himself down onto an old stone horse-trough, holding his head with his hands.

Haunting memories of Margret as a happy child, collide with the desperation in his mind of just wanting to hold her, embrace her, if only he could do it right here, right now, he would do anything the Gods wanted from him to make it a reality… But the empty reply to his heartfelt pleas, only serve to enrage him; he wants to scream at the Gods and damn them all as frauds as the pain relentlessly torments his mind, untill tears flow unbridled for his loved ones. He tenses his fists so tightly, they become white and bloodless, then he looks up to the heavenly sky thinking that Margret too had looked at the same sky, the same clouds, the same… but now, now she's dead, murdered at the hands of the English peacekeepers, for what reason he will never understand. He winces at the thought that she is now hidden away, cold, lifeless, unattended and hastily buried somewhere in a stinking peat bog in remote unconsecrated ground, suddenly, he's disturbed by loud shouting and hailing coming from the gate-port. "Ranald, come over here and look at this, come quickly..." Steadying himself; Ranald looks over to where the source of the hailing had come from, then he sees that his loyal ghillie Cormack is frantically waving and beckoning him to come over. He slowly stands up and tries to compose himself as Cormack calls out to him once more. "Ranald, hurry up, get over here quick, for there's a group o' riders comin' right for us along the auld Tongland highway... Wait, ah can see that they're trailin' wie' them a train of about twenty or thirty moorland hablars."

Ranald quickly dips his hands deep into the nearby trough and scoops handfuls of chill cold water onto his face, them he brusquely wipes himself down, while mumbling desperately... *'Please God don't let me break...'* But Ranald struggles to keep his rampaging thoughts at bay, he takes a long deep breath, composes himself as best he can, then he walks briskly towards the gatehouse whilst grasping the hilt of his sword. He calls out to Cormack, "Can you make out who it is that's approaching us?" Cormack replies, "There's four riders ah reckon, one o' them seems to be a knightly lookin' fella and the three others look like Gallóbhet..." Cormack hesitates a moment; then he calls out to Ranald, "I recognise them now, it's Hector, the chief of the Buidhe (Boyd) clan with his son Rab, and it looks like Chief Sean Cinneidigh (Kennedy) and that's Sir Bryce Blair wie them as well... And Ranald, I think that's yer nephew Eddie óg Little, he's riding with them too." Ranald prepares himself to meet with his kinsmen, though he had desperately hoped it was William that was returning from the north. He can't understand where his nephew might be; he knows he must be somewhere in the shire, for he himself has already met with Bishop Wishart at the Glasgow council where he gained vital information obtained from William from the Bishop. He knows that William must have met with Leckie mòr by now too... His thoughts are distracted as the riders thunder through the gates of Crosshouse then come to a halt at the nearby paddocks. As the riders dismount, Ranald walks forward to warmly greet them...

"Good day to yiez ma' friends," But there is no immediate reply forthcoming from the weary looking riders, it's then that he sees the grim countenance on the faces of his kinsmen. As they dismount and tie their horses to the corral posts, Hector reaches out and clasps Ranald's open hand firmly, he says, "We've come away to see yie Ranald, initially it was only for to gain any news from the council deliberations, but then we heard of your losses, we would wish to offer you our deepest condolences ma friend."

"Aye," says Bryce, "It's a bad business old friend."

Eddie óg Little, walks forward, he is clearly upset, "Ahm so sorry too uncle..." Ranald puts his arms around Eddie and comforts him, he says. "I know yie were very fond of Margret Eddie óg... and our wee Maw too." Eddie looks at the ground and sobs. Ranald continues in a gentle tone of voice, "Don't you think it's about time you went to see your mother Aunia and make yer peace with her now boy? Time sure is plentiful abundant when your young son, but in these uncertain climes, ah reckon that it's best we all make our peace with our loved ones, for ah do know she misses yie so..." Eddie replies eagerly, "I'll be doin' that soon now Ranald, for ma apprentice time in the border marches is now done and ah'v come up here to join the fight." Ranald looks at Eddie curiously, then he enquires, "What do yie mean boy?" Eddie replies "Ah'v run away to join wie' uncle William, I've heard that he's raised an army to fight against the English, so ah'll have to be meeting with ma Maw to get her blessing." Ranald is quite taken aback upon hearing these words from

Eddie…"What are yie talking about boy, Williams army?" Bemused, Eddie looks at Ranald then he says joyfully, "I've come to join with uncle William like ah said… don't yie know? Everyone is talking about how he defeated an English army up in the north, now many of those who hate the English for what they've done, they are all talking about joining his army."

Ranald glances at Sean, Bryce and Hector, who smile in resignation at the impetuous nature of Eddie óg. Rab Buidhe, a tall young man of similar stature to his father Hector, steps forward and says, "C'mon you Eddie óg, let's get goin' and we'll help to feed n' graze the horses with Cormack." Ranald says, "Aye Eddie óg, I'm expecting your uncle William to be here in Crosshouse very soon, so you'll be getting a chance to ask him about this fine army of his then, or yie'll get the very truth of it all." Eddie replies, "Well ahm goin' with him uncle…" Ranald smiles and says, "Ah can see yie have yer mind made up already son, but you would be better coolin' yer heals till William gets here, so away yie go wie' Rab and get yie to the horses."

As Rab escorts Eddie away to the horses, Ranald and his kinsmen leave the tower yards to discuss more pressing problems in the first-floor chamber of the Crosshouse tower. Soon they are all sitting down around a table. Ranald is preparing their fare when Bryce speaks…

"It's been a terrible business for yie Ranald, with the demise o' your kinfolks at Ach na Feàrna, Glen Afton and now what's happened away up in Kilspindie too, aye, a terrible business indeed." Hector agrees, "Aye, the English are fair tearing our country asunder and there seems to be naught we may do to stop them." Sean enquires, "What's happened to good King John, where is he? It would seem that we're now to be governed by English constables and governors, while our own King bobs back and forth like a salmon float and more interested in saving his English estates than paying any heed to our mortal plight." Bryce sighs "Aye, the English are sorely destroying us Ranald, I've just recently came back from the Stirling salt markets, and ah tell yie, away up there I was witness to some English lord callin' himself Cressingham, he was presiding over the flaying of a hundred peasants and their families, for the non fuckin' payment of English taxes would yie believe." Bryce looks down, "Ma friends, ah will tell yiez this, ah'v never witnessed such a thing before, ever. Nor could I have imagined seeing such a distressing sight as that was, where men, women, children, all were stripped naked, shamed and herded to the markets square, then they were flayed to death in front of my very eyes… yet none there would or could raise any objections to what was happening, for fear o' the most severe reprisals, myself included… much to ma own shame."

"Ma friends," says Ranald, "I know not yet what we may do, for King John is betrayed and confounded by many of our own nobles, men who once showed him equal respect as a lord of this realm, but now that he's our King, those the same nobles turn their backs on him and run cock-a-hoop to King Edward and showing outright disloyalty to our very own rightfull King." Hector enquires, "Where's our King's council?" Ranald replies, "King John is sorely counseled by factious nobles such as Moubray, Cospatrick, Menteith and the likes, Longshanks has removed all loyal Scots from Baliol's side and surrounds our king with men who show him nothing but contempt." Bryce says, "Ah'v already seen the recent scripted annals o' Saint Alban's Ranald, it publicly declares that King John dare not be speaking on behalf of the people o' the realm of Scotland, as he is naught now but a fattened timid lamb lost amongst a pack of starving worm-infested wolves, our own fuckin' nobles would yie believe... It goes on to say that if he dares to show his face amongst the populace, he fears that they will trample him to shit as a raged mob."

Shaking his head in despair, Ranald listens intently as Bryce continues, "Aye, our beloved King is as popular as a captain o' a fuckin' plague ship." Hector says, "Your choice of words at one time would have brought us great mirth Bryce, but the situation we now find ourselves in, ah reckon' your words are bloody accurate." Everyone nods in agreement. "It gets worse for King John," says Ranald, "Wishart has already confirmed to me that Longshanks is now making demands upon our King to attend English courts." Hector enquires. "How can that be?" Ranald replies, "Supposedly he's a respondent to hear appeals from disenchanted appellants from Scotland, who object to the legitimacy of legal decisions and judgments made against them in our very own courts. Ah also heard from Wishart that King John has only just recently returned from Newcastle assizes, where he was forced to reply to an appeal from Roger Bartholomew, the burgess of Berwick, and would yie believe it, the burgess now declares that he and the burgh worthies wish to secede the shire into English dominion, his reason being that the taxation in Scotland is much too high for the burgh traders thereabouts to sustain."

"This is nigh unbelievable." says Sean. Ranald continues, "When King John sought to apply the detail of the legality o' the treaty of Brigham, *'that no man of Scots birth is required to plead in legal proceeding outside the realm of Scotland...'* Longshanks simply tore up the treaty in front of King John and declared that henceforth, no hindrance from Baliol or his estate would be tolerated, nor allowed to effect or interfere in any way with Edward's overlordship as the Magnate

Supreme of Scotland." Hector rages "This is preposterous..." Ranald says, "There's known to be at least one hundred such outstanding appeals made against King John now waiting to be heard in those English courts over the next few months, and that doesn't include many more appeals and claims from traders in Gascony and the low countries, they're all claiming remuneration and financial reimbursements for broken trade agreements against the Crown Exchequer of Scotland. Yet it's Longshanks very own English fleet that is blockading our ports and seizing all moveable trade goods for the English crown, unless tax is paid through English ports, then taxed again upon exit or entry to Scotland."

"I don't understand?" enquires Hector, "What does that mean?"

"It means," replies Ranald, "That all of our exports are now being forced to go through English ports. Then they are taxed twice upon arrival. First, they're taxed for using their ports to send our goods from, then they're taxed again on the profits from such goods; and that state of affairs is also meant to give the impression to foreign traders that we Scots are too small, too stupid or too expensive to be trading with, while it gives vim to the lie that England's trade flourishes."

Slamming his fist into the table, Bryce is in a fury; "The English treasury taxmen in charge up here in Scotland are employing upon us a taxation at breaking point too! They say it's in order to pay for their voracious army that steals our seed corn and barley — then they leave our barns bare of all our winter sustenance. Their fuckin' tax collectors are now demanding at least four times that declared from our last annual returns to Alexander's exchequer. But most heinous of all is that they murder, rape and plunder all the simples and serfs of this realm at their leisure, for supposedly non-payment of these taxes. And should any, including nobles of birth, who cannot pay these fuckin' new taxes and didn't sign up to the Ragemanus roll, make any attempt at complaint, they're harassed, stripped of rank and property then sent to some fuckin' prison. Ah tell yiez this ma friends, many more are just being disappeared or they're getting' fuckin' executed publicly." Hector says, "The only reply the English have to our just complaint is to accuse us of sedition, then they apply to us without any mercy, the lash, axe, sword or gibbet. Jaezuz Christ Ranald, Ah'v already gotten two o' ma eldest sons that are now languishing in the dungeons o' Ayr castle, and they've had their backs opened up by the lash, simply for not looking to the feet of common English soldiery in the passing… Ranald, you're the Sherriff of this shire, what is to do? I beg o' yie to have ma sons released."

"I'm Sherriff in name only Hector." says Ranald, he sighs, "It's Lord Henry de Percy roosting in Grey Rock castle near Glasgow who's the law here now, I'm just another name in an empty tabard, just like our King. But I'll do what I can to get your sons released."

Hector says, "I'm pleading with yie Ranald, will yie at least go and speak with this de Percy fella on my behalf to have ma sons sitting back at ma hearth, for I've failed them otherwise." Ranald says, "I will give it my utmost priority Hector, for I must meet with De Percy in a few days time anyways to be giving him an account of young William." Bryce enquires, "What's that to be all about?" Ranald replies, "Apparently ma nephew is accused of killing a master Selby, the son of the Constable of Dun Dèagh, he's now being sought as a willful brigand chief, for raising a mob with his gang of outlaws and the murdering o' English soldiers at will." Bryce laughs aloud, "At least that nephew o' yours has hog-hair on big balls." Ranald, who appears somewhat annoyed, glares at Bryce, then Bryce explains himself, "Ach, what ahm really tryin' to say is, I may not know the truth of young Wallace's exploits yet, and when I spoke out of mirth there but a moment ago, I immediately felt shame upon us all, as we sit around this table in idle chatter. But I know by rights we all should feel shame when a youth such as William, at least by all common accounts fights back, while we and many like us just sit about and talk a good fight." Hector says, "Ah agree with yie there Bryce. It may be that young Wallace and others like him will help us raise an army and free us from this English bloody tyranny."

Ranald speaks, "I don't know what the actual detail is of it all yet, nor what's happened to William since he went to see lord Moray, but I do know that he's back in the shire somewhere, for he's delivered to Wishart important writs and also passed on some verbal information from the Lord Moray. Bishop Wishart in turn has informed me o' the contents and what Lord Moray said to William, and ah must be telling yiez this too, it's very grave news indeed ma friends that ah will be revealin' to yiez all in a moment, but as far as William leading some army of revolt up in the north is concerned, naw, ah'm afraid it's nothing of the truth, but we'll not be knowing all the facts till we hear from his very mouth what's really happened."

"And what about Glasgow council Ranald?" enquires Bryce, "Will yie tell us then of the council minutes and was there any news there is for us?" Ranald replies, "I've never been to such a council as this, not since the parliament before the invasion of Harold Håkonsson's Norsemen many years ago. But then, that was a council of war held in Ruther's great castle halls, led by a noble King of Scots and the honoured lords of the Garda Rìoghail, but this council, ah can only say that this council inside the Bishops Palace was led by block-headed oxen seeking only to fill their purses."

Hector enquires, "What dyie mean? Was the meetin' held in Bishops own private Palace?" Ranald replies, "Aye, the meeting was held in secret and for safety in the bishops own personal compartments, just a few miles northeast of Glasgow castle. The palace was surrounded by former members of the trusted Garda Rìoghail to protect the meeting, they stood guard around the palace, with a second line around the moat and a third guarding the bishops loch and surrounding area, all to protect us from any English approach to the volatile assembly." Hector says, "It sounds like the only army we have in Scotland exists solely to be protecting or escorting the self-appointed fuckin' elite?" Bryce sneers, "and not to be giving' us any protection from the English usurper it would seem, maybe it's our own fuckin' nobles who fear a wee folk's rebellion against their petty rule that's got them all scurrying for English protection, but maybe they're right, for it'll be against our own fuckin' nobles that we will go to war against, and no' the English, if changes are not made damn soon."

Sean enquires, "Tell us Ranald, what was the content o' the meeting?" Ranald replies, "It was just a cacophony of many enraged trader and burgess' voices, all shouting at the same time with no thought to any propriety, it was a disgrace. Everyone there demanded answers about the state of the realm's trading, they only came to silence when Wishart broke his Crosier hammering the heel of it into the hard oak floor of the great hall." Hector enquires, "Were there not any decisions o' merit reached at all?" Shaking his head in dismay, Ranald replies, "To placate the English, the council has declared that William is to be marked down as a wicked and felonious Brigand Chief, then they offered up a substantial reward for his capture. The English too are also offering the same weight in silver as the weight of his head, and that of his Irish commander, Stephen ua h'Alpine, a notorious Irish villain." There's a gasp if incredulity from everyone. "What the fuck..." exclaims Hector, "Our own fuckin' council has sold out two of our sons, just to appease the English King?" Bryce runs his fingers through his tussled hair in exasperation. "I don't fuckin' believe this..." says Sean while clenching his fists white knuckled, "Ah can hardly believe what ahm hearin'. These self-appointed pie-faced fuckers are supposed to be meeting to discuss the rape and ruination of our realm... and all they can come up with is to be greetin' about their loss of profits, then they declare our kinsman and the mad Irishman as outlaws, without a single witness other than the fuckin' Sudrons themselves?" Hector throws his chair back in a rage and barges across the floor of the chamber, wrenches open the door, almost breaking it off its hinges; such is his wrath. He storms outside and takes in a deep breath of fresh air to clear his head.

Everyone in the chamber is greatly perturbed at this news, then, Sean turns to Ranald and enquires, "Surely such a gathering of important personages as this with such a great burden upon our realm, must have reached decisions greater than this?" Ranald, despondent and partially distracted while grieving for his daughter and family, tries to remain loyal to his rank as Sherriff and dignified for his friends. Hector, still outside, notices the stillness and silence coming from the chamber. He glances back inside and is dismayed when he sees the pallid expression on Ranald's countenance.

Returning to the chamber, Hector speaks with a care, "Ranald ma old friend, please forgive our impetuous wrath." Bryce says, "Aye Crauford, we plain forget ourselves, and you with your own grievances weighing so heavily upon yer shoulders..." Ranald smiles weakly then says, "Please, be seated Hector, for I do have other news from the council of Glasgow..." Hector takes his seat once more while glancing at the tired and wretched features of his kinsman, he says, "All o' our families have suffered badly Ranald, but of a'late, you've suffered more than most I know. This evil pestilence gnaws at our very gut and turns us into fools who now direct our anger upon each other, rather than against the cause of all our grief, will yie forgive us our foolish tongues?"

"Ach ma friends," replies Ranald, "there is naught to forgive yiez for, though it's a sore fact that the price of living in these turbulent times has never been such a feature in our lives before, but our expression must now find an out, and as you say, we must not be foolish enough to lay our anger and frustration upon each other, for all this would do is aid the cause of divide and conquer set by this English usurper." They collectively nod in respect of Ranald's words; then Sean enquires, "So what other news do you bring us from the great council of Glasgow's lamentable meeting?" Ranald replies, "No' much news and even less good news, in their wisdom, the Burgesses are all of one mind and thinking to appeal for Glasgow, Stirling, Perth, Dundee, Berwick and Edinburgh to be accepted as part of the English crown estates too, just like Rosbroch."

There's a gasp of outrage as Ranald continues, "Remember that I had said to yiez earlier about King John's required attendance to all Scots appeals in English courts, well he tried to employ his crown authority in defiance, when MacDuff of Kilconquhar sited a claim against the Scots treasury and lost. MacDuff appealed against our King's ruling in the English courts and won his case. It was then that King John finally found grit and refused to make any further appearances in England, he also refused to appear in any other appeals held against him in any English court, be it a local or royal court." Bryce exclaims, "What? That will no' be pleasing the English King." Hector sighs, "It's about time Baliol stood his ground."

Sean enquires, "So what's the outcome in Baliol's regard?" Ranald replies, "The expected reaction, Longshanks threatened Baliol with land and title forfeiture if he did not appear in person at the royal courts in London, to which, King John relented and did make that attendance. Longshanks then threatened to seize and confiscate all of the territory owned by King John in England, France and that of his family too, unless he bends the knee to English authority in perpetuity." Sean exclaims, "Fuck, so what happened?" Ranald replies, "Fair play to King John, he dug his spurs deep and made his pleading that he could no longer reply to any citation or legal writ placed upon him from England, not without proper and legal consultation with the Magnates and Bishops of the realm of Scotland first." Sean exclaims cheerily, "Fuckin' good on him," Bryce declares, "Aye, fuck Longshanks."

Everyone laughs; then Bryce enquires, "So what was Longshanks' reply to that wee belter?" Ranald replies, "Not good, as you would expect. The English King immediately ordered the remaining Scottish treasury confiscated and had it deposited in his London exchequer. Also, the principal castles of Edinburgh, Glasgow, Dundee, Inverness, Stirling, Ruther's glen, including all major towns such as Rosbroch, Berwick, Hawick and Jedburgh, they are to be keys-delivered to him by Sassine, henceforth these bastions are now protectorate property of the English crown, at least till all debts to England for the expense of employing a peace keeping force in Scotland are paid to them in full, and with interest. That's why the foolish burgesses of Glasgow mistakenly believe that by joining Northumberland, they may avoid these punitive taxation measures being applied in Scotland."

Hector exclaims, "This is grave news indeed Ranald, If the English have seized our treasury and taken all our food stocks, grain, livestock and then deny us the right to freely trade with Europe, how the fuck can we ever pay any debt owed to England under such perilous circumstance?" Ranald replies, "King John found a way, his answer was, if Scotland is no longer a sovereign realm but merely a province of England, then it falls that a new province cannot be responsible nor be expected to pay for past debts incurred by a realm that no longer exists."

"Ha!" exclaims Bryce, "Well said King John, if the English are to declare us as a mere province of the English crown, then by Baliol asserting his right as the lawful king of a new province, we therefore cannot be indebted to the English crown. How may they have it both ways?" Ranald replies, "The Lawmakers of Longshanks laughed at king John's application, then they reminded him of his oath given as a subject of the crown of England, next he was reminded that all the signatories on the Ragemanus who swore fealty to Edward as their liege superior, are therefore tax subordinate and personally liable for all expenses and provisions to sustain an English army in Scotland." Hector growls, "The fuckers, all o' these noble bastards who signed the Ragemanus who have lands both in England and Scotland, simply see our sovereign realm as a mere source of pasture and profit. Their seed is fresh planted here and no more than a generation grown at most, then the rest of their freebooting friends are brought here, solely to expand their existing holdings in England, but how is it that they may then dictate to our native blood such wickedness?" Suddenly a voice calls out from a corner stairwell… "RANALD…."

Everyone turns to see a tall young man appearing from around the corner of a darkened spiral stairwell, his appearance is as though he has just risen from slumber. He walks forward carefree and cavalier, his longsword sheathed over his back, while sauntering arrogantly into the chamber proper; his léine lazily flowing open without a care and his legs free and bare of clothing. Ranald smiles, then he stands up to make an introduction as the tall handsome young stranger joins them at the table. "My friends," expresses Ranald, "may I introduce to you Sir Gilbert de Grimsby." Jop smiles confidently as he sits down at the table. Ranald continues "Gilbert, this fella here is Hector, chief of the Buidhe, and beside him is Chief Sean Cinneidigh, and I know that you and Bryce here had met during the Glasgow council the other eve." Bryce acknowledges Jop warmly, while Sean and Hector are obviously suspicious. They scrutinise him closely. Hector enquires, "Don't I know you from somewhere Grimsby? You're lookin' se' well bred, yet yer dressed in attire as some fanciful Gallóglaigh?"

Jop smiles then he brazenly pulls Hector's bowl of porridge across the table and scoops out a mouthful with Sean's spoon. Before the two kinsmen can properly react, Jop replies, "It's likely so that you do recognise me Hector, for I know you well enough, and you too Sean Cinneidigh." Hector exclaims, "What the fuck, did yiez hear that bloody Sudron accent? He's a fuckin' Englishman." Instantly Sean grips his sword, preparing to free it from it's scabbard, he exclaims, "What trickery is this goin' on here Crauford… yie have a Sudron spy here who sits among us, and no doubt he's been gone and heard our entire conversation? Then the bastard defies us with spoonin' Hectors porridge?" Hector scowls, "Aye, and with your very own ladle Sean." Jop casually lifts a flagon of milk and takes a long drink to quench his morning thirst. As he places the flagon back upon the table, he winks at Ranald… Hector and Sean are both perplexed. "I am sorry good fella's…" laughs Jop. Sean, still clenching his sword, demands an answer, "Why are yie se' fuckin' sorry Sudron, tell us now, why are yie here? For I wager soon enough that yie sure will be fuckin' sorry, real sorry that yie ever showed yer burnt fuckin' face toward us." Sean glances at Ranald; he clears his throat then enquires, "Eh, well, what ah mean is, if that sits well enough wie you Ranald, this being your house after all…" Jop laughs, casually ignoring the implied threat from Sean with a seemingly defiant attitude, he grins and leans close to the red blustering face of Sean, "I'll tell you why I'm sorry, I'm sorry to see that your memory is no longer capable of serving you so well in your twilight years old man." Before Sean can respond, Jop turns and looks closely into the eyes of Hector, "And you too auld fella…" Hector and Sean can barely contain themselves.

Bryce smiles at Jop but says nothing.

Both Ranald and Bryce desperately try to hide away their humour during the momentary silence in the chamber, then Jop lazily raises the flagon of milk to sup once more. Hector, who can no longer take this impertinence, pulls his sword free as Sean knocks the flagon out of Jop's hand. He deftly jumps to his feet, simultaneously pulling out a secreted dirk and instantly presses the blade firmly under the jaw of Sean, then, just as quickly, he withdraws the blade, slams it back into the scabbard and sits back down as though nothing had happened. Hector looks at Sean completely bemused; then they look at Ranald. Sean demands, "Tell us what fuckin' trickery is this Crauford… why does this brazen Sudron bastard freely wave his prick in our faces as though we're both shipyard whores so desperate for his service?"

Grinning, Ranald replies, "You'd better be telling them Gilbert, before your gizzards are breathing through a few new extra holes." Jop laughs aloud; then he says… "A few new extra holes? Then I'm sorry for the ill-thought humour my old friends, but clearly my darkened complexion has shielded my youthful good looks away from your memory.

Perhaps you may remember me when I tell you that my name hereabouts, is Jop of Riccartoun." Hector and Sean glance at each other, still completely baffled. Sean points at Gilbert, "Naw…" he exclaims "you cannae be young Jop?" Hector takes his seat then leans forward, "You're Jop… Jop o' Riccartoun, naw it cannae be you?" Jop replies with an impish grin. "The very same." Hector and Sean look at each other; suddenly Sean's eyes light up, "Jop… Jop o' Riccartoun?" Grinning infectiously, Jop replies "Yes… Did I not just tell you that?" Sean looks at him closely… "Your father is auld Jop, the smithy of Riccartoun?"

"Aye, so ah'v been told." laughs Jop, Hector laughs heartily too then slaps Sean on the back, "Sean, would yie no' just believe it, that's auld Jop's boy… remember, he's the farrier to Richard Wallace o' Riccartoun and Alain Wallace frae down in Glen Afton, may the Aicé bless his soul. Do yie no' mind when Jop here was just a wee toaty boy, do yie no' mind when he used tae shoe all the auld nags for us on the cheap, very badly though if ah mind right enough." Hector's eyes light up, he exclaims, "You're really young Jop's boy?" Jop laughs then replies, "For fuck's sake, aye, it's really me."

Sean slaps his thigh; "Well ah never would o' guessed it boy. Though ah thought that ah knew yer face from somewhere, ya young feckr… now I remember yie." Hector grabs Jop roughly by the neck and pulls him close then he slaps him hard on the back, as does Sean. Hector grips Jop hard by the shoulders then he gazes intently at him, "My my, would yie look at you now boy, a head taller than all of us and yer built like a bull standin' on its hind legs, and we're no' chittlin' chickens ourselves. Ach now, it really is you ya young pup. Here, listen up Jop, ma son Rab is outside at the corrals with Eddie óg, they're seein' to the market hablars, feck me, he'll be more than pleased to be seeing yie again." Sean says, "Aye, but you just wait a wee bitty Jop, what is it yie have got goin' on wie' this annoyin' English accent o' yours, what's that bein' all about?" Ranald stands up from the table and says, "While you're all catching up, I'll be getting' some more fresh cooked breakin' fast vittals sent up from ma kitchens."

Ranald leaves them while Jop explains what has happened to him since he left the shores of Scotland to seek his fortune. He tells of how he has served and travelled far in King Edward's service, first as a soldier of fortune, then rising through the ranks by merit, to now being highly regarded and esteemed in the English military machine as master pursuivant in war and earning the privileged position as personal Royal standard-bearer to Longshanks himself, honoured by carrying the sacred Flag of Saint John of Beverly into battle.

A short while later, hot vittals are soon brought to the table where they all eat and talk about the situation of the realm once more. After a while and well satisfied with their morning vittals, they all sit back in their chairs; then Jop speaks, "Regarding the state of our realm ma friends, I must say this to you all, in your strictest confidence, that I and many other Scots who are in the service of Longshanks, shall remain so for as long as we can maintain it, or till we're caught." Curious at these words, Bryce and Hector glance at each other; then Hector enquires, "What do yie mean Jop, explain yourself?" Jop replies. "My brother Scots and I shall deliver intelligence about English numbers and tactics back to Wishart and Bernard of Kilwinning. Should the Scots here at home take up arms against this usurper and his tyranny, then we'll serve Scotland best where we're already stationed." Sean, Bryce and Hector appear unsettled... "Ah don't know," says Hector, "Would it no' be best yie all return to help us re-establish our army here?" Ranald says, "You must listen carefully to Jop's words, for he and others witness private remarks made in the court of the English King that otherwise we would have no ken at all." Bryce, says, "Aye, tell us everything Jop, for we were never prepared for what has come upon us, and we need time to bring our wits and forces together." Jop replies, "Time is what you don't have, though opportune is upon us with the English distracted and facing a likely war with France. Longshanks is secretly gathering all his allies to launch an attack on King Philip in Flanders." Sean says, "Then we may catch this moment to resurrect our armies to drive the English out of Scotland." Jop says, "My friends, I must depart soon for England, so, with your blessing, I will relay all the information I know to you here and now." Hector says, "tell us everything yie know Jop, for it's true that the English have sure caught us unawares and they now kick us hard on the down. We desperately need all the time we can get to be organised… ah tell yie, if the English let slip their grip on us for only but a fleeting moment, then ah swear by the lion of Scotland, ah will tear their guts asunder by return. Aye Jop, you must stay where yie are."

Sitting up in his chair, Jop says, "I will tell you all later what the commanders of the English army and the comfort women of Edward's court say when they are free and loose with their tongues, though some of it is hard to discern between fact and fantasy, we must consider it all." Sean eagerly enquires, "Tell us all yie know then Jop, be it a fact or a fancy, we will be grateful for any forewarning." Jop, says, "I will do so now, but first I must tell you that I met with Bishop Wishart, Bernard of Kilwinning and Duns Scottus in the Bishop's palace long after the Council of Glasgow had dispersed. They are secretly colluding with Lord Moray of Avoch, Comyn of Badenoch and many others, all in order to bring together the surviving Ceannard of the Garda Rìoghail and raise our armies back to arms." Hector rages, "This is preposterous. Why were we not made notice of these intentions Ranald?" Before Ranald could reply, Jop continues, "This was discussed but two nights ago, and as we speak freely now, I would have spoken to you all thus before nightfall in front of your own hearths. There are many spies and tongue-twisters abroad here, aye, even amongst our own people. It's only kin and kin of kin who may be privy to this information."

Hector and Sean nod in understanding as Jop continues, "It's well known that Longshanks is provoking and antagonizing King John with great vigour, as is easy for all to see. He intentionally makes a fool out of our King which our lord is hard pressed to escape. But as Longshanks employs such base insults upon our King, Philip of France has seen this too and seizes the moment to abase Longshanks, he has now summoned the English King to Paris to answer for acts of outrageous aggression employed by his sailors, in their zeal to blockade Scot's trade in French ports. It's there in Paris that Longshanks must explain to Philip why his English freebooters are raiding French Crown ports from the safety of English territories. Longshanks initially refused to appear, instead he has called for a treaty with Philip, but I believe that Philip now intends to confiscate all the territories of the Plantagenet house in France and rid himself of the Plantagenet broom once and for all. Now there's the nub of a potential for war between the two realms." Sean sighs, "Ah... so this is why Longshanks intends to go to war with France?"

"Aye," replies Jop, "Philip has publicly declared that Longshanks' is afolist, contumacious and has publicly pronounced a forfeiture of all his holdings in France, but it's also well known by Philip that while Longshanks pursues a fake parley, he is in fact preparing for a war that he cannot fiscally afford." Hector says, "Then this is indeed the moment for us to rise as a nation." Jop continues, "Longshanks requires a large and indentured army that he need not pay, an army that he will have no compunction in sacrificing in war simply to drain King Philip of men, that is one of the reasons Longshanks has summoned Baliol. Another reason is that he wants Scots levies, our senior magnates and their retinues are to join his forces this fall for an attack on Philip, he wants to use the Scots as cheap arrow-fodder." Bryce exclaims, "Incredible, if our bonnie King John can stall our forces from joining the English King long enough, then Philip may subdue Longshanks on the fields of France?" Jop smiles, "Unknown to Longshanks', King John has made a secret alliance with Philip and also Eric of Norway, offensive and defensive." exclaims Hector, "Fuck," "this really is good news, and opportune for our own army to assemble and end this rape of our realm."

"There is also more news to our vantage," says Jop, "the Welsh now rise and intend to fight against English domination, led by the forces of a powerful warrior Chieftain called Madog, the son of Llewellyn ap Maredudd. If the Cymrans are successful in driving the English back, and with France and Flanders causing Longshanks much grief, I've also heard that the O'Connor alliance in Ireland intends to rise up against Edward too, that's why we must take this opportunity to unite all the realm of Scotland now, before we are naught but a memory. So you see, you do not have time, for that time you seek is upon us now..." Sean sighs, "It all sounded fine till you spoke of uniting this realm Jop, we've so many English lords in control of our major trading ports and Shires, and worse still, Longshanks has too many Scots subordinates who lick his arse and that of his minions." For a moment, there is silence at the table, then Hector says, "These fuckin' nobles use the rule of martial law and Edwards powerfull army to set a great lie against our small truth for their own greed, there are only a few Scots nobles left who would rally to such a cause." Jop says, "I understand, that's why it's imperative we unite all now, before it is too late. What I tell you next is not from Longshanks, but directly from Bishop Bek of Durham, John de Warenne the Earl of Surrey and Hugh de Cressingham, Edward's new treasurer in Scotland." Jop looks into the faces of the men, who all listen intently… "The purpose of Edward's humiliation of King John is to seize all of Scotland's trading assets for the English crown without an act of war. He has no use for the likes of Carrick, Galloway and the lands north and west of Moray, it's there that the English intend to bleed these areas dry of the entire populace and then replace them with hoof and forestation."

"What exactly do yie mean by hoof and forestation?" enquires Hector. Jop replies, "We have been told that any common Scot who looks directly at us, other than those who has signed the Ragemanus, must be goaled or killed on the pretext of them being seditionists. Particularly the folk in those lands that I previously mentioned… hunters and trappers are a good example, for they have all been deemed as outlaws and are now to be hunted down. It would appear the intention and design of this English strategy, is to remove all who dwell in those lands by any means necessary and within God's law, and I mean everyone that is not in martial service to the English crown. So my friends, other than prime woodlands, Edward's sheriffs will fill the vacated land with Oxen and sheep. He then intends to confiscate all the lands and territory on the trader east coast from Berwick to Inverness, then plant English settlers there from the north of England. He will also grant landed estates to his supporters here in Scotland or to English Barons. There are also moves afoot, that any Scots lord can be dungeoned, their lands confiscated, and women folk of station or substance are to be sold off to barons in England for breeding, the daughters of serfs are to be sold off as inn-whores or used as plantation slaves." Everyone is completely stunned at this direct information.

"But what of those who signed the Ragemanus?" enquires Hector, Jop replies, "Come the next generation of Scots, the original Ragemanus will be conveniently 'Lost' then only a fake facsimile will survive for posterity, legally binding Scotland to the English crown by the chains of slavery as a mere territory. These false deeds are also to cause confusion and legal argument betwixt native families here for a thousand years to come. I should say betwixt those that are left alive after completion of the death lists."

Hector blusters, "Death lists, what death lists?"

Ranald replies, "This is the grave news I mentioned earlier that I was going to tell you about." Sean exclaims. "Death lists? You mean that the English intend to kill us all… but, but that's impossible?" Jop replies, "Not all, but kill most, that is their intention. England needs our lumber, coal, fish, beast and wool; these are the five most important trading assets in Christendom, other than wine. My friends, England runs ravenous and is near bereft of all these assets, whereas Scotland flourishes. Longshanks desperately needs these assets and the monies gained to feed and pay off his Barons and his army. He will then levy our youth for his army as he did to the Welsh and Irish. If we don't act now, the glens of Galloway and the Highlands where thousands of families now dwell; will surely be empty of children's laughter and forever lost to the sound of sheep. Soon it will come to pass, only one man of authority who wears the English crown upon his sleeve will lord over these lands, and any Scot who rests upon that same land, will either be a slave… or dead."

Everyone goes silent, almost in disbelief. Sean exclaims "Naw... I cannae believe that their plan is the extermination of our entire people." Jop shakes his head, "Believe me not, then you will all die. Look you to the Ragemanus; only the signatories who share land in both realms are unscathed. Those who are native Scot with only an interest in the land of his birth has already been redacted from the rolls, they and theirs will not last another ten winters. Longshanks has already removed Scotland's records of antiquity and sunk most of it in the sea just east of Newcastle." Jop continues, "If it were mere fantasy my friends, then look only to the Jewry, for there are none left alive in England. Or look to the extermination of the entire Cathar peoples of the Languedoc. Soon there will be no Flemings, Welsh nor Irish who will ever again be freeborn. I ask you all, who is there in Scotland to stop this brutal visitation being brought upon us by violence, slaughter and arson, none I fear unless you rise up the common people of Scotland, there my friends, there is your army of freemen and women, the folks who will fight for their land, not for the nobles."

Ranald gasps, "I cannot think these actions of a Christian King could ever be possible, but my own family and many others are now feeling the first wave of this great evil." Bryce says, "We've fought off all invaders in our history, if King John gains an alliance with France and Norway, then with the French and Norse as our allies, we could stop this English King dead in his tracks."

"Or stop him dead in his bed." says Hector.

Everyone laughs heartily at the thought. "So tell us Jop..." enquires Ranald, "Do yie know what the status is of this alliance?" Jop replies, "I know that King John has already sent his younger brother Edward to marry Philip's niece, the daughter of Count Valois, but Longshanks' spies have already alerted the English King. From what I have heard so far, is that Longshanks plans to counter this potential alliance, he has also issued King John with another summons, and that is to forcibly expel all the French, Flemings and Jews from Scotland entirely, all under the pretext that they are potential enemies of England, otherwise Longshanks will annex all betwixt Stirling Castle, Edinburgh, Berwick, Jedburgh and Rosbroch. As I said before, the planned future for the border marches, Galloway and the Highlands, is to be running to the footfall of sheep and cattle, not of men, that is the full intention of Longshanks and his English Barons." Sean says, "I had heard rumours o' this, but I thought it was nothing but a drunkards scurry."

Ranald scratches his chin, then he says, "That must be why Wishart and the council of magnates are urging that the ancient bull from Pope Celestine be brought to the fore from His Holiness, where absolution to Scotland paying homage and fealty to England can never be blessed, as we're the sole *'Daughter'* of Rome." Hector says, "Aye, but I've also heard that Longshanks counters this claim with a command that all goods on such lands are protected solely by English peacekeepers as there is no Scots army, and those said goods are the chattel of malingerers or seditionists, so he's ordered that all those goods and assets to be seized and sold, with all the revenues raised to be sent to his own personal exchequer in London." Bryce nods, "I have heard it so, the merchant princes of Berwick have already organised riots against the sale of goods for such purposes." Bryce says, "It's already begun, the Berwick Scots and Flemings rose up against English Bailiffs and drove them back into England." Hector says, "To recall the subject of the greatest merit my friends, I cannot resolve my senses as to what was said a moment ago by you Jop... To think that Longshanks plans the entire annihilation of all who are Scots born… naw, it's too great a crime of magnitude against God." Despondently, Ranald shakes his head, "I believe every word Jop has delivered ma friends." Jop says. "Heed me, it is well known by the common English soldier that the treatment to be meted out to any native Scot of any station who dares to look directly at even the basest o' English knaves, is to be brutally beaten or killed with no recourse." Hector says, "I've seen many o' our fellow Chief's sons, even daughters of noble birth much abused in this fashion, then they were stripped of their inheritance. Particularly those that had chosen not to sign the Ragemanus Rolls. Even my good friend Phelim MacEierick of Kerne and Cumno, all that is left of his clan are now skulking in the Wolf and wildcat hills with many other dispossessed and dispirited people."

"Hector's right," says Bryce, "We've got no more winter provisions left anywhere for it's been requisitioned by the English, now my kith and kin wander starving in the fallow fields, eating root, winter nuts, worms, mice and rats. They cannot hunt for food, for like yie said already Jop, that's been outlawed under pain o' death, our lands now lay barren and fallow and we've no' got any seed to be planting for next year's crops." Sean says, "Jop's right, we must do something, if we don't rise now, then we're fucked, but how, we cannot even feed our army nor pay to arm them, our realms coffers are empty, and all our arms have been taken by the English?" Jop says, "Not all arms, there are still major stores of the Kings armoury hidden away from the English, the three main armoury caches are securely stashed between Bourghtree, Knadgerhill and the Irvine sands harbour fortalice."

Bryce says, "Then we must do something soon, for I too find the words of Jop chilling and ringing true to my ears. Many of my Clan kith and kin are already dead, murdered most foul after being accused of sedition or treason by the English." Hector says, "Or those like my sons who now languish in a filthy dungeon, sent there by false pretext. Yet, when we as meek fools abide by this imposition of martial law, the answer is always the same. We have no power to change what's happening, but it's not too late to bond with all our realm's kinfolk and allies to gain ready everyone we may trust, for when King John does make the call to arms."

"Aye," says Sean, "we can no longer sit idly by, we must rise now." Hector says, "We must, look you to these death lists and what has already fallen upon your own blood Ranald, and that of your daughter's kinfolk, the Wallace." Bryce says, "We must act now, for it would appear the die is now cast. If we abide by English law, then that same law is designed to murder us, so what else are we to do but fight back before it's too late? I tell yiez, if any o' these fuckin' English bastards insist on tugging my beard just one more time, I swear to yiez that I will bathe my sword deep in their blood and ne'er will I lay it to rest till I am dead." Sean says, "Then let's waste no more time here; make the call to arms this very day."

Hector and Sean draw out their swords with grim determination and fortitude. Ranald says, "Yiez must hold your swords yet sheathed ma friends. Aye, go and make all preparations to rise, but share this information with only that of your own blood, for I fear that there is none other who would hold so precious to our own lives, those who do not value the lives of our kin, they would soon be informing the English of our intent for a gold reward. Anyways, I'll be travelling with Jop in the morn up to Glasgow to be seeking an audience with Lord de Percy. I'll find out as much as I can about what his plans are here in Scotland on behalf of Longshanks." Hector enquires, "Will yie be seeking a pardon for William and ma boy's Ranald?" Ranald replies, "Aye, that

I will Hector, ah hope to be bringin' yie back comforting news upon ma return, for this lord Henry de Percy has gained ma respect on more than just the one occassion, and ahl tell yiez why, for some reason that ah cannae yet fathom, and despite all that has been laid against ma nephew, I've had notification from de Percy that he may yet grant William another pardon, but only if I once again put my lands up as surety for his behaviour, and Hector, I'll beg for your sons release too, on my knees if I must."

"Naw," says Hector, "I dearly wish my sons to be free Ranald, I need them back with me to be hidden safely from this English injustice that kills so many and all on a whim, but do not do this treaty with de Percy by giving him your title as bond, for it is obviously a trick with a hidden agenda. Young William is fair and strong, and the English will easily find a way to make his impetuous spirit retaliate, then you will surely lose your lands and he may lose his life anyway, perhaps both of you may lose your lives. Naw, I would rather my sons lay forever imprisoned than you and yours risk all for their freedom."

For a moment none speak, then Ranald replies, almost hopefully... "I only risk property and title Hector, not my life. I have met this de Percy on but a few occasions, but he appears to be more than fair under the circumstances." Hector shakes his head and almost laughs, "Naïve nor fool you are surely not Ranald, but I think it so that it would also be your life you most certainly risk too." Jop speaks, "I've known lord Henry de Percy a long time. He's a cold, humourless bastard, but he's a fair man too. Though Hector is right Ranald; de Percy's gesture will be for purposes that are surely not magnanimous. William may simply be bait used to trap you for reasons yet to be seen. It may be though, that in my presence, de Percy does give to you his word on a sworn oath. I reckon his chivalric honour will over-ride any mischief or maliciousness to trap you immediately, though I wouldn't set my..." Suddenly a large clay water butt crashes to the floor behind the table, sending shards of broken pot and water splashing everywhere. Everyone jumps up and immediately stands to guard, pulling their swords to drawn in defence while looking for assailants.

Unexpectedly, Eddie óg calls down from the rafter gantry, "Ahm sorry, ah was just leaning against it, and it fell..." Ranald and his guests look high up into the dark cruik-beam ceiling gantry to see Eddie óg appearing petrified...

After a brief moment trying to gain a better focus in the dimness, much to their surprise, they see that Stephen of Ireland and William are standing beside Eddie óg, both leaning on the gantry rail and watching them all intently. "William..." exclaims Ranald, "How long have you been up there?" William replies in a sullen voice, "Long enough uncle..." Everyone below the gantry stands in silence simply looking at each other. Ranald enquires meekly, "Are you fella's coming down?"

Stephen and William stare down in apparent defiance of their elders. A seminal moment when young men realise with a stout heart and stoic conviction, that they may challenge their elders eye to eye as equals. William replies, "We didn't mean to be listening to yiez like spy's uncle, but ah'm glad that I heard what I heard, rather than be part of that conversation, for looking down on the situation I can see everything, I see it all clearly now..." Hector calls out with authority, "Wallace, Mac h'Alpine... you fella's come down here, now." Ranald dwells on William's words as the young men continue looking down upon them, almost with contempt. He calls out, "William, what is it that you see?" William clenches his fists tightly on the rails of the gantry.

"I'll tell you that I now see why le Brix came to Scotland all those years ago to start a feuding war between Baliol and the Comyn. I can see why English bishops are now rewriting our history, I see too why the few now in power here in Scotland are favoured by Longshanks and that the many who till the fields unto death, are but worthless slaves and bred only to serve new masters." Ranald enquires, "And to what end do you see these things?"

William exclaims, "What end yie ask me? Naw, this is just a beginning, for I see that I as a common man, would make cause for war against the English with my fellow countrymen of all station, regardless of their ages and sexes, that I would make it for this moment in time, right now, this day, this week, this year and forevermore, I would fight them without pause or mercy till they leave us in peace. We should fight them with our minds set in both light and darkness, using all that we may gain to task and destroy this evil spectre who calls himself the King of England. We must fight and keep fighting hard and mercilessly, untill the English are driven from our realm with such a force, they may never return except in fear. I see too that Longshanks is preparing not for a war against us, but to set a morass of plagues against us that no honest man can ever fight against. He sends into our land many different plagues against us, seeping into our very souls, like a fungus, creeping for years and rotting all that's good in us till our own house falls upon our heads, leaving naught but a barren wasteland as hunting grounds for his avaricious elite. These English lawmakers may cynically call this travesty a 'union' of our two peoples, but it is naught but treason against the very being of Magda Mòr."

Jop looks up at William, something in his gaze and the words he uses makes the hairs on the back of his neck prickle. "I see it too…" exclaims Jop, "For years Scotland has thrived under a just and righteous King in Alexander, where none knew strife, and all knew elevation through honest endeavor. But now, without firm guidance, Longshanks knows that by sowing the seeds of distrust and division, that we Scots will tear ourselves apart, and in the end, no war will be necessary to subdue such a cheaply bought a realm as this. Soon, there will be none capable of war who will be left alive to fight for Scotland, only those famishing hyena's who plan to send others of honest endeavor to do and die for their bidding will be left alive, all in order to fatten their already overweight and famishing gut, William confirms to me that we must all be prepared for a total war."

"I see more than that Jop." says William, "If I look through the eyes of Longshanks, I can now see why Canmòre and his offspring had to die. I can see why the maid had to die. I can even see why my family and others like us have had to die, for Longshanks and his minions know that many of us will never submit to foreign rule, perhaps we may, for just a moment in time, but then he also knows that if we do rise and drive him out, this great King of Christendom would be forever shamed to face his peers, and now that he has made his move, he can never back down or he will lose not only the assets and wealth he has already stolen from us, such loss of face he would suffer would end his rule in England."

Hector calls out, "Come down boys and we will talk." Stephen backslaps William and nods towards the stairwell. "C'mon Eddie," says Stephen. "Time for us to have a wee feast and drink after that bonnie oration from Wallace there." They begin walking towards the stairwell when William pauses. Stephen looks at him, "That was feckn odd there Wallace." William enquires, "What dyie mean?" Stephen replies, "Well, wit' us listening like little Gods sitting on a cloud looking down on them all talking, and then the scheme of things was all bein' laid out before us, aye, and that was quite a speech there too brother." Scratching his chin, William says, "Feck Stephen, that really was an odd moment right enough, it was like still bein' in that dream we had about Leckie in the cavernous labyrinth underneath Carlibar. And how is it we could both dream the same dream? And then there was us listening to our kinfolks and all o' Jop's revelations, it's like it's still all a bad feckn dream, yet it all seemed to become clear to me what's happening… and why." Stephen replies, "To be sure that was bleedin' weird that visit o' ours to Leckie mòr's place. So you be tellin' me now brother o' a different mother… that wee speech o' yours, it was though a wee roman emperor was makin' a comeback, but speakin' through you, so tell me, when did the real part end and when did the dream begin or is it the other way about… that's what I want to bleedin' know. I remember everything 'ceptin how the feck we ended up outside the feckn place, and now we're here?"

"I'm feelin' the same about the state o' our minds just now Stephen." replies William, "I just don't remember us going from the forge inside the Carlibar, to us waking up outside the place, and then as yie say, us standing up here like a trio o' wee Gods… Ach, fuck it Stephen, maybe it was the drink that Leckie gave us that's muddlin' with our heads, let's go down and talk wie them."

Shaking his head in bewilderment, Stephen says, "Well, if you don't know, I sure don't have an answer. But I tink' to me'self, that was your true Tam moment there Wallace." Glancing at his friend, William laughs then slaps him on the shoulder. He says, "Fuck me, don't be saying that we're unwitting prodigies o' true Tam Stephen. For as much as I like the auld fella, he's definitely a few nuts short of a squirrel's banquet for sure." Stephen says, "Then me bonnie mental friend, like your very own self there, I tink' true Tam tinksyour one tit short of a cow's full udder." Stephen laughs again, then he sees the blank expression on William's face, he says, "I'll wager you tink' the same about yourself too, don't ya?" William ponders for a moment, then says, "Let's just go down and find out what's best to do next, now that we know that I'm a brigand chief with a gang of one, you, ma wicked wanton commander, Stephen ua Mac h'Alpine, the notorious Irish villain, and now the whole English army is looking for us both." Walking down the stairs, Stephen stops then enquires, "What the feck do yie mean Wallace, the English are lookin' for, 'US'…?" Both friends laugh at the thought as they eventually gain the main floor of the chamber. Waiting for them there is a great and warm welcome shared by all.

William feels almost uncomfortable at this unusual adoration. He says, "These are for you uncle." and passes Ranald the parchment rolls he picked up at Leckie's. For the next few hours, they all talk intently about the state of affairs in the realm. Rab, Cormack and Eddie óg join them at the table to hear William relaying orally and in great detail, the information passed to him from Lord Moray, and also what had happened with the killing of Selby and the English soldiers up in Dun Dèagh.

"So, there's no army?" enquires a despondent Eddie óg. William looks at his young nephew. "Naw Eddie, there's no army, well, not yet anyway, the first thing I'm doing when leaving here is headin' for Lammington to see Marion." Ranald speaks, "You cannot be doing that William, not yet anyways, if the maid is seen in your company, you may put her at risk of death, and that too of Sir Hugh and his household by association if you're caught by the English as a wanted felon and outlaw." William exclaims, "What I did Ranald was in defense of my life, never in malice." Jop says,

"Ranald's right Wallace, you surely risk the lives of anyone with you if you're apprehended. Wait just a wee while yet." Ranald, says, "Bide yer time a wee bit longer William, Jop and I are to meet with the Governor of Grey Rock castle up in Glasgow the morn. We'll be but a few days up there and I'll be asking for your pardon, or at least a license for you. But you must promise me you will keep out of trouble till all is settled in the country. We just need somewhere safe for you to dwell till I get back with the writ for your peace." Hector says, "I have an idea to keep Wallace here out of trouble till yie get back Ranald. The grand horse market is in Ayr in a few days time and the horses of Kilmaurs forest are all gathered and ready to be taken to the Laglan corrals, just a few miles northwest of Ayr town. The woodland there is vast and near impenetrable, it's thick and dense with miles of gorse and needle thorn, at the centre is a maze of our hawthorn and broom stock enclosures, it would be perfect for him to shelter in there."

"Come with us Wallace?" says Cormack, "it would take an army many years just to get near to you in the Laglan. There are so many boltholes and hidden armed sentinels in that dense woodland, you could never be taken by surprise… Fuck, you could never be taken at all in there." Rab agrees, "Cormack's right, you and Stephen should ride with me on the morn when we take our herd of cobblar's down to the Laglan, you would easily pass for a wrangler if we're stopped by the English." Eddie shouts out hopefully, "Am coming with yie too uncle, I have finished ma apprenticeship in the borders and ah would like to be seein' me Maw…"

William looks at Eddie óg, "I was going to say that you should go and see your Maw, but she's away up at Loch Lomond shores with your aunt Uliann and the Gallóbhet just now, but she will be back in the Wolf and wildcats soon enough... Aye Eddie, you may come with us too." Eddie whoops with joy as Stephen enquires, "Hector, see this Laglan woods yer all talkin' about, I've about fifty of the finest souls you could ever wish to have on your side in a scuffle. Would they go un-noticed in these Laglan woodlands ya all speak about?" Laughing, Hector replies, "The Laglan is no' the Wolf and wildcats for sure Stephen, but it's almost as big as the Carrick itself, and it backs onto the Wolf and wildcats. Yie could hide the whole o' fuckin' Ireland in there and never find it in a hundred years." Stephen replies, "That's it sorted then, I'll accompany Wallace down to Laglan, then I'll travel back up to loch Lomond and bring me merry men down and we'll make shelter there till we're all in bleedin' favour wit' the English... or more satisfying oi do believe, till we bleedin' kill them all." William laughs, "Are yie sure Stephen? I mean, me bein' yer Brigand chief, don't yie think that I might want a wee say in the matter?" Stephen replies, "Aye, yee might be wanting a say right enough, but while your tiny mind is still working out what to do and what really matters, I'll get everything organised..." Everyone laughs at Stephens humour, breaking the tense atmosphere of the meeting.

Cheerily, Stephen continues, "Sure now, me foin big friend who's still working things out... Doesn't every Brigand chief need an army o' the finest bleedin' Gallóbhet cutthroats you could ever wish to meet, and for them to be on call for ya should yee need them?" Stephen continues, "And being wit' you se' long me boy, I will tell yie this, you really do need an army beside yie. And wouldn't the Laglan be just the right place to bring the Bonnie Marion to tryst wit' ya in safety, wit us by yer side?" William thinks long on the words of Stephen, Jop and Hector. It would appear that if he does not consider their advice, what alternative would or could he pursue. Ranald is also correct when he said that the life of Marion and her family would be seriously jeopardised if he did not think out carefully his next move. Stephen says, "For fecks sake Wallace, it's no wonder you need me," he continues "So Ranald, as the thinker for me brain-dead Brigand chief here, it's agreed, Wallace here will be going to the Laglan wit' me, I'll watch out for him while you get his pardon sorted out, and mine too if ya don't mind." Everyone laughs out loud at the diplomatic skills of Stephen. Jop says, "Wallace, with such a friend as you have in Stephen, I would carry no such worries as a burden if I were to share this world with such a fine fella as he is." Stephen grins, "Why Jop me fine fella, I couldn't agree wit' ya more, dyie hear that Wallace? So let's get our heads together, take up Hectors offer and be moving ourselves and that string o' fine horses down to the Laglan for the duration."

It appears to William that Stephen and Hector's suggestion is really a good idea, there is no other place he can go at this moment till his pardon is issued. Jop speaks, "You should go to the Laglan Wallace; it'll offer you great protection till we procure a pardon for you from De Percy. And you'll have the Wolf and wildcats at your back." Hector says, "Aye Wallace, there's bands o' dispossessed men in Galloway and Carrick, you could bring them all together and have a force ready when we need it." Rubbing his hands together enthusiastically, Stephen says, "I'll bring me Gallóbhet down in a couple of days, and if we contact your uncle Joannie Wallace, with MacLelland o' Bombie and the remainder of the Gallóbhet down there too, you would have near on a few thousand good fightin' men and women at your disposal." William exclaims, "Whoa there everybody, just feckn hold your horses, ahm no' a Brigand chief, nor have I any desire to be. When Ranald comes back with the pardon, then that's it for me, I am going to marry Marion at Saint Kentigerns." Stephen scoffs, "It very well might be the last bleedin' thing you do then Wallace. I thought when you spoke up there in the gantry that you really understood what's happening and what will happen to your country if you Scots don't make a stand, or was that all horse-shit for the rest of us to deal with?"

"No Stephen," says Ranald, "Every man must make his own decisions and live by them and the consequences. And I must add, it would be best for us all to keep the peace, for this English army is the greatest fighting force in all of Christendom, a small band of hero's, no matter how empowered they may feel by having righteousness on their side, would only enflame them. And as Hector says, the English may only be looking for the one single excuse to unleash the full might of their army's wrath upon us all." Looking at Ranald, William says, "Tá uncle, for ahm no' a hero, and I've given ma word on oath to wee Maw and Marion. I'm putting behind me my desire for vengeance upon the English for all they've done to us. I know what I said up there from the gantry, but I also see now that time moves on, anger one day relents to resignation the next. The one true thing that's in my heart, is my love for Marion and what that love may bring to us if I mind my business and keep the peace." Ranald puts his hand on William's shoulder…

"You affirm the faith I have in you William. I'll have no lost sleep putting up the surety required with de Percy, for I truly believe your heart talks when you speak thus." Jop speaks, "You may be right Ranald, but many would not agree with you nor have the same liberty that Wallace has as a choice, even though you may not think it." Unexpectedly, Ranald says, "Eddie óg?" Looking back in surprise, Eddie replies, "Aye what is it?" Ranald continues, "Go you now with Cormack and ready all my guest's horses, for they'll be leaving here shortly." Everyone looks at Ranald, completely baffled by the immediacy of his words. Ranald commands, "NOW..." Eddie óg appears bewildered, but his orders are plain enough, he gets up from his seat and leaves the chamber. Cormack says, "C'mon wie me." The silence in the chamber is broken only by the sound of both Cormack and Eddie's footsteps running down the wooden stairs outside the chamber. Ranald stands in silence with the opened writs in his hands, he's been reading them while Jop had spoken with William, and he'd seen enough to realise the serious gravity of the contents. Sean, Bryce and Hector look curiously at Ranald, who sits down in a sombre mood.

"What is it that ails yie Ranald?" enquires Hector, "your words with Eddie óg there were curt, what is it yie see in those writs?" Glancing at William, Ranald replies, "These writs confirm all that Jop has said. But William, you must tell us what is not written in these writs sent here from Lord Moray, and be leavin' no name out. When yie have spoken your word and this is all done, you must leave us immediately and make for the Laglan, for there will be no safety for any of us till you are secure in that fastness." William looks around the chamber and sees all with a cautious trepidation written upon their faces. He sits down beside Ranald, then he says, "I will tell you the complete detailed account on the death lists the English have for each shire of Scotland." Hector says, "Our names are on those lists, aren't they?" William nods his head in agreement; then he tells them of all he knows about the death lists, and how he knows...

When William has finished delivering this grievous news, an ominous and foreboding silence falls in the chamber. A little while later, William and Stephen are sitting on their horses with more than thirty fresh wild-caught hablars tied in train, all ready to travel from Crosshouse to the secretive woodland corrals of the Laglan. Cormack, sitting on the lead horse, turns to William and enquires, "Are yie ready Wallace?" William enquires, "What way are we goin'?" Cormack replies, "We'll be taking the hunters route south then stopping for a rest and vittals at old Symons Clachan o'Loccard, his place sits on the remote west side of the Kelmernoke forest, if that's sound by you?" William agrees; then he looks down at Hector, Sean, Bryce and his uncle. Hector says, "Go in safety Wallace." Ranald speaks, "Remember William, once you get into the Laglan fastness, stay there till I send word for you, do not be tempted to travel to Lanark or Lammington, for you will surely risk all and the life of the bonnie maid if you are to be so reckless. Bide your time just a few more days, then God willing, you will be free to join her soon enough." William replies, "I'll do as yie bid me Ranald, though my heart aches to be with Marion, I understand the perilous situation abroad, I will no' be risking it nor be the cause of it… no' yet, I'll wait." Ranald slaps the rump of Warrior…

"God speed son."

William nudges Warrior to follow on behind Cormack, while Rab closes in behind dragging the lead horse, with the rest all tagged nose to tail. As Stephen passes Ranald, he speaks quietly, "And you be takin' great care dealin' wit' those there English yerself." Ranald smiles, "Will you watch out for William Stephen? I hear his words, but I feel more the strength of his hearts impetuosity, but it's obvious he's badly conflicted betwixt love and vengeance." Stephen leans over from Fleetfoot and holds out his hand… "Ya have sure got me word on that." Ranald shakes Stephen by the hand; then steps back as Stephen spurs Fleetfoot into a gentle canter behind the small train. Hector and Sean stand with Ranald as they watch their youngblood kinfolk disappear into the forest on their perilous journey to the Laglan.

"What's to become of us…" enquires Ranald, Hector replies,

"I don't feckn know, but I fear we will all fall into a spiral of hell before this business is over. The killing of our people by the English is all at their whim and fancy without recourse. They don't even have a care to make false charges now; they simply kill us because they can. And as it's been declared by Lord Moray, backed by this news of death squads from young Wallace; we're dead men already if we don't make a stand. And you ask what will become of us Ranald? Young Jop has said it plain enough, the English are determined to make this a land of their seed, hoof and root…"

Suddenly Sean calls out, there's a rider closing in on us fast from the east." Hectors says, "That fella's sure in a hurry?" As everyone looks towards the rider, Jop says, "That's one of my men, that's Harry, one of my dispatch riders. I wonder what's up?" The rider soon arrives at the gates of Crosshouse. Jop sees the horse leathers foaming on the flanks of the horse, he says, "Co'nas Harry, what brings you here with such urgency?" Harry dismounts and hands Jop a writ, he says, "I've just ridden from the Bishops Palace Jop, this writ here is from Wishart himself, it's for your urgent attention." Jop takes the writ from Harry, breaks the seal and opens it. For a few moments he reads it, then he says, "My friends, again this is for your ears only. After I tell you of this news, you must go back to your homesteads and make sure you and yours are prepared for any eventuality, speak to none about this till next you hear from me."

Ranald, Bryce and Hector look at each other concerned as Jop continues… "It's as I said before, but now it's a fact. Longshanks has ordered King John to raise an army of levied Scots to be fighting with the English in the forthcoming war with Philip, but as yie know, King John has already made a secret alliance with the French King who is raising an army of Scots exiles abroad in that realm, with exiled Irish too as we speak, John has no intention of joining the English. One month from now, when Edward attacks France, King John requires all the Scots in pressed service within the English army, to move quickly and join forces with Philip' then lay a combined force against Longshanks in Northern France. At the same time, King John will attack all English forces entrenched here in Scotland and drive them out, he intends to rally all Scots who can fight for this realm, then he will invade England and seize all as far as York. Eric of Norway will set his fleets to wage war against the English fleets all along our coast..."

There is consternation upon hearing this news, but there is also a feeling of great relief amongst the small gathering. Jop continues, "I also read from this writ that Lord Moray has gained the support of many nobles in the north and east, more than we could have thought possible. He intends to raise his standard and all of his forces in the north and join our King as soon as possible on the fields of Scone, this is vital information my friends, at present, none other than our native nobles and chiefs must know of this." Ranald turns and looks for William and sees him riding away in the distance, Jop says, "We will need him soon enough Ranald. Lord Moray has confirmed to me in this writ that your nephew Wallace is to command the southwest Gallóbhet vanguard for King John. Though Wallace doesn't appear to know it yet, he'll soon be leading the Gallóbhet army as a warlord into a full-blood battle against the English." Ranald is surprised, he says, "That is a time-honoured position held by the Gallóbhet Jop, as is their right to be directly in front of the Scots King, but William doesn't have the battle experience nor the mettle to lead the Gallóbhet army?" Jops says, "Lord Moray must have seen enough in Wallace to make this his decision, and we know that Lord Moray is no fool."

Wolf and Wildcat

Death in Ayr

As they leave for their fastness destination, William rides up point with Cormack, Rab and Stephen bring up the rear of the horse train, while Eddie óg canters freely, wrangling the few wandering strays and foals on their flanks as they traverse the eastern edges of the Kelmernoke forest, consciously staying well clear of the main highways, drove roads and most importantly, any English patrols and port blocks. The day wears on uneventfully and they're all looking forward to a rest as they close on Symon's old smithy Clachan of Loccard, but it isn't long before they recognise the familiar stench of death in the air and slow their train pace to a cautious walk. William signals his companions to be prepared for anything and anyone who may be nearby, and far from friendly. As they walk on through the dark woodlands, William notices Warriors ears prick forward, they all pull their bows and nock arrows ready to react, but nothing interrupts their slow movement till they pull to a halt at the entrance to a clearing in the dense woodland. William stands up in his stirrups and raises his hand high.

Stephen low whistles to Eddie óg, halfway up the train, signalling for him to halt. Stephen whispers to Rab, "Let's move slowly up towards Eddie óg, we can send him to the back of the train to keep him safe, then we'll go forward and see what Wallace and Cormack have seen to find out why they've stopped." Stephen and Rab slowly and silently make their way up the line of horses to Eddie and order him to the rear of the horse train, telling him to keep a watchful lookout for anything or anybody out of the ordinary. They wait till Eddie is safely at the rear of the train then they re-notch barbed hunt arrows, pulling tension and ready to loose, then they make their way slowly forward, halting a little distance away from William and Cormack. There they dismount and move forward stealthily on foot. As they gain close using the undergrowth shadows on each flank of William and Cormack, they become acutely aware of a heavy pungent smell of death coming from the clearing.

Without turning his head, William speaks quietly, "I reckon we're too late..." Stephen and Rab step from the undergrowth and are immediately repulsed by what they see. "What the fuck..." exclaims Rab, he turns away and begins to wretch. William dismounts cautiously as Stephen comes up beside him, "Jaezuz Wallace I thought my eyes had seen enough killing and I would never flinch again from death... but this?" Rab clenches his eyes tight shut; then opens them again. After a few moments of gazing stupefied and in utter disbelief, he says, "There must be at least a dozen o' Symons wain's bodies scattered all around the place."

Becoming accustomed to the initial scene, Rab exclaims, "My fuckin' lord... who could've done this to those poor wains, they've been gutted, and they're mixed up with all those dead dogs n' hogs." He pauses then enquires, "But where are their heads?"

William and Cormack grip their bows, both tight notched, just taught enough on their strings to loose in a second. They spread out and walk cautiously forward into the clearing, where the smithy Obhainn's still smolder from deliberate arson. They walk silently around the edges of the clearing, stepping over limbs savagely hacked from young bodies and human detritus mixed with dead human and animal offal. William and Cormack come upon four adult women and two older men hanging by their necks from the boughs of trees. "Man, look at them…" gasps Cormack, "they've been butchered, and ah mean butchered."

A little distance away, William could see the hanging bodies have had their eyes gouged, ears cut off and all have been disembowelled, their guts strung outside their bodies and hung around the nearby branches like bunting at a fair, but this is not what Cormack is focussed upon. William hears a short signal-whistle and turns to look at Stephen, who nods in a particular direction. He walks forward a pace and sees what has stalled Rab and Stephen. At first he thinks he is looking at a large wild Boar or woodland deer that has been hung up, gutted and skinned on a gibbet to wind dry, but Cormack points toward the centre of the gibbet, he whispers, "Ahm certain that's the remains o' auld Symon? Fuck, those are his daughters too…"

In the middle of a large gibbet meant for bull hacking, skinning and meat stripping, auld Symon has been hung up naked by his ankles. Tension on ropes has pulled his legs wide apart unceremoniously towards each corner of the gibbet; on the floor just below the remains of his head is a large pool of blood, gore and hanging entrails. Nearby lay a great butchers cleaver that has obviously been the crude tool used to hack his body down the spine, stopping short beneath the top of his rib cage. "Fuck…" exclaims Stephen, "He must have still been alive when they hacked him near in half, he must have seen everything happenin' to his kin before he succumbed." As they gain closer, William sees that it's not Boar or beef hanging beside old Symon… Cormack is correct, it is the bodies of two teenage girls who have also been cleaved in half, decapitated and left hanging to resemble butchered swine on a market meat rack. William covers Stephen as he approaches the smithy workshop, where three large cauldrons simmer beside a glowing forge. He notices Stephen peering inside and glance at the contents. Stephen immediately spins on his heels, tearing his eyes away from the macabre scene. He looks at William, in an instant they both know that the death of Katriona, young Stephen and his unborn child is foremost in their thoughts. Stephen screams in primeval rage…"The fuckin' vats are filled with the heads of the Clachan children…"

"Wallace, Stephen…" calls out Cormack in a croaky voice. They look at Cormack who points to the blacksmiths forge, much to their revulsion, they see the half-burnt skulls of more children stacked in a pyramid, pitch has been poured on them then set alight. "Fuckin' de Percy…" rages Stephen in a fury. Cormack, his face grey with the experience of his witness, says, "Naw, no' De Percy, I don't think so."

Stephen demands an answer, "Who then if not de Percy, for I'm more than fuckin' familiar with the mark of his trade?" Cormack replies, "I watched an English lord execute all the prisoners in Ayr town about two weeks ago by cutting their heads off and stacking them so, but his name wasn't de Percy." Stephen urgently enquires, "Do you remember the name o' this brave English lord yie speak o'?" Cormack replies, "I'll never forget it as long as I live, his name is Sir John de Warenne, the Earl o' Surrey. He's an old man by the look o' him, but I'll never forget the expression in his eyes and what he said as they led over a hundred souls to the market square in Ayr. He read out a proclamation to the local people who were forced to listen." William enquires, "What was in the proclamation, do yie remember?" Cormack replies, "Aye, ah remember it well, for none who heard it could ever forget, if they do so, it's at their peril. De Warenne read out that the punishment for sedition or any act deemed to be an insult to King Edward Plantagenet, lord superior of Scotland and any of his lords, knights or soldiers who act on his behalf, that any malefactors apprehended in such an action, supported by sufficient witness before two English men of the crown, shall suffer public beheading within two days of judgment." Rab says, "It's right enough what Cormack is saying, I witnessed that same proclamation bein' read out." Stephen spits on the ground and looks at William, who just shakes his head in grim countenance. Stephen says, "Well, I still think this is the work of de Percy." He looks at William and enquires, "What do we do now, hide away like it didn't bleedin' happen?" Cormack says, "We should collect all the bodies and set them to the flame." Rab says, "Shouldn't we give them a decent burial? We cannae leave them like this…" Stephen replies, "We haven't time to bury these poor souls or pyre them… if we do that, we may give away our presence. Sure now, haven't we learned that by now?"

"Naw," replies, William, "We must go on in the hope these wretches gain blessing from another, for Stephen's right, we cannae be stayin' here any longer. We must continue on to the Laglan." William walks over to Warrior and mounts, all the while scrutinising the Clachan. He stares trance-like at the scattered mutilated remains of auld Symon's family, then he gently nudges Warrior forward and away from the scene towards the woodland bridleway. "Let's get out of here." commands Stephen. Rab and Cormack look at each other and reluctantly follow Stephen out of the enclosure and back to their horses, they halt when they see young Eddie standing wide eyed, open mouthed and paralysed seeing the scenes of wanton butchery in the clearing. Stephen demands, "What the fuck are you doing here Eddie óg?" Eddie stammers,

"I... I..." Stephen snarls, "You wanted a war Eddie óg... well, here's your fuckin' war." Stephen approaches Eddie, then, without warning, he slaps Eddie hard across the face, knocking him to the ground. Eddie holds his face in shock as tears well up in his eyes. Stephen growls, "I thought I fuckin' told you to stay at the back of the feckn horse train ya witless little bastard. Do ya tink' I gave you an order just to hear me own fuckin' voice, pretty as it is?" Stephen makes to viciously backhand slap Eddie óg, but he stops short as Eddie curls up, cowering to avoid the blow. Stephen shouts at Eddie, "Get up ya little fucker, if you're to ride with us, you do exactly as you're bid... Do ya hear me boy?"

Eddie óg looks toward where William, Rab and Cormack sit impatiently on their horses watching the scene. Eddie searches their faces for a sign or something that will make him feel justifiably victimised by Stephen, but they remain expressionless. William stares at him coldly, he says, "You do as you're told in future boy, for all our fuckin' lives depend on every man doing his duty. I can see the man in you grow, so let Stephen's chastisement be a reminder to yie... or go to your mother now and suck on her tits, for this is no' any fool boy's game that we play."

Leaning forward, Stephen gives Eddie a lift back to his feet, then he gently brushes the bewildered Eddie down... "What will you be rememberin' o' this day then Eddie óg me boy tell me?" Eddie nervously replies, "The massacre of Loccard, and you slapping me to the ground..." Stephen smiles, "Good, then half your wits won't ever be distracted ever again by what you see, now git on your bleedin' horse and be ready to leave before I boot yer fuckin' arse too, we'll ride together and talk plenty more about yer responsibilities." Stephen puts his hands on young Eddie's shoulders, as a father does when nurturing a son. "Eddie me boy, I remember when I was half your age, me auld fella did the same to me'self, but in his excitement in delivering to me such an education, he taught me wit' a big feckn whackin' stick instead of the flat soft side of his hand that I used on you. And would yie know it, didn't he not just go and break me bleedin' jaw. So, think yourself lucky that you only have half a swollen red face. Now you be remembering this lesson…" Eddie replies nervously, "I will."

Grinning, Stephen says "You remember this Eddie óg, always do the fixin' o' the required askin' and do it exactly as it's put to you, do you be understanding me ma young friend?" Eddie looks at Stephen then he glances at the clearing of old Symons Clachan. Surveying the carnage, he turns and replies, "I'm sorry Stephen, I'll be listenin' and I'll be doin' the fixin' o' the askin' in future." Stephen breaks into an even bigger grin, he says, "That's the spirit Eddie me boy. Now git on yer horse and wait here till I come back, have yie got that? And you be thinkin' about all I said." Stephen mounts Fleetfoot and nudges him into a canter, knowing that his action has served many purposes that may possibly save not just Eddie's life in the future, but maybe everyone else who may rely on him. He smiles to himself, knowing that although he didn't want to strike the boy, the hefty slap across the face and lecture had broken the spell of death converging Eddie's young mind, a spell that has driven mad many older and more experienced folk than Eddie óg. Stephen rides up beside William who is keenly surveying the route forward; he notices that William appears extremely agitated.

"Nuthin' we can do," says Stephen. He speaks quietly, "Wallace, there's nothing we can do for auld Symon and his people now. I wish there was, but leaving this place now is the right thing for us to be doin'." Looking down at his saddle, William shakes his head, "Is this who we are now Stephen? It wasn't so long ago I would have run for my crib, greetin' like a wain to hide below my mantle if I'd seen a dead man. Now we leave the dead and their families scattered like a meat feast for vermin to eat their fill. Now we deem there's no time to waste burying someone beyond a care."

"That's just the way of it Wallace..." replies Stephen, Rab rides up beside them; "We'd better get goin', it won't be long till it's nightfall and we're barely halfway to the Laglan." Stephen enquires, "Who's on point?" Rab replies, "I'll take point, for I know the route best from here." Rab nudges his horse forward and skirts the outside of old Symon's Clachan. Turning Fleetfoot, Stephen nods to William then rides to the rear of the train to walk on with Eddie. William grabs the lead horse rope and says, "C'mon Cormack, let's make for the Laglan. We need to get there before darkfall or we'll never find the place." They pull their horses into the course of a shallow burn running around the Clachan of Loccard to continue on with their journey towards the Laglan.

After a while riding in silence, Cormack speaks, "Wallace, I can barely believe what my eyes have seen this day, those poor families... fuck, we should have carried them to a pyre and sent them on from the hands of their own folk with a care and a prayer, not leave them defiled I..." William interrupts, "We had no choice." Cormack exclaims, "But such barbarity, why do the English set themselves upon us so, the flaying o' people regardless of sex or age and their use of rapine, guttin' and beheadin' for the slightest transgression against them as they see it. Why Wallace? I don't fuckin' understand why?" As they traverse their way carefully through the forest, William thinks long on Cormack's questions, "I don't know why Cormack, that wee word has haunted me for years. All I know is that if we do not fight back against the English soon, there will be none of us left in our realm and Scotland will be but a mere fable in a child's story some day. Fuck, I don't want to fight anyone, I don't know what the fuck to do." Cormack looks at William, "Ranald told us of what happened at Glen Afton and Ach na Feàrna. I don't know how you can keep a sharp wit or not rise up against the English with all others who have suffered as you have…" William sighs, "I've wondered that ma'self Cormack, believe me, I've thought long and hard about retaliating and tearing raw vengeance from the hearts of every English bastard I meet… but always there's a greater threat to those I love by any action I may take, and my love Marion who's with child awaits my safe return." William pauses, then says, "I just want to be left alone Cormack… can yie understand?" Cormack is dismayed by William's answer.

A few moments pass, then Cormack replies, "Naw Wallace, ah don't understand… you tell me we're fucked if we don't fight back, yet you say that you personally won't fight. You say to me this English yolk will not be here forever and you'll find a way to live with them. Which is it Wallace, fight back or hide away to let others suffer on your behalf? Ah thought better o' yie than this…" Glaring at Cormack, William spits out the words, "Don't you fuck with me Cormack, all I want to be doin' is live in peace, and I think that it may yet be possible. I ask yie this Cormack, who the fuck in their right mind would want to live as an animal hunted by hungry wolves, day and night?" Cormack replies, "None, and ah agree with yie, but you're already hunted like that hungry animal Wallace, and if Ranald doesn't gain you a pardon, what will yie do then? You can't be going back to Ireland, for all Scots there have been outlawed, you would be arrested or executed if found without a warrant from an English lord. So where else would you go? Flanders? Longshanks wages a war on the Flemish for their trade in wool, so where else then Wallace… France? Longshanks prepares to war with Philip too, so what will you do without your precious pardon?" Pulling Warrior to a halt, William glares at Cormack; "Why do yie goad me Cormack? We've been friends since childhood, yet yie ask me questions and prod so deep that it sorely does vex me. It's as though you act as an agent for another, what is it yie want from me?" Cormack exclaims, "What the fuck do I want from you, don't yie see Wallace, don't yie get it ma friend? If you alone raise your standard, many will follow. Folk look to you in the hope that you take up arms against the English and drive them out of Scotland." Cormack sighs in frustration, "What the fuck is it you're talking about? Wallace, ever since you defeated Longshanks' lackey forces of Angus Óg at Invergarvane, then your adventures in Ireland as a Gallóbhet chief, your battle with the English garrison at Dun Dèagh and Saint John's then driving them into the sea, and now, after you now being declared the most wanted brigand chief in all of Scotland..."

With anger evident in his voice, William replies, though taking great care not to completely lose his temper with his old friend, "Cormack, at Invergarvane my naivety cost the lives of many of my dearest kinfolk, in Ireland I learnt much from the Gallóbhet as a Ceitherne, not as a chief. And up at Dun Dèagh and Saint Johns... For fucks sake Cormack, all that happened there was a drunken English squire tried to kill me, but he got killed in the affray. I fled the place disguised as a pilgrim for fucks sake, there was no battle, and certainly no English were driven into the sea." Cormack turns in his saddle and points at him... "Wallace, it doesn't matter the truth of it, what matters is what the common folk believe, and believin' in you gives them hope. I..."

"Ahm warnin' yie tae fuckin' shut it Cormack," curses William, "you're testing me dearly. I've already told yie, I won't be raising any fuckin' thing except a family, now you keep yer mouth shut and we'll get on fine for the rest o' this journey." Cormack appears dumbfounded and embarrassed by the outburst. William sees this and feels a deep shame that he has spoken to an old friend in such a base rage. But he has his own thoughts about what they had just encountered, everything he has experienced is flooding back to him about his own family tragedies.

For the next few hours, they ride on in silence. It is not long before dusk descends over the high Carrick when Cormack notices the silhouette of Rab on the skyline stop abruptly. "Look…" exclaims Cormack, "Rab's stopped and holding his hand up." William looks up and scans the skyline, he sees Rab about half a mile away, his black outline standing proud against a blood red winters evening sky. William raises his hand to signal Stephen, he waits till he's acknowledged, then he hears Cormack say, "It's all right… Rab is waving us on." William looks at Cormack who is still watching Rab, he thinks of his harsh words spoken to him earlier and how he might have offended his friend in a manner that still makes him feel shame. He thinks too of how he had known Cormack as a friend since childhood, yet only now is he really getting to know him. William looks around then he says, "Check this out behind us Cormack."

Cormack turns and looks at him, "Check what out?" William nods his head towards the Northeast… "Fuck," exclaims Cormack, "Isn't that no' just se' beautiful?" William turns and sees Stephen is pointing for young Eddie óg as they too gaze up at the sky. Cormack speaks softly, "A good omen Wallace, that's the lantern o' the Aicé Luna with us this night." They all sit awhile looking up at a most beautiful glowing full moon as it appears to be hanging low in a dark blue Scottish sky. "Amazin." sighs Cormack. "Yie feel as though yie could just reach up and touch it." William looks at his friend, the beauty of the nightfall scene collectively soothing their hearts. "Will yie accept my apologies for ma earlier ignorance o' decency towards yie Cormack. I didn't mean to…" Cormack raises his hand, "Ach Wallace, it's fine. I think that no matter how we think we feel, the terrible greeting we were met with at old Symon's Clachan has sure got to us, even if we didn't think it so at the time." They both look up again at the heavens, Cormack says, "Aye, and there's the full moon to remind us of the Cruathnie chóinn." William says, "An auld expression ma wee Maw always used.", Cormack, smiles as he replies, "Aye Wallace" "how many years have we known each other and all the other folk of the Cruathnie, yet we have never raised a hand in anger towards each other, nor have we spoke ill because o' that teachin'?" William says, "Aye, accepting with respect that others see the same things differently is good." Cormack grins, "You mean like earlier on between me and you?"

"Aye…" replies William with a grin. They both laugh and shake each other's hands, then William speaks, "We'd better get the train goin' for I see that Rab is getting' agitated and turnin' his horse away." Cormack is curious, "It looks as though he's cantering back toward us?" William turns and waves to halt once more. Stephen and Cormack bring a stop to the train. It isn't long before Rab rides up and pulls to a halt. "What's happenin?" enquires William. Rab replies, "About a mile from here where we have to cross over the main drag to Ayr, fuck…" Cormack enquires, "What is it?" Rab replies, "There's been another massacre up ahead, everyone up there's been murdered and flung into the ditches at the side o' the drag or hung from trees. Their auld vanner horses lie dead all over the fuckin' place, it looks as though…" Rab falters briefly. William enquires, "Is it families again?" Rab replies, "Aye, it looks like there are many more this time, maybe hundreds. It would seem to me that everybody is fleeing the countryside for the safety o' the towns with all o' the killing going on, the number o' bodies up there stretch as far as I could see in both directions." Cormack lowers his head, "How much longer can we be taking this Wallace?" But William doesn't reply. Rab says, "It looks safe enough for us to be crossin' over the drag, there are so many tracks where we can cross that our own tracks won't be noticed." William enquires, "How long ago do you think that it happened up there?" Rab replies, "It looks as though they were all killed no more than a few days ago, so it's no' se' fresh and the stench is fuckin' terrible. Yiez should be covering your breathing when we go through, and get a grip o' the horses tight, they may spook bad, for there are also packs o' wild dogs, night wolves and rat packs skulkin' and fightin' about the feastin' up there too."

Looking up at the darkening sky, William says, "We'd better get goin', it's maybe a good thing it's gettin' dark, for young Eddie óg has already had a baptism that would shake the wits o' most men." Cormack says, "Rab, you rest and ah'll take point." Rab replies, "Naw, it's no' se' far tae the Laglan now Cormack, I know the best way through that maze o' bracken thorn into the depth of that fastness, and the guards there know my signals anyways." Cormack says, "Tá mo chara."

Rab spurs his horse on and rides forward. When he reaches the hillcrest, he waves for them to follow. William turns and signals to Stephen then the horse train moves slowly onward till they finally reach the Ayr drag road. As they move through the scenes of death on the long drag, the stench is unbearably vile and stomach churning, "Fuck," exclaims William. He douses a cloth from his water bladder and puts it to his face, covering his nose and mouth. He sees that Stephen has already made a wet breather for both himself and Eddie óg. William looks at Cormack and enquires, "How many do you think are up here Cormack, for the stench is fuckin unbearable?" Cormack replies as William hands him the bladder, "I don't know, I reckon maybe there's a couple o' hundred... more?" Cormack shakes his head mournfully. "Men, women, wains, dogs, livestock, even the auld horses too." Cormack is almost in disbelief.

"Fuck, what's happenin', am ah fuckin' dreaming all o' this has happened? I cannae believe what my eyes are seein'?"

William shakes his head, "I wish you were dreamin' Cormack, and I'm wishin' ah wasnae in yer dream." Cormack covers his face as they cross over the main drag road to Ayr town as they weave their way through the bloated and part-scavenged bodies. They see scores of grotesque, frozen, mutilated bodies, as though torn asunder by some frenzied demons from the otherworld, but they know this terrifying scene was not made by demons, but by men.... English men. Tentatively they make their way through the macabre scenes till they get some grace from the stench of slaughter by crossing a small ford, then before long, they finally enter the Laglan forest, where a feeling of relief and security sweeps over them as they make their way deep into the vast woodland...

"Cormack?" enquires William, "Ah'v heard o' this place, yet I have never entered it before, how big is the Laglan?" Cormack replies, "The main woodland stretches from the edge of Ayr town boundaries and away eastward across the Carrick hills to the north face o' the Wolf and wildcats, then away as far south as am Magh Baoghail and the north-west side of the black monk's lands of Crossraguel." Curious, Cormack looks at William, "Have you never trapped the Laglan?" William replies, "Naw, mainly trappin' the Wolf and wildcats then on down into the Ettrick and fringing the border marches. Though ma auld Dá used to tell me the Laglan was a bountiful forest to trap in." Cormack grins then says, "Aye it is Wallace, maybe no' as big a death-trap for the unwary as your Wolf and wildcats, but it's been well adapted by beast over many hundreds o' years before man was ever here. It's an intricate maize o' grand thick thorn bush and dense hawthorn coppice, wie many a' cluster o' tall oak, elder and pine forestation too. It's so full of game, the hunters over the years have created a myriad of twisted pathways, secret hunt-runs and corrals for the hunting o' deer, wolf and the great monarch stag, and there's plenty o' mad wild boar in here too." Sighing, Cormack continues, "Aye, it's some place, but since the English have outlawed all o' the free hunting in Scotland, it's now become the home o' dispossessed men, cut-throats, robbers, thieves… and folks like us." William laughs out loud.

Immediately Cormack exclaims, "Fuck's sake Wallace, keep it down, these are desperate fella's hidin' in the Laglan, if they hear yie they don't take any prisoners." William smiles then says, "I thought you had just described the nobles of Scotland and all the clergy had infested the Laglan?"

Cormack laughs at the thought.

"Wallace." says Cormack, "We'll need to be dismounting now, there are face and gullet traps o' wild thorn that'll rip your face off or open your throat in the blink o' an eye. They're set up to catch the unwary in the dark of night, so we'll need to be walking the rest of the way to get to the corrals." Before he dismounts, William signals Stephen and Eddie óg to dismount. He sits motionless for a moment watching, just to make sure that all is well at the rear of the train; then he too dismounts. William and Cormack gather their reigns and walk forward, following the secretive wynds behind Rab who is now forging well ahead of them. "Wallace ma auld friend?" enquires Cormack. "Aye, what is it?" enquires William. Cormack continues, "Tell me this, see when Jop said the plan o' the English is to kill all the people in the lands of Galloway and north o' Moray, do you really think that could ever be possible? Ah mean, to kill everybody and put sheep and cattle in our place. Ah just cannae even consider that someone could think like that…"

"Ah don't know," replies William, "It would be hard to imagine walking the glens and finding no neighbours there exceptin' sheep. But ah'll tell yie this though, I've seen many hundreds killed in Galloway and away up in the north-east, likely even thousands, so I reckon ma reply would be aye, the end result could easily be what Jop said, an empty land fit only for wool, lumber merchants and Longshanks' Sheriffs." Cormack says, "Hoof an' root he said. By jaezuz it makes yie wonder though doesn't it, if auld de Brix hadn't started that feckn civil war, there would be thousands of fit and fine warriors ready to fight against the English, but now, now they all lay dead somewhere, and for what, a feud between two Norman bastard barons?" William replies, "Those Norman nobles hold the power of the ruling elite like little bastard Kings, then they set their laws upon us all, yet they never set foot on the land save to collect rents and taxes, then they sign away our realm to some English King, it sure does look like Jop could be right, there's a bad plan unfoldin' for us."

Cormack enquires, "But Wallace, why would the English King want Scotland though, there's nothing here that he doesn't have tenfold in that great country o' his?" William replies, "I'm no' se' sure about that, ah know the English desperately need our lumber. Ma Dá and uncle told me that England has near been bankrupted by Longshanks, all because of his eternal need for war and strife, and he desperately needs new land for England's growin' glut o' Baronial sons. Aye Cormack, ah reckon that Jop is right, for lumber, fish, Wool, coal and hides are the major trading items in all of Christendom, and Scotland and Flanders produce the best quality wool and lumber in abundance." Cormack enquires, "But what has that got to do with clearing people away from the land?" William replies, "I suppose it's as Jop said, there's coming a time when one man wears the crown of England on his sleeve, and he'll sit upon swathes of vast empty estates as a solitary master to the great glens of Scotland where thousands used to till the land, and it will only be land for him and his King, for we Scot's will be long dead like old Symon back there, or livin' in some form o' slavery to that same King's man. But if it comes to it, we will rise up against them, but that will be a costly affair, whereas sheep won't rise up against them… or maybe they might." Cormack exclaims, "Sheep instead o' men? Fuck that." William replies. "Aye Cormack, fuck that…"

Walking on, they see through the thick forest canopy, dawn beginning to break. Long hours pass as they make their way through the seemingly endless claustrophobic walkways, William, now getting very weary from all the travelling he has been doing over the last few weeks, enquires "How long dyie reckon before we reach the corrals?" Cormack replies "Ach it'll no' long now, we should be there before mornin'." William mutters, "Ah fuck, ah hoped yie might have said we're almost there." Cormack replies, "Naw, we're no' there yet…" They continue to trudge deeper through the Laglan forest when William notices his face, arms and legs are a mass of bleeding scratches; he enquires, "Are we nearly there yet Cormack? I'd sure hate to come through this feckn place with someone who didn't know the way?" Cormack laughs, "Wallace, Ahm near sick of the number of times you have asked me *'Are we there yet?'* Yer like an annoying wain on a cart going to the fair." William grins, "Aye, that may be so, but I'm worn out, bleedin' to death, and all I want is to get my head down, so

Cormack… are we there yet?" Before Cormack can answer, a head pops up nearby startling William; then he sees that it is Rab grinning him. Laughingly, Rab says, "So you're here at last Wallace, ah thought yiez were lost."

"So did feckn I?" replies William.

He looks at Rab; but he can't see a way through the thick high thorn bush where Rab's head has popped out. Both he and Cormack walk a little further, when a great slab gate made of stout trellis and thorn bush is pulled back, revealing a large enclosure with great obhainn's and a large charcoal fire-pit burning in the centre. William's eyes light up as he enters the corral then he stands aside and watches as Stephen and Eddie óg bring in the last of the horse train behind him. They tend to the last of their duties by corralling and laying feed for the horses; eventually they sit down around the central campfire, tired and very weary. Rab has a big hot and steaming cauldron of mutton stovies ready for them.

"Where have yiez been?" enquires Rab as he ladles out great bowls of stovies. Cormack laughs, "Wallace kept me talking and we got lost a few times. Fuck, all I heard all night was, *'Are we there yet, are we there yet…?'*" William exclaims, "What th' fuck ya cheeky feckr?" He pushes Cormack so hard he falls off his stool and onto his back, where he lay laughing and choking on his stew, much too tired to raise himself up from the ground. Looking around the great Laglan corrals, William says, "This is some place you fella's have here, if you didn't get ripped to death coming in, you'd walk past and miss it totally." Cormack replies, "Aye, it's a good place to be in these climes, and with so many other good fellas around about us in similar corrals yie would never see, even an army couldn't take this place without losing thousands of their own men and still no' take it, that's if they were very lucky, even a great forest fire couldn't shift us from here."

Stephen yawns long and weary, then he enquires, "Cormack, ah need ma crib and Eddie óg there has fallen asleep sittin' upright, where are we going to crib down?"

"Over there," says Cormack, "see that grand obhainn by the side o' that great elm... that's for us." Rab says, "Ah'v stuck a wee peat fire on in there and there's loads o' skins to get buried under. Ah'll check the horses are down then ah'll take first watch, ah'll wake yiez up about mid-day." The weary friends gratefully retire to their obhainn and lay down where they drop then quickly falling asleep, blissfully lost into the planes of dreams and far from the world that has changed so dramatically beyond their ken... or worst nightmares.

* * *

Two weeks pass agonizingly slowly in the Laglan fastness as William paces the corrals like a trapped wolf, while Stephen has long left for Loch Lomond and has not yet returned. Rab has departed with a message for Marion, but he too has not returned, and there was still no news from Ranald regarding a possible free pardon for the killing of Selby, leaving only William, Eddie óg and Cormack in the Laglan wood fastness. William sits sharpening his father's dirk with a leather strap till the edge is keen enough to shave off his growing unkempt beard. He sticks the blade carelessly into a nearby tree then takes off the two talismans to polish for the umpteenth time, then hangs them on the handle of his dirk, suddenly he stands up raging and cursing, "I can't fuckin' take this no more..." Cormack looks round in surprise from his watch guard, "Jaezuz Wallace, I understand how you feel, but what can we do? Yie have to be waiting here for news to come, there'll be some good reason why everyone's late. Fuck, I'm no' even an outlaw and I'm stuck here with you." William starts to pace back and forth, "I've got to do somethin' Cormack, for ma mind is going feckn witless being stuck in here." He then walks over to where Warrior grazes and begins to tack him up. Cormack rushes over and enquires "What the fuck are yie doin' now Wallace?" William curses, "What the fuck does it look like I am doing? I'm tacking up Warrior and I am going to see Marion." Cormack grabs the reigns, "Don't fuckin' do it Wallace… yie'll fuck up everything if yie get caught, why don't we send Eddie óg up to Crosshouse and see if there is any news about yer pardon?" Wallace says, "Ahm going to Lanark Cormack, I must see Marion, she's with child, fuck, ah don't even know if she's given birth yet. She may not even know if I am alive or dead with so much rumour being spoken about me."

Releasing his grip of the reigns, Cormack says, "What will I say to Ranald if he comes and sees that you're no' here?" William mounts Warrior and pulls on the reigns, "I'll be back in two or three day's Cormack, I only wish to see Marion, after that I'll return. Fuck, ah pray that the pardon has been granted though, then I'll be free to return to her for good." Cormack looks at the expression of his friend's face; he can see the despair in his eyes. "Go careful then Wallace." Pondering for a moment, Cormack then says, "Why don't you cut through to the Wolf and wildcats south of here, for it's known the English don't frequent those hills, there are too many brigands and cut-throats thereabouts, so they leave it well alone." William laughs, "Aye, and me bein' a Brigand chief as well, I shouldn't have much problem with any outlaws there either, eh?" Cormack laughs, "And you being dressed in haggard leathers, bull mantle and a brat, wie a torn green léine, no' shaved and yer hair halfway down your back like a molting wolfhound, I think the English being so superstitious will run for their lives when they see the green Ettin of the woods." William laughs, "Pull the gate-trap Cormack, the longer I talk I'm just wastin' time." Sighing, Cormack goes to the trap ropes and pulls them, dragging the gates open. William nudges Warrior on towards the opening trap when Cormack calls out... "Stop, Wallace... Stop..." Bringing Warrior to a swift halt, William, looks down at Cormack, who's examining Warriors back legs. "Not good Wallace," says Cormack, "Warrior's cast a shoe and another one's loose. Yie cannae take Warrior out this day till yie re-shoe him, and we don't have any shoes here." William groans and dismounts, then he examines the hooves of Warrior and groans again. Cormack, who is looking at the front hooves says, "These front two need shoeing as well and his hooves need trimmed. Wallace, you should have had this done already, yie can't ride him out like this..."

At that moment, a sharp whistle could be heard just outside the stockade, "That's Eddie óg..." says Cormack, "He's up in the lookout tree, that's his signal for strangers coming." William and Cormack pull shut the gates and secure them, then they run for their bows and position themselves behind two hidden murder holes in the thorn-bush thicket, waiting for the strangers to arrive.

After a few tense moments, two men in forest green léine' rust brown hauberk' appear, casually leading their horses and packers. William whispers, "I think I know those two fellas..." Cormack says, "I do, that's MacAlasdair and MacRuaridh from the Rhinns o' Galloway, they must be up here for horses from the fair." Cormack drops a side-trap to greet the two friends. William steps out and says, "Seamus, Alain, I have no' seen you fellas for a few years, what brings you two worthy rascals away into the Laglan haven for villains?" MacAlasdair replies, "We've come tae the right place then?" William calls out, "Open the gates Cormack and let these two stragglers in." The gates open and the friends greet each other proper. MacRuaridh says, "I have got some good news here for yie Wallace," William is puzzled, "What do you mean, yie've got good news for me?" With a grin, MacRuaridh replies, "A pardon for yie from yer uncle Ranald." William exclaims, "You've brought ma pardon, yie mean ma uncle actually got me a pardon... for real?"

MacAlasdair pulls out a rolled velum note from his saddlebag and hands it to William, he immediately snatches it from MacAlasdair then scrutinises every word. He exclaims, "It has Ranald's seal on it and that of De Percy too. How the fuck did he manage to get me a pardon?" William turns, whoops with joy and shakes his fists in the air, he looks at Cormack and shakes the pardon at him, "Cormack, ma pardon is here at last, I can go to Marion a free man... right, ahm going to feckn Lammington right now."

MacAlasdair and MacRuaridh look at each other then MacAlasdair speaks, "No' yet yer no'... you're to take the Kilmaurs horses as cover to Ayr first, then pass a message to Boyd's wrangler for his chief Hector and Sean Cinneidigh, then yie can go wherever yie please," MacRuaridh hands a sealed parchment to William, he exclaims, "Fuck, what are you two doing?" MacAlasdair replies, "We have to get down into Galloway, we've heard the English are sweepin' up from Taigh Mhàrtainn in the south and we've to get back to move our families to safety." Cormack says, "Wallace, let's get the horses to Ayr as fast as we can, ah cannae manage that lot wie just me and Eddie óg. We could be there by midmorning; you can take ma white stallion Loach and ride him into Ayr, pick up shoes then ride back here and shoe Warrior. You could get over to Lanark or Lammington by later this eve." William enquires, "How will you get back?" Cormack replies, "Ach, I'll take a train horse, stay overnight in Ayr then ride it back here the morn." MacAlasdair says, "Wallace, any other time we would have done this for yie, but we cannae wait about any longer, me and MacRuaridh here need to get going. Ranald says the message for Hector and Sean is important and it needs to get to them this day." William says, "Sorry fella's for askin' but ah thank yiez for the thought."

They all agree to meet again soon; then MacAlasdair and MacRuaridh leave on their journey southwest towards Galloway. Cormack leaves Eddie óg his camp duties and orders; then both he and William train the horses and leave the Lagan enclosure. They travel quickly through the Laglan forest and soon they are entering Ayr town. The journey has passed quickly and been uneventful for the two friends. William is euphoric at the thought of being a free man with no one searching for him, now he is at liberty to travel back and forth without a hindrance and as he pleases.

"Look at you." Says Cormack, "You've been grinning since we left the Laglan woods Wallace, it's good to see yie smilin' again, but you better no' be lookin' so happy or the English will think you don't fear them." William, still grinning, replies, "I don't fear them... Fuck them. I'm a free man and can and do as I please..." Cormack shakes his head forlorn, "Wallace, are yie fuckin' witless? We can't afford any trouble... especially you. I'll wager that your uncle has put everything up as surety on the merit o' you keepin' the peace, his home, land, his title, as he did for you once before." Slightly shamefaced, William replies, "I'm only funnin' with yie Cormack, there will be no causin' o' any trouble from me. I'll deliver this message for Boyd and Sean... and his horses; then I'll be getting back for Warrior, and then, then I'm going home to ma Marion, for that's been a long day in coming, and now that it's here, I can hardly believe it." Cormack smiles seeing the joy in William's expression, it's like the William of old that he rides with as they pull the horse train into the main market square in front of Ayr castle. Within a few moments they are at the auction stable yards. William says, "There's a hell o' a lot o' English soldiers going to and fro from the castle… we'd better be minding our business." Taking the saddlebags from his horse, Cormack replies, "Aye, and thank feck they're paying us scant attention Wallace, so let's just be keepin' it that way. I'm going over to speak with the wrangler about our train, if you can lead them into that empty yard over there, then look about for some shoes."

"Ah'll just wait here with the horse shit and mind ma own business Cormack." Says William, "Here, you take the message for Boyd to his wrangler."

William hands Cormack the sealed message. Cormack leaves with the message to meet with Boyd's wrangler, while William leads the horses into a corral and lay's out feed for them. He sits down beside the corral gate and watches the hustle and bustle of the busy market, he then takes bannocks and poddynox out of his saddlebag and chews on the vittals, while he observes the weavers and dyers hanging up their wares, fishermen laying out fresh catch and hanging fish out to dry on long lines, shipbuilders and craftsmen working on crafting furniture.

'Ayr sure is a busy little seaport' thinks William. He looks away down to the busy riverside piers and sees fine fresh animal skins, hides and wool being loaded onto small ships, while large wine barrels roll ashore down rickety gangplanks from other ships. His vision is interrupted by a gaggle of Dominican Blackfriars scurrying past him on their way to preach to the unconverted. He chuckles as he watches them wind their way in and out of the busy market like a raft of ducklings following their hen duck wee Maw. Rummaging about in his bag for some more vittals, William glows in the thought that he carries his pardon and is now free from strife,

soon he'll be riding back to Lanark to see his Marion without a care in the world. He's about to take a large bite of his poddynox when a booming voice shouts in his ear...

"On your feet, you louse infested beggar..."

The loud voice startles William, he looks up quickly and is met with the stern face of a large tough looking English soldier glaring down at him, with his hand on his sword grip. William notices about a dozen more English soldiers also staring down at him. The soldier angrily commands, "On your feet I say beggar, or by all the saints, I will run you through where you sit." Slowly, William raises himself from the ground. As he stands up, the English soldier swipes the vittals out of William's hand when he hears a voice speak nearby, "Another slovenly Scotch oaf I see." William sees two knightly soldiers approach him, the senior looking knight enquires, "Who is the owner of the white stallion there you fetid atavistic oaf?" William feels slight relief it's not a warrant for his arrest on hearing the question, he thinks to comply and cause no trouble, despite the provocation.

"The Stallion belongs to my master, I'm the man-servant of Lord Crauford, his tacksman is over there with the auction wrangler." The knight sneers, "Oaf, quickly, go on, run along I say, tell your master that Sir Cecil de Romille of Skipton wishes to ride-out on the white stallion." William replies, "At once my lord." Suddenly the Knights steward slaps William hard across the face, "When you speak to your superior, never look into his eyes or I shall have you hung from the castle walls." William immediately looks at the ground, "Aye Sir, sorry Sir, ah beg yer forgiveness Sir..." Raging inside, William walks the short distance to Cormack and tells him of the knight's request, he rages, "Ahm gonnae kill those bastards..." Cormack looks him in the eye, "Don't you fuckin' do anything stupid Wallace, just you wait here, and you keep lookin' at the ground, or ah tell yie, you, me and everyone else here will be well and truly fucked." Seething with anger, William can barely hold his temper, "Aye but…" Cormack glares at him and appears extremely concerned. He waits till he's well satisfied that William will hold his temper; then he turns and walks over to speak with the knight. Despite Cormack's instructions, William is seething at being treated like vermin by English "Peacekeepers." Meanwhile, the soldiers of Romille have brought forward the white stallion and the knight mounts him, he says to Cormack, "I may wish to acquire this fine steed Scotchman, but first I will ride him to measure up his disposition." Cormack nods in reluctant agreement, when William notices something; he closes on the knight and raises his hand… Immediately he's grabbed by four soldiers and forced to the ground, his face buried in the freezing shit covered mud of the corral.

"You dare raise your filthy hand to an English knight?" screams the steward at the top of his voice. William struggles to talk. Spitting out the filthy mud, he utters, "No Sir, it's just that I noticed the Lord is wearing spurs, this spirited stallion has never been spurred, it could be dangerous… he may bolt." The knight laughs then says, "Hold these two until I get back, they both dared to look me in the eyes, then they insult me by telling a knight of good King Edward how I should ride a flea-bitten animal such as this." William and Cormack are manhandled against the corral rails and held securely under guard, they watch as the knight pulls hard on the reigns of the white stallion and brutally digs both spurs into his flanks, Loach instantly rears up and bolts into a crazed uncontrollable gallop. "Sir Cecil…" gasps the steward. William and Cormack glance at each other as chaos and panic tears through the market square, they watch Loach gallop wildly along the castle walls, desperately trying to scrape the rider off his back, then they both cringe as Loach gallops completely out of control and then back into the market place, bucking and rearing, knocking over stalls and stands alike, trying desperately to throw off the knight who strenuously pulls and jerks on the reigns, ripping into the sensitive inside flesh of Loach's mouth. In a panic, the English knight digs his sharpened silver spurs even deeper in the Loach's flanks and gut, causing Loach to try and flee the inescapable pain being inflicted on his body. William shouts aloud, "HE'S A SOFT MOUTH…"

The steward quickly looks round upon hearing the warning. William shouts aloud with great urgency, "Tell him he is soft mouth… stop spurrin' him…" The steward is also in a panic, but he takes William's advice and calls out to the hapless Romille, but the horse keeps bucking and kicking wildly, knocking fleeing locals and soldiers to the ground. Loach suddenly stops, double-rears and throws the knight high into the air, as he falls unceremoniously to the ground, Loach viciously back-kicks the knight with both hooves. Romille flies through the air and lands on hard ground where his head strikes a boulder, stunning him, as Romille tries to sit up, Loach kicks back again, striking Romille viciously on the side of his head. A loud sickening crack is heard above the noise of the crowd as the knight flops over, his body shaking uncontrollably. "Guard these two…" screams the steward.

English soldiers begin pouring out of the castle as the steward runs quickly over to Sir Cecil and cradles his shaking body. More soldiers rush from the castle to gather around the knight, then all goes silent… English soldiers slowly move aside revealing the steward, who looks completely bereft. He gasps, "Sir Cecil, my lord Romille… he's dead." The steward stands up and orders nearby soldiers to raise the body of the Lord Romille and take him into Ayr castle, then he marches directly over to William and Cormack, followed by the knight's faithful retinue and some soldiers from the castle. William can see the English are beyond enraged and knows both he and Cormack are now in a grievous and perilous situation. He discreetly reaches for his dirk but can't find it, he looks down then curses, he remembers he stuck it into a tree. In his excitement on receiving the pardon, he'd forgotten to sheath it when he left the Laglan.

The incensed steward stands in front of William and Cormack, glaring at them as though lost for words. Then he speaks with venom… "You two shall lose your heads for this foul murder of my lord Sir Cecil." Cormack gasps. William looks at him and could see absolute fear draining Cormack white. He fares no better himself as his mind races. He had thought often that he may die in battle or as an old man… but never in his wildest imaginations did he ever consider being beheaded. The cold shock of fear flows through his body and strikes at his very soul. Desperately, William looks to escape, he wants to run, but the experienced soldiers hold him fast, their mood enraged at the death of their lord. Cormack reaches out and pulls the steward by the shoulder to try and explain, "My lord I…" The steward glares at Cormack; in an instant he pulls out a long blade dagger and sticks it deep into Cormack's throat, he pulls it out then steps back and waits. Cormack grabs his throat looking entirely bewildered, unsure of what has just happened.

William is stunned and sees his friend grasping at his throat as blood begins to pump and pour from the lower part of his larynx. Cormack tries to talk, but only garbled sounds come from his mouth as crimson bubbles and frothy spatters of clotted blood exits his mouth. The steward nods to one of his men who draws his long sword while other soldiers grab Cormack's arms, pulls them back and forces him down onto his knees. "NO..." screams William. Cormack stares at William, bewildered and completely unaware as the soldier behind him viciously swings his long sword in a great arc, he swiftly brings it down and cuts cleanly through Cormack's neck; the torque force spins his head into the air.

"NAW..." wails William as he looks to the sky.

A dull thud is heard as Cormack's head hits the ground, followed by guffaws of laughter coming from the English soldiers while they watch Cormack's body jerk then collapse beside the head and gaping mouth, the body pulsing blood into a great pool at William's feet. A soldier picks up Cormack's head and holds it close to William's face where he can't help but stare into the eyes of Cormack, certain that he could still see a flicker of life shine in the eyes of his friend. William, held securely by English soldiers, drops to his knees in disbelief as the soldier holds Cormack's head high and shouts to the gathering mob. "So dies another Scotch felon for the murder of Sir Cecil de Romille." Immediately sensing a moment of ease in the grip of his captors, William quickly moves to his feet, pushes back, power-drives his knee into the groin of the soldier closest to him, head-butts another and boots the Englishman between the legs holding Cormack's head high.

"Kill the Scotch bastard..." screams the steward. But it's too late. William pushes forward, grabs a dirk out of its sheath from the body of Cormack, flips it over, catches the blade and throws it with all his might. The blade spins through the air and pierces through the steward's tabard to stick him in the heart. The steward looks down at the dirk sticking out of his chest, he gasps, "He has done for me..." He then staggers back a few paces and falls onto his back, dying as his blood pumps profusely from his body. William takes advantage of the moment's confusion. The soldier who was Cormack's executioner, swings his sword, but William is too fast and moves in towards the strike, he catches the soldier's wrist, foils the power of the blow and smashes the soldier full on the chin with his forearm, knocking the soldier senseless. He quickly wrenches the sword from the soldiers grasp and viciously swings the sword down, catching the soldier on the left ear, cutting through his eyes and exiting on the right side of his head. At that moment, two more soldiers bull-charge into William, knocking him to the ground, at the same moment he feels an excruciating pain and sees a halberd spear point has entered his body between his skin and his ribs, pinning him to the ground. Wrenching the spear tip out, William staggers to his feet, but more English soldiers quickly surround him and raise their weapons to strike him dead, when a shrill voice is heard over the chaos.

"DON'T KILL HIM…" screams the castle captain. William weakly swings the heavy long sword once again, but a mace smashes down, catching his arm and snapping the bone above the wrist. Instantly. the pain of the wound and his broken arm cause him to drop the sword to the ground. Swarming English soldiers begin to beat him with cudgels, he tries to roll into a ball, but then he feels an enormous and unbelievable pressure on his shin, suddenly sheer pain sweeps through his body. For a fleeting second, he sees a soldier pounding at his lower legs with the steel butt of a pole arm, then he hears the bone snap, causing incredible pain to surge throughout his body.

The captain shouts at his men, "Take him alive you fool's or you shall suffer execution in his place." but the soldiers continue pounding William with cudgels, boot and fist. The pain is so excruciating all over his body, he begins to convulse and wretch. The vicious assault continues till he feels faint and loses consciousness. William lies in a pool of his own blood and vomit, his leg and arm broken, his face swelling so badly, he is unrecognisable as the young freeman who stood so proud only moments before. The captain and English soldiers stand over his broken body, glaring at him with hatred and contempt, believing that he is the cause of their lord's demise and that of his loyal steward. The castle captain commands, "Drag him by a horse to the castle then throw him in the lower dungeon, he shall suffer greatly for these foul murders."

Drifting in and out of consciousness, William feels himself being dragged over rough ground that tears and rips at his flesh, but he is beyond pain and completely passes out. He comes to once more, only to find that he is naked and languishing on a wet cold stone flagged floor in what appears to be a dark stinking dungeon. He struggles to try and understand where he is, where he could be, but the searing pains now wracking his entire body is almost too much to sustain. He can barely move, he can barely see, his eyes are swelling near shut. William tries to raise himself up from the stone-flagged floor, but the intensity of pain from his broken limbs, cause him to pass out once more. Stirring, he tries to raise himself again, when a head shuddering crack on his jaw knocks him back to the ground, he tries to sit up once more, when a soldier kicks him full on the face, knocking him senseless.

He didn't know how long it was he had been unconscious when he hears an English voice enquire, "Is he still alive?" then he feels a deep stinging sensation in his back as the English soldier drags a razor-sharp dagger down his spine cutting deeply into his flesh, making him groan with the searing white-hot pain, then he feels impacts about his head as soldiers brutally beat him. He passes out, free from the pain of many wounds and broken bones in his body.

For two days William lay under guard. When the dungeon door opens, and the head jailer walks in and looks at him. He immediately goes into uproar upon seeing the condition of William. He shouts to the guards, "You fools, is he still alive?" The jailer pulls William's head up and holds his hand over his mouth, he pauses a few moments, looks at the two soldiers and shakes his head.

"He's not breathing, give me your dagger."

One of the soldiers pulls out a dagger and hands it to the jailer, who immediately sticks the blade deep into William's shoulder, but there's no reaction, not even a flinch. The jailer pulls the blade out and sticks it in his other shoulder then he begins to rotate the blade viciously on its point in the shoulder blade, but again there is no reaction, no blood nor any bleeding. The jailer looks at the guards and shrugs his shoulders… he slashes deeply into Williams back, but again there is no response. "He doesn't bleed." says the Jailer.

He continues, "The magistrate is here to trial and execute all the prisoners, this one here was supposed to give us a particularly entertaining spectacle, and you have let him die you reckless fools." The Jailers pauses for a moment, then he says, "Take him to the barracks garderobe and throw him down into the cesspit below, then I want you to take the rest of these prisoners out to the square and prepare them for trial and execution… and do not kill any more or them you fucking idiots, or you will take their place." The soldiers immediately grab William by the hair and drag him up rough stone stairs, across the castle courtyard and then into the barracks garderobe, there they drop his lifeless body on the floor, walk over to the large wooden bench seats the castle soldiers use for defecation, pull them up and lay them against the wall. The soldiers drag William over and push him over the ledge, where he drops and tumbles almost forty feet down into a rat-infested pit filled with the rotting bodies, piss, shit, vomit and detritus waste from the soldiers stationed in the castle barracks. The soldiers slam the bench seat of the toilets down as one laughs...

"The shithouse is too good for that Scotchman."

Meanwhile, the visiting Magistrate Hazelrigg; sits in the sumptuous royal apartments near the top floor of Ayr castle, reading the lists of condemned prisoners, when the jailer enters. He says, "All the prisoners are prepared for their trials and executions my lord, but one has succumbed and we've disposed of his rotting carcass."

The magistrate waves his hand, "T'is nothing but an irk, we have enough to be entertaining us this day." The jailer coughs, then he hands the magistrate a writ, "What's this?" enquires the magistrate. The jailer replies "I found it in the dead prisoners bags my Lord." Curious, Hazelrigg opens and reads the document, then he speaks aloud, "This is a free pardon for some fellow called William Wallace of Glen Afton, and the seals of authority in attendance are from Sir Ranald Crauford, the sheriff of Ayr and Sir Henry de Percy of Alnwick, Governor of Ayr, Galloway and Cumberland." Hazelrigg pauses for a moment, then he says, "William Wallace, hmm... I'm sure that I recognise that name from somewhere. Ah, is he not the Brigand Chief that was responsible for the murder of Lord Romille... and you say that he's dead?" The jailer replies, "It is most certain and without any doubts my lord. His body was badly broken by the soldiers, and he had many malignant wounds. I stabbed him several times myself just to make sure that he was dead." The jailer replies... "My Lord, I can assure you, William Wallace the Brigand Chief, he is most assuredly dead...

Death in Ayr

BEAUMARIS COUNCIL

Situated in the Island of Anglesey on Northwest Wales, Maitre Jacques de Saint-Georges, otherwise known as Master James Saint George of Savoy, the King of England's French architect, walks along the unfinished battlements of Beaumaris Castle. He views with pride, this new state-of-the-art fortification, with its stunning cloud high towers punctuating along thick curtain walls and staunchly fortified circular castellated corners that expound the impregnable features of this formidable structure. He scans the great moat that has a long sea channel linking the castle to a fortified sea-gate that opens onto the Menai straits to access the Irish Sea. He smiles, knowing the primary function of Beaumaris is to quash any uprising from native Cymrans and also thwart any seaward invasion of by Scots and Irish armies upon England's northwest flank.

Jacques recalls many heated meetings with Longshanks, who is convinced a combined force of Scots and Irish will at some time use Anglesey to attack England, then try to split his realm in two by driving from west to east through Chester to Newcastle. Any invasion of England by the Scots and Irish would be stoutly repulsed from this impregnable location. Edward approaches the castellated platform of the unfinished chapel tower to stand beside his favoured architect. From this magnificent viewpoint, he survey's the fabulous structures of a new military town being constructed around the castle, then he scans the morning waters of the Menai straights. Glancing towards the mainland of Wales towards his great war-fleet anchored in the Straits, Edward is pleased. "Jacques... this stalwart of Beaumaris will finally complete the Iron manacle around the neck of Wales, never again will the Welsh raise an army of rebellion against the crown of England." Jacques enquires, "My Lord, may I show you the final plans for the completion of this wonderfull castle." He quickly lays out the technical plans on a nearby table. Edward scrutinises the plans while Jacques stands aside, nervously awaiting comment.

After a long pause, Edward proclaims, "A master plan Jacques, sheer genius I say, a castle within a castle. And with these outer walls angled all askew, I see too that it will improve the angle of fire from the multitude of arrow slats, covering every inch along the base of the curtain walls. Again Jacques, I am greatly impressed with your diligence." Jacques replies enthusiastically, "My lord, observe that I have also included a succession of hidden murder holes covering each of the three portcullis, including all access from the barbican. I interjected them to the towns defensive walls with overhanging parapets, projecting corbels and more murder holes, these features will allow your archers to target specific attackers upon entering the exterior base of the perimeter walls." Edward points at the plans, "Explain the purpose of this particular?" Jacques replies, "My lord, I have designed this unique juxtaposition of the outer and inner walls in the event that any enemy who breaches the outer defences, would be forced unwittingly into a funnel trap, there they may be slaughtered with broadsides from the numerous arrow slats, murder holes and stoop traps, long before they could ever reach the inner gates."

Studying the plans, Edward then looks around at the actual construction of the castle, he frowns, "Then tell me Jacques, what of my personal compartments, the castle halls, granary, kitchens, stables, why is it no one labours upon them? My household does dwell in drafty pavilions while my need to accommodate the steward of Wales, the sheriff of Anglesey, royal officers and constables are great. Explain to me why these structures are not yet completed?" Jacques swallows nervously, "My lord, there is fifteen hundred craftsmen and apprentice's... but there is no money left to pay them, nor is there any monies available to bring forth the materials I so desperately require." Longshanks glares at Jacques, "We have over four thousand Welsh prisoners here who need no pay, why do you not use them?" Jacques replies, "We do use them for labouring Sire, but they do not have the skills required for important tasks, also, the Welsh are not fed and the only water they receive is by licking the dew of the grass in the morning, they are but simple peasants who are sorely weak with hunger and many maladies."

Edward looks across the Menai straits, his face darkening with rage. Jacques offers a solution of sorts... "My lord, it may be more prudent to consolidate the castle in its present state of construction by using what materials we have left... may I also suggest Sire, you have defeated the Welsh in the whole of this realm, perhaps the Castle would best serve as a hunting estate, as it is no longer apparent the requirement for such a bastion..." Edward looks north towards Scotland and west towards Ireland, then he says, "Jacques, you are a most talented architect, but ignorant of the needs of a King. You think by subduing the Welsh that we will slumber in our chambers easily, with naught a concern for the willful machinations of others who dwell upon our borders?" Jacques listens intently as Edward continues, "It is not just the damned Welsh Jacques, should the Scots revolt before we subdue them, then by opportune they ally with dissident Irish, I have it on good authority from my agents they will attack England through Anglesey, whilst my northern army awaits the heathens at the border marches of Scotland. I am aware that should the Scots unite with the Irish, they will strike us from this seaboard and attack Wrexham, Chester then Newcastle in an attempt to trap my northern army betwixt them and Scotland, then destroy it. And should that happen, those heathens may move freely upon London. No… we cannot ever allow those Scotch and Irish heathens to unite." Jacques flushes upon hearing Edwards reply. "Sire, if we let the Welsh peasants shelter overnight in the Castle precincts, rather than out in the open where they die of cold in their hundreds, we could proceed with limited construction till funds are available to pay the craftsmen and materials."

Glaring at Jacques, Edward says, "You should know Jacques that all Welsh are forbidden to enter any Bastide. (Fortified town) Nor may they conduct trade within its walls or surrounding precincts. I've issued writs that if any Welsh are found within any town walls after sundown, they are to be taken to the castle gates and hanged… furthermore, if any Scotch or Irish are found the same, they are to be hung by their beards and their throats opened as a warning to these lesser creatures, that none of their kind may grace the same footpads as any loyal yeoman of England." Edward turns away from Jacques and studies in great detail the plans for the castle and township. Jacques notices two heralds riding fast towards the castle from Royal pavilion encampment. He says, "Sire, heralds make speed and approach us from the pavilions." Edward looks over the parapet and sees two heralds trailing a white stallion into the cobbled courtyard then dismount. He smiles when he sees they have brought with them his companion steed, the famed Bayard. The heralds hurriedly run up the outer stairwell and present themselves before their king, breathless from their exertions.

"My Lord..." gasps the first Herald. Longshanks commands, "Speak, lest you test my patience." The Herald replies immediately, "Sire, good Prince Edmund and the Bishop of Durham Anthony Bek, Sir Hugh de Cressingham, Walter of Lanercoste, Sir Walter of Amersham the lord chancellor and Sir John de Warenne, the Earl of Surrey, they have arrived at the royal pavilions." Edward smiles upon hearing this news. The second herald speaks, "My lord, they are also accompanied by a Scotch delegation, comprised of his imminence William Fraser, the Bishop of Saint Andrews. Lords Cospatrick of Dunbar and Sir Robert Brus of Carrick, also in attendance is the steward of Wales, Sir Tudur ap Goronwy and his entourage. They too await your pleasure in the royal pavilions." Edward takes in a deep breath of Welsh sea air then he walks to the head of the stairwell, followed by his heralds. He stops and turns toward Jacques...

"You shall consolidate Beaumaris for me Jacques, I want you to pick the finest of craftsmen you require to complete the works, reward them with estate portions forfeited from the Welsh. Oh, and use the Welsh prisoners as you deem fit, work them to death if needs be..." Edward pauses, then he continues, "Select fifty Welsh prisoners, bind their hands behind their backs tie them face to face in pairs by their beards, then have them thrown them into the moat. This should inspire the other prisoners to work diligently for you... I am sure that will amuse you..." Jacques gasps at the thought of such horrific actions to be committed on his order, he stammers as he tries to object, "But, my lord..." Edward notices Jacques hesitation, he waves his hand frivolously, "What... fifty is not enough? Then make it one hundred., that should suffice to get the rest of them working with the vigour of conviction. Now make it so, for I shall be watching from the pavilion's, do not disappoint me Jacques." Edward storms off in a flurry with his heralds, leaving the mild-mannered Jacques to ponder over his macabre duty. He thinks for a long time, considering the consequences of disobeying his master. Finally, Jacques walks in a daze towards the parapet walls and orders two guards to go and select one hundred Welsh prisoners…

Sweeping in through the doors of the royal pavilion at a brisk pace, Edward welcomes everyone, "Fair morn my lords…" he walks towards his royal seat and halts abruptly beside Robert Brus, the earl of Carrick. He says, "My regrets and sympathies upon the death of your father lord Brix, he was a consistent and extremely loyal man, I shall miss him." Brus replies, "Thank you my lord, I only hope that I may provide the same dedication and devotion to you Sire as did my father." Edward studies Brus of Carrick, then he replies, "You most certainly will good Sir, have no doubt about that."

Edward walks casually through the pavilion, deliberately scrutinising everyone the gathered council, then he takes his seat at the head of a large, round and ornately decorated oak table. Edward, inspired by Arthurian legends, has had the magnificent circular table constructed with a face of twenty-five alternating-coloured segments of pastel-greens and wheaten-whites, running from a single pointed rose centre to the outer edge circumference, where bands of ebony white walrus ivory circumnavigate the grand table, gratuitously inlaid with gold symbols of Plantagenet heraldry. The grandiose table setting is complimented with ornate chairs, all situated at the broad end of each segment span. "My lords…" says Edward, "I require my Scotch delegation here to retire to the appendix pavilion awhile, as my honoured guests of course, do rest there awhile after your long and arduous journey, and please, do partake in the food, wine and refreshments provided. I have also provided washed Welsh girls and boys for your pleasure. My friends, I must first take urgent council with my advisers, when I am done here and you are much rested, I will send for you, then we may talk." Bishop Fraser coughs, "My Lord, may I beg a moment?" Edward beckons Fraser to his side where the bishop whispers in his ear for a few moments, he then kneels before the king, kisses his ring and leaves to rejoin the delegation. Edward scratches his chin thoughtfully in reaction to what the bishop has just said.

Meanwhile, the Scots delegation, led by Bishop Fraser and Sir Cospatrick Dunbar, bow and make exit to a place of rest and nourishment. "Be seated my lords," commands Edward, for we have much to discuss." As the council of advisors all take their seats, Edward looks at a vacant chair nearby and sighs, "Robert Burnell is greatly missed my lords, for there are none here today nor in all of merry England who has the legislative mind to match his keen wit." Edward shows slight emotion upon reflection of his friends passing, and everyone is aware it was a terrible blow to the heart of the King.

"Now," says Edward, "With our loyal friends de Brix and Burnell gone by the will of God's grace, they are a great loss to this realm..." he pauses a moment, his steely character momentarily displays another hint of emotion at the passing of his loyal companions, then he looks up and continues, "Nevertheless, the realm must live on without them, so I would ask you to dwell on the business in hand. My dear Bishop Bek, do convey to me the status of the tax on the clergy." Standing up from his chair, Bek replies, "Sire, since the Pope elevated Robert of Winchesley to the archbishopric of Canterbury, the archbishop has since obtained a Papal

Beaumaris Council

Bull, namely the Clericus Laicos, prohibiting the clergy from paying any taxes to your exchequer without the necessary consent from the Holy See. Winchesley is using this bull to defy our tax collectors by upholding the Bull." Edward replies sharply, "Then Winchesley shall have a dilemma of faith to deal with, for if he should choose his Pope above his King, I will have those of his flock who refuse to pay taxes, imprisoned and wracked, then I shall have his head my lords, for these are desperate climes." Bek continues, "My lord, I have spoken with Winchesley about this possibility, he responded by leaving the decision to the conscious of each individual clergyman. I have pleaded with him over many days, and we may have found a solution, whereby both the Crown and the Papacy may save face and you may still raise religious taxation."

"How so?" enquires Edward. Bek replies, "A solution may be by the issuing of a new Papal Bull, the Etsi de Statu, which will allow the crown to apply clerical taxation in cases of pressing urgency or a threat to the realm." Smashing his fist onto the table, Edward rages, "A threat to the realm? Philip of France has seized my lands of Aquitaine and Gascony, impounded my fleet in French ports, confiscated my wine and wool assets both in France and Flanders, the Welsh and Irish have bled us dry of monies because of their damned rebellions and uprisings. My lords, I press upon you with great urgency, our realm is indeed under a threat most severe, we must raise these religious taxes now, or we surely may be undone." Bek replies nervously, "Sire we await confirmation of the Papal Bull first, otherwise Winchesley threatens call for your excommunication, with the approval from the His Holiness." Edward partly regains his composure, with a cold hard glare; he looks around the faces of everyone sitting at the table. Lord Amersham speaks, "Sire, it's true that our realm now faces the greatest fiscal crisis of your reign, for our commitments exceeds our resources as chronic debts are being accrued in preparation for wars in France, Flanders and Sire, the Florentines say they are no longer willing lend us monies till all past debt is recovered."

"My dear Amersham," enquires Edward, "I trust you have a solution, for your bloated head remaining attached to your body doest surely depend upon it. If you seek vantage in replacing a great man in Burnell, you must pray most fervently that you match his mark." Amersham pales as he replies, "My Lord, we would have the monies to fund an expedition into France if the council of Barons agrees, but they do not, for they see no gain in warring the French. They also say Philip does pose no threat to this realm, only your personal estates in France." Edward clenches his fists, "And what would the Barons want in exchange for their support, for I gain weary of placing a gentle hand on these traitors who fore-swore to serve me and the cause of England."

Raising his hand, Cressingham replies, "Sire, they do not refuse as such, they state instead that they are merely reluctant to contribute to any more expensive and unsuccessful military policies. they believe England is bleeding dry by unwarranted taxation. The Earls of Hereford and Norfolk do brazenly state the baron's council will not serve in France, instead they have presented a formal statement of grievances, whereby you reconfirm their Charters, including a revision of the Magna Carta, and only then will they present monies, men and equipment required for any reasonable campaigns." Edward enquires, "Amersham, my lord chancellor, what say you?" Amersham clears his throat nervously, "Sire, the hesitance of the Barons council is based upon a series of grievances focused on an instrument they term as the Remonstrance's, their first objection is your right to demand military service without council. Sir Roger Bigod, in his capacity as Marshal of England, informs me that the Barons council will object to all royal summons of military service untill all these grievances are agreed upon a sealed charter. He also states that military obligations can only be extended to service for the crown if you yourself are not present at the source of any said threat to the kingdom, otherwise the barons may not be obliged to serve in any expeditions other than in direct defence of the realm."

Amersham trembles as Edward glares at him… "My lord, the Barons express concern regarding the crowns design for incessant warfare, subsequently putting great financial demands upon England's subjects. My lord, the Barons state that previous lay subsidies have raised a hundred thousand pounds for the exchequer, they also demonstrate a serious conviction it has all been squandered and do baulk at the burden of prises, seizures of wine, wool, hides, fish and with the addition of the Maltolt. the Barons believes the realm flounders and does not flourish due to your excesses. They also add Sire, by the crown instituting income and personal property taxes simultaneously, they now seek reaffirmation of rebate in a revised Charter of the Forest."

"Sire," says Cressingham "Baronial land taxes and the demand for one half of all clerical revenues is meeting with much resistance throughout the entire Kingdom, the Barons council state that the fiscal demands placed upon your subjects is causing resentment amongst all the Barons, they say these new taxes will lead to dissention and possible insurrection throughout the realm, and should the Barons leave their shires on fruitless foreign wars as they see it, they also express deep concern that they may have no estates left by their return." The pavilion goes silent, as all dwell on the alarming peril of fiscal ruin and the possibility of another

Barons revolt, threatening the Crown itself and security of all England. Edward appears statuesque as he sits in his chair deliberating. Walter of Lanercoste speaks, "Sire, if we do not strike at King Philip in haste, then you will certainly lose Aquitaine and Gascony, along with support from the northern brotherhood of Kings for the Great Cause."

"Ah, the Great Cause…" sighs Edward, "Adolf of Nassau, Wenceslaus of Bohemia and Albert of Habsburg have informed me that unless we send them immediate fiscal aid for their armies and demonstrate that we can chastise Philip, they may withdraw their armies and contribution from the Great Cause." Edmund says, "My lord, emissaries from Sir Guy de Dampierre informs me that he would support your attack on Philip. He will launch a war against him from Flanders upon landing our army on French shores." Edmund continues, "Sire, when our army was repulsed at Bordeaux, we returned with but a fifth of our expedition, and though they now rest short of food at Plymouth docks, they are still of stout heart and eager to join with the second army to embark for France."

De Warenne speaks, "Sire, I have stripped Ireland and Wales of most of their resources, including clearing all gaols in the Pale and southern shires of all available serfs, and yeomen, leaving only a token force in each of your territories. As we speak, the armies are now gathering from Tilbury to Plymouth. Sire, we have nigh on thirty thousand knights and levies awaiting your orders, when King John of Scotland arrives with twenty thousand Scotch and Lord de Burgh attends with ten thousand Irish, we may have at our disposal sixty thousand men for war on the French." Stroking his beard, Edward enquires, "Amersham, you say that Bigod informed you the Barons council would rally if England were attacked or threatened?" Amersham replies, "To a man

Sire, their loyalty is not in question, it is their concern for the state of the realm." Edward enquires, "How many yeomen, men at arms and knights could the baron's field if required?" Amersham replies, "Collectively, forty thousand or more Sire." Walter of Lanercoste says, "Sire, with an army of nigh on one hundred thousand men ready and willing to attack the French, this would surely impress the Northern Kings Alliance and bring them joyously to your side to implement the Great Cause. With the armies of the brotherhood joining our crusade, this would be the greatest army the world has ever witnessed, and all at your disposal. Sire, in our moment of despair, this may truly be God's intervention, we must surely strike the French now and be done with them." Edward feels an enlightened mood arise in his council.

"Perhaps Walter you are correct," says Edward. "this may be the time, but there are two problems, one is money to launch an attack on Philip, and the second…" There is a tense silence as Longshanks studies the faces of his council, he says, "The second, is the heathen Scotch, I do not trust a single one of those dogs." De Warenne enquires, "How so Sire, your demand for Baliol to bring an army was delivered personally by my own hands?" Cressingham speaks… "Sire, the taxation levies and monies we confiscated from the Scotch are secure in King Henry's treasury in Westminster abbey, a very substantial amount indeed, and they shall be doubled by the end of the year." Edward sits back in his chair, completely surprised by Cressingham's comment, he enquires, "How so, why was I not informed of this; and to what worth do you say is secured in the exchequer?" Cressingham, somewhat embarrassed, replies, "My Lord, I thought my journey to this council was to inform you of these acquisitions. It's not certain the exact worth yet, but it exceeds a few shillings short of two hundred thousand silver pounds."

The surprise news of this windfall amazes the council. Turning to De Warenne, Edward enquires, "My lord, what is the cost to transport our army to France and keep their bellies sustained, before we let them loose upon the land to feed themselves freely and make booty in the French countryside?" A surprised de Warenne replies, "Less than one eighth silver pound per man Sire." Edward appears extremely confident, "Good Walter, perhaps a miracle has been sent from above and born to life in your words. A true revelation has come to me through you, Gods willing servant." Walter replies, "I know not to what you refer Sire? Edward rises from his chair and beckons a guard, who immediately responds. He is required to bring food, wine and refreshments, then summon the Scots delegation.

Before the guard leaves, Edward whispers in his ear, the Guard acknowledges his king and quickly makes exit. Edward returns to his seat… "My Lords, I have requested some fine fare be brought to you and I have also invited the Scotch delegation to join us. But before they arrive, I must tell you that I truly believe God has shown me the way. I also believe the thorny problem of Scotland and France will soon be eliminated then we must inaugurate bring the Great Cause. Very soon, then the annihilation of Philip and imposition of Papist influences will be sent scurrying back over the Pyrenees, then my good men, the Great Cause of the Northern Christian Kings may rule directly as ordained." Walter of Lanercoste professes, "The divine right of Kings Sire, it is true that you are subject to no earthly authority, deriving your right to rule directly by the will of God and not subject to the will of the people, nor any other estate decree by the nobility of the realm or any false prince of Rome." Walter declares, "Only God may judge a King Sire, for any who would attempt to depose a king or restrict his powers, does preach contrary to the will of God." Edward hints a satisfied smile, then says, "The Great Cause must begin in Scotland and conclude in the great Palace of Blachernae on the Bosphorus. My lords, the elimination the Scotch problem is truly the beginning of a new Christian empire, and the Scotch fools will deliver unto me the instruments of our success themselves." Cressingham enquires, "Pray tell us Sire the detail of this Scotch problem, other than their subjugation?" Edward smiles as he raises a goblet of wine and gazes at the mosaic beauty of the glass, he says, "Before the Scotch delegation took their leave earlier, Bishop Fraser told me that Baliol has raised an army in Scotland, but instead of joining us to invade France as intended, the Scotch puppet king and Philip have both agreed to an alliance, to which they shall fight together, simply put, if one is attacked, the other becomes an ally."

The gasps and protestations of the council are considerably audible. Edward raises his hand, "My lords, the Great Cause, as good Walter has said, now begins, but not in France as we first thought, but it shall be in Scotland, I see that now. Our miserable Scotch vassals who scurry about their shit ridden realm while blowing out their chests out in pathetic protestations, do serve my purpose better than I could have planned, it is surely God's will these scurrilous Scotch are brought to heel or eliminated." The council glance furtively at each other, completely bemused by Edward's apparent good humours. Edmund enquires, "Brother, if the Scotch have raised an army and pledged themselves to ally with Philip of France, do tell us why your humour is so gay, I completely fail to understand?" Edward drinks from his goblet, smiles, then he enquires, "Amersham, did you not say that the Barons by their sworn oath would be obligated to stand by my side if England were to be attacked?" Amersham looks around the council bemused, then he replies, "I did Sire…" Edward continues, "And Bek, did you not tell us that the Pope through the prompting of our gracious Archbishop, is issuing a new papal bull the Etsi de Statu, which will then allow us to apply clerical taxation based upon any threat to the realm?" Bek replies, "That is true Sire, but…" Edward slams his goblet on the table, "Then my lords, we shall invite the Scotch to attack us, for I have a mind to remove the seditious King of Scotch in the same manner that we have destroyed the Welsh royal house of Llewellyn. By removing the royal head from Scotland for daring to raise an army against us, we must lure them into invading England, for only then will it bring the Baron's to heel by my side when the Scotch launch an attack upon our sovereign realm. By that single action of the Scotch my lords, I will have all the justification I need and is required to eliminate them, then, as the French come to their aid through treaty, I shall attack Philip with our Brotherhood allies. When Philip is dead, the Great Cause will be sweep through the Balkans and on to Constantinople." Edmund exclaims, "But Sire, the Scotch have not attacked us?"

"Not yet Edmund," replies Edward, he says, "but soon they most certainly will. When the Northern Kings alliance doest see how I bring these islands into submission with such ease and then witness the multitude and might of my armies, they must surely honour all their pledges and follow me on this the most Holiest of Crusades against both the Papacy and the Saracens." Edward looks into the eyes of his council, all of whom are stunned into silence. He continues, "My Lords, this morn we had faced another possible Barons revolt with the potential destruction of the realm, as was suffered previously by my father King Henry at the hands of De Montfort. Don't you see, with the Scotch raising an army and rejecting my authority, their sworn Lord Magnate Supreme, they have unwittingly offered us the opportunity to inaugurate a new Christian empire to be ruled by Kings, not Popes." Walter exclaims, "It is God's blessed work Sire. I now see your vision with great clarity. I also see why the Scotch must be lured into attacking our realm, therefore in our defense, the Barons and Church must finally rally to our cause." Bek says, "Sire, you are truly a master tactician and visionary, surely blessed by doing God's bidding. Now the unwitting Scotch must play their part to the fullest." De Warenne says, "We have been waiting for this moment for ten years or more Sire, good Walter does play Gods willing conduit and indeed facilitates your revelations, a united crusade with the mightiest Christian army ever to leave these shores... Sire, I bow to your great wisdom."

Edward sits awhile as the others gleefully converse, then he speaks, "My Lords, this is what is going to happen, De Warenne, you are to leave at first light to meet the Sheriffs of Chester, York, Lancaster, Westmoreland, Northumberland and Cumberland. You are commanded with authority, to summon all who owe the realm military service within their jurisdictions, they are to rendezvous with their retinues prepared to war with the Scotch at Norham castle by long Friday." De Warenne replies, "It shall be so Sire."

"So, my Lords." says Edward, "We shall bait the trap by using the enemies of the lord Brus. When the foolish Scotch cross the western border like sheep into the fold, we shall attack Berwick in the east. For other than London, Berwick is the richest city in these islands, with a revenue return according to my friend Burnell, near one third of England's entire annual treasury income." The gasp from all upon hearing this information amuses Edward, he continues, "I have recently entertained emissaries from Bishop Wishart of Glasgow, who in good faith, has delivered to me the antiquated repertory of the primitive state and rights of Scotland's estates, demonstrating the total accounts of ecclesiastical taxation and benefices raised under Alexander's reign, which does confirm the account of Burnell to be true."

"Sire…" gasps Bek, "my spies have searched for these codex' for nigh on ten years…" Edward glares at Bek, then he laughs, "Dear Bek, you are most certainly not I…"

Bek looks at the table shamefaced as Edward continues; "I have given my life in the service of the Holy See, now Scotland's revenue doest show the fiscal vantage of an independent church, solely in the service of a King. Wishart pleads with me to grant autonomy to the church in Scotland in exchange for their loyal support, I have granted him this one concession. It would seem to me that the religious establishments of my own realm live a life of luxurious entrenchment at our expense and protected by Rome my lords. Something I shall remedy in due course." Bek enquires, "But Sire, how will we control Scotland if their church is separate from the state?" Edward replies, "Only separate from your avarice Bek. I have sent word to the Scotch bishop that only I as his liege lord shall be his superior in that land, and it would serve you best to remember this."

Edward observes Bek's consternation then continues, "Never fear Bek, in time we shall destroy all Scotch self-belief and they will soon be sucking at your imminent teats." Bek enquires, "But how may you trust this Scotch bishop Sire?" Edward smiles, "He is a brother Cluniac and is most forthcoming with vital information, all in exchange for a promise of a consideration in regard to Scotland's independent religious sanctity." Longshanks continues, "Wishart has also informed me in great detail of their late King's wish to join the Varjag and Dudesche Hanse."

There are murmurs around the table then Bek says, "I have heard of this Hanse Sire, but what does a confederation of market trader guilds based on the herring fisheries from Baltic Germania and..." Longshanks interrupts, "From the Baltic states to the North Sea and Scotland my dear Bek. These benign traders as most do see them, may become a greater threat to England than the French or Saracens could ever be. If the Hanse gains a foothold in Scotland, then another dire threat to England is born, so much greater than we have ever faced collectively from Danes, Norsemen, and the French. Mark my words my lords, we must crush the Scotch completely before they gain a union with the Baltic league. I am well informed the Scotch intend to conclude the Hanseatic treaties by the twenty-seventh day of April next year." Bek says, "This Hanseatic configuration was created simply to protect their economic interests, they have no standing navy nor army Sire?"

"That is so my dear Bek," Edward replies, "but they have the power to establish diplomatic privileges independent of kings, which makes them potentially a greater threat in martial strength than any King's army on the continent, for they have at their fiscal disposal, a most powerful mercenary army and fleet." Longshanks continues, "This union is fast becoming the wealthiest league in Europe, for their merchant fathers solemnly do declare and make known to all, when any member of the Hanse is attacked, be it by piracy or by a sovereign King, they can and will fund an army of professional mercenaries for mutual protection. Since Emperor Frederick declared Lübeck an Imperial City, the merchants of that city have pursued quite singularly their own interests to preserve their herring industry, but they desperately needed access to salt, which allied them to Novgorod, Hamburg and Lübeck in a bond of trade and mutual protection, they now expand this unique opportunity to other important principalities, including Cologne, Rostock, Bremen, Visby and the Wismar, all joining this confederation, which if the Scotch do join, would certainly threaten our Great Cause, for what need they of Kings then my lords? That is why Scotland must be brought to its knees now." Cressingham sighs, "Now I fully understand Sire, should the Scotch be allowed to join this European Union, potentially we shall have the largest army in Europe on our borders. Even greater than the Northern Brotherhood of Kings, I see what a dire threat Scotland may be to England. Sire, does Wishart declare the progress of negotiations?" Edward replies, "Alexander's death and unrest that's plagued Scotland during the interregnum, delayed the agreement, but I have it from Wishart that king John and the council of Guardians intend to meet with Hansa emissaries in Berwick by April, that they may establish a Hansa Kontor major in the Scotch seaport. Balliol's intention is to formalise membership in Lübeck early in May. That my lords is why we must attack the Scotch before the twenty seventh day of that month."

Edward continues, "The Hansa now has over sixty city states in the Baltic basin in league. They call themselves the thirds or the Rhennish and Wendish, based in the Rhineland for transport shipping out of Lübeck and trading Prussian grain from the Teutonic Order. Now they flex their muscles and wish to become a qaudrancy, bringing Bergen, Bruges, Inverness and Berwick into their fold." De Warenne enquires, "But Sire, forgive me, but why would Scotland joining the Varjag Hansa be any threat to England?" Edward glares at his council, "Must I spell it out to you? Then I shall make this plain for all. Should Scotland ally with this European Union or whatever, we will have an extremely powerfull enemy at our back door, with the capacity to bring an army against us the likes of which Kings could only dream off. I mentioned Bergen earlier, which means Eric of Norway could easily impose a war with England, for he is sworn to support Scotland should England declare war with the French. My lords, not only do we need Scotland's resources for our own purposes, if Scotland is reduced to a mere territory of England's crown, then none can then treat with them. For it is England who shall be the leading member in the Hansa of the fourth quadrant… not Scotland."

"Then Sire, what is your will?" enquires De Warenne. Edward replies abruptly, "The annihilation of Scotland's ability to remain a sovereign realm my lords, that is my will. We shall bring the port of Berwick into the realm of England's peace by utterly destroying the Scotch population of that city, then we shall plant our own loyal yeomen in there from Newcastle and the Northern shire's in their stead, then my lords we shall control the two most important and wealthiest seaports in England, and it will also serve as a warning to all Scotch that we will not tolerate any dissent or rebellions, no matter how great their palaces towns and cities may be." Bek enquires, "What is your will Sire after we have secured Berwick?"

Edward replies, "Quite simple Bek, once we have repopulated Berwick, we shall repeat this mark throughout Scotland, till it is truly a single English shire. We must then eliminate all those miscreants and their families in Scotland who did not sign the Ragemanus nor swear loyalty to me as their rightfull King. We shall remove for all time any thoughts the Scotch may have that they are a sovereign realm or that they may ever survive without being in servitude and dependent upon England." Cressingham gasps, "Sire, that number may exceed over five thousand nobles and thirty thousand lower officials do you wish it so that we should prepare for a pogrom on the Scotch, as we did the Jewry?" Edward laughs aloud, followed by everyone enjoying the mirth of Cressingham's analogy. "A pogrom upon the Scotch?" smirks Edward, "By my leave Cressingham, I say yes... And you will be entirely responsible for the seizure and confiscation of all the Scotch realms monies and moveables." Cressingham enquires, "All of their monies Sire? There are also many wealthy Lombard's, Jews and many Fleming's Guild houses in Scotland too." Edward grins "All monies dear Cressingham." Edward continues, "Walter, Bek... you shall both rally the house of God to collect all taxes due under the pretext of this threat to our realm. You must also insist upon a prompt delivery of all payments due. The principle of the Etsi de Statu must be enforced, under pain of death and damnation."

Bek and Walter reply, "Sire." Edward says, "Edmund, you are to meet with Roger Bigod, Humphrey de Bohun, De Gray of Codnor and Hugo de Courtenay, then you must call to arms the earl's council of Wessex. I want them prepared for war against the Scotch. Then you personally are to travel to France and continue to make false parley with Philip, insist that we shall settle our differences without need for war... for the moment. Once we have annihilated all Scotch rebels and dissenters, we will turn the fury of God's chosen warriors upon Philip." Edmund replies, "Sire."

"You Amersham," continues Edward, "You shall collect all monies from the Church estates in Scotland, I will also require an accurate accounting of our Scotch adventure to date. Soon, when the Scotch are lured into attacking us, they must be smote down quickly and forevermore be dependent on England as their sovereign master. We shall never allow them to gain time to ever think of raising their heads from servitude or imagine they could ever be independent again without the handouts from our treasury. We shall foster a culture upon the Scotch that does survive Cressingham's pogrom, an education of servile dependency under the guidance of our chosen crown representatives as we have done so in Wales and Ireland." Edmund enquires, "What are your thoughts on attacking Scotland brother?"

Edward replies, "We shall take that realm by fire and sword Edmund. If the Scotch gain any momentum, they will be a much tougher nut to crack than the damned Irish or Welsh. We must look upon this Scotch adventure with the passion of a crusade." Edward continues, "Though I shall not execute Baliol, I shall merely strip him of his crown and put him in the tower, there he may rot his life away in contemplation, certainly not as a martyr to his misguided Scotch tribes. Bek, you must ensure that all remaining records of Scotch antiquity are destroyed completely. I have personally overseen the removal of their treasured Lia Fáil on which Scotch Kings are inaugurated. The crown of the Scots and their holiest of relics the Black Rood of St Margaret and the Lia Fáil are to be placed beneath my throne, situated below Talaith Llywelyn, demonstrating the subjugation of those basest of races." De Warenne says, "But Sire, should the Brus, Comyn, Stuart, Moray and their allies all unite, including bringing their Garda Rìoghail together with those Highland Norsemen and savage Galloway armies of infamous Gallowglass; and Sire, as you have mentioned previously, the dissident Irish rebels, we may yet have a war that will surely set these islands towards total destruction."

"Nay my lord," replies Edward, "Lord Brus awaits an audience nearby in some vain effort to gain a mere crumb from our table. Prepare de Warenne, for when this business is done, Scotland shall be naught but a backwater vassal. I hereby appoint you as senior warden of the kingdom of Scotland, and you Cressingham... you shall be my treasurer de facto." De Warenne is astonished, "My Lord..." Edward continues, "I know your sister Isabella is the wife of Baliol, but fear not, they shall share grand apartments in the tower, and when this business is settled, I will exile them in good health to Baliol's ancestral estates of Helicourt in Picardy, then your house shall receive all of Balliol's lands in Yorkshire." De Warenne grins, "Sire." Edward says, "Now my lords, we shall discuss the finer details of this venture and make refreshment before the meek Scotch attend us."

The council eagerly discuss Edward's plans and continue deliberating in a hearty mood, feasting and dining, when they hear the sergeant-at-arms call out... "Sire, the Scotch delegation begs an audience." Edward waves his hand and the Scots delegation enters, accompanied by the Steward of Wales, Sir Tudur ap Goronwy and a former Welsh ally of Longshanks' Madog ap Llewellyn. As the delegations enter the pavilion, the King's council welcomes them all, then Edward notices a young squire walking beside Lord Brus. He exclaims, "Is that you young Robert Brus, or should I address you as Robert thee Bruce?" Robert smiles with relief upon hearing the jest. Edward greets the young Bruce...

"My, look at you, a fine young squire and make no mistake Sirrah. Do tell me Robert, how did you fair under the wing of my Lords Wessex and de Burgh, did you learn much from these fine men?" Bruce replies with a wry smile, "It was more than a little educational Sire." Laughing heartily, Edward replies, "More than a little educational, how curious?" He then puts his arm around the shoulders of his young friend, "My boy, you have a way with words that demonstrates a diplomatic future in my host." Edward looks at Robert the Bruce and taps the end of his own nose, he says, "No doubt someday you may make a fine King of Scotland..." Everyone falls to silence upon hearing Edward's words, while Robert the Bruce at simply gazes open mouthed in disbelief while Edward walks back to his seat, he gestures "Be seated my lords, for we have urgent business to discuss."

"Sire?" enquires Robert, "Would you wish it that I leave your council to the business in hand, for I have not yet the wit to be understanding affairs of state?" Edward looks at Robert for a moment, then he says, "No Robert, I want you to hear what is discussed, for I do believe your very future will benefit from keeping your ears open and your mouth firmly shut. Now you take a seat at the table Robert, for here you may begin to learn the subtle art of kingship."

The astonished council, sitting equally spaced in the seats of the round table of Plantagenet, hurriedly move to allow Robert the Bruce a seat. Edward brings the council to order, "My lords, I shall get directly to the business in hand. Bishop Fraser, I shall require you to make plain all that you inferred in regard to the state of the realm of Scotland. Do speak candidly, for there is no court formality here."

Bishop Fraser replies, "Sire, the situation in Scotland is very grave indeed, many of the native and lower nobles of Scotland believe themselves to be subdued by a foe, and they now prick up their ears upon the withdrawal of English troops from Scotland, but thankfully, Baliol's undermined position could not unify all the factious nobility of the realm. The lords Comyn, Douglas and Moray chiefs of Scotland's most powerful houses and clans, dread complete subjugation to you from Baliol, but when you demanded that the Scotch King raise an army to join our solemn cause in the war against France, these same nobles held a secret parliament at Scone, then elected twelve guardians to act on behalf of their King to manage the affairs of Scotland. Four bishops, four earls and four barons were put in charge of the secret government of the realm." Glancing at lord Brus of Carrick,

Edward enquires, "I trust that no Brus was a party to this group of traitors?" Brus replies, "Why, no Sire." Edward says, "Continue good bishop, my appreciation of your forthright account does favour you." Fraser continues, "Sire, my lords, these Guardians immediately renounced all allegiances to you. An instrument yet to be delivered to your court, contains an account of the grievous injuries committed upon Scotland to the rights and property of John Baliol the King of Scotland. Already they have dispatched ambassadors to France and have secured a treaty pledging Baliol's son Edward to wed the niece of Philip, princess Marguerite de Taranto of Anjou. They have also broached Eric of Norway, Sire, both Philip and Eric have pledged ships and an army in support of Baliol, should a war with France and Scotland become enacted." Edward laughs, then replies curiously, "At least the Baliol's boy has a fine name."

Everyone laughs at Longshanks' humour.

"Sire," says bishop Fraser, "The Guardians under the name of King John, intend to exile all English from Scotland, already the Scotch have raised two armies to defend Scotland's borders against any future English invasion." De Warenne stands up in anger, "Sire, this is outright, treason we..." Edward raises his hand, "My dear Warenne, of course it is treason, and it shall be dealt with in due course. Lord Dunbar, what say you?" Cospatrick replies, "Sire, the resentment of English authority, the constant humiliation of their king, and by your courts finding Baliol guilty of manifest contempt and disobedience toward the Crown of England, does foster constant talk of rebellion against what the Scotch deem to be a foreign takeover of their realm. When King Philip of France seized your territories of Aquitaine and Gascony, the Scotch now see your call to arms against France as a fortuitously brief respite, providing a real opportunity to claim their realm back as they see it. When you commanded King John to raise Scots military support, they did indeed raise an army, but as our lord Bishop has stated, it is not to ally with England, but to defend its borders from your armies return." Edward says, "The Welsh, there is something I admire about the Welsh Goronwy. When you mistakenly supported Madog in the recent rebellion, it was your use of the Longbow that appealed to me, I have a job for you as my steward of Wales."

Everyone listens intently as Edward speaks freely with his former adversary, "Goronwy, how many men are there in the Welsh army?" Goronwy is surprised at the question, he looks around the table then replies, "None Sire, none other than those who serve in your army now, and perhaps those held as prisoners on the shores of the Menai?" Edward continues, "You may have noticed that I spared your rebel army the knife when I subdued the Welsh. Now Goronwy, I ask you, how many Welshmen are in vinculum awaiting sentence betwixt Caernarvon and Beaumaris?"

"Perhaps fifteen to twenty thousand Sire?" replies Goronwy. Edward rises from the table and focuses on Goronwy, "Then my lord, I do hereby elevate you Sir Goronwy, Marshal of Wales. You are to raise a Welsh army for me and must put all to the sword who refuse my hand. For those who do step forward, you are to make them ready for Scotland. Furthermore, you shall have my blessing and my authority to do what you will to achieve this, do you accept?" Goronwy and the others are again in disbelief that Longshanks has bestowed such an honour upon a former enemy. Longshanks continues, "The Welsh have risen twice against the tides of fortune, do you and your Welshmen so wish to be forever in bonded servitude, or would you rather share in the glories of England as we march forward?" Goronwy falls on one knee, then he clasps the hand of Longshanks "Sire, by my unswerving loyalty to your crown, I shall serve you unto death." Edward replies, "Have no fear of death, Lord Goronwy, your good fortune and reputation shall grace our history by the decision you've made this day."

Goronwy says, "My lord, I will ensure that the Welsh army will be ready and prepared to march upon Scotland at your very command." Edward smiles, "So be it Sir Goronwy, gather all our loyal Welshmen on the border marches of Llangybi Castle in the shire of Monmouth, there, both Sir Bogor de Clare and brother Brian le Jay shall provide for all your martial needs. I shall send a herald ahead of you to inform them of their duties and to assist you and your men, does this my lord Goronwy, demonstrate my good faith in you?" Goronwy replies, "My lord, your very command gives to me all the faith that I require." Then he takes his seat, contemplating the incredulous strategy employed by Longshanks that has also taken everyone by surprise.

A growing sense of something bigger than they could ever imagine is beginning to foster excitement at the Kings pleasure. Edward turns to the Earl of Carrick, "Now Sir Robert, do tell me all about Scotland. I had heard that Baliol has confiscated your lands and has then given them over to the Comyn, am I right?" Brus replies, "Sadly it is so Sire, our support for you has cost us all of our lands and estates in Scotland, but it is nothing compared to the service to which I am sworn to in regard to your Great Cause." Edward grins. "Do you hear that young Robert the Bruce? I saw from your grandfather, and I now see it from your father, the wit of politic is forever sharp in your blood." Edward continues, "Sir Robert, I hereby make you paladin constable of Carlisle and warden of the Northwest marches. I require you to staunchly defend Carlisle and all the northern approaches to England. And should you gather such a force and wish to reclaim Annandale across the border, I shall be sending you a Welsh army of support, but only if the Comyn, Graham and Baliol's resist you."

"My liege Lord, I…" stammers Brus, "I cannot thank you enough for your kindness and understanding. I humbly accept your decision with humility and gratitude, and I too will defend your realm onto the death from all who would seek to do you an injustice." Edward replies, "Good, it is all settled then." Edward continues, "My lord Brus, I require you to man Carlisle Castle immediately; then I want you to send foragers into Annandale and prod at the Comyn's, Graeme's and Baliol's, in that they may feel that honour can only be served by launching an attack upon you in Carlisle. When they have crossed the border marches, this will be deemed an attack on the realm of England, we shall send a Welsh army to support you to crush these rebels once and for all. Then my friend, all the lands that you have lost, including estates and territories of our collective enemies, shall be yours once more."

Brus enquires, "My lord? May I take all steps that I deem appropriate to stir up that nest of vermin, ensuring that they fall to your whim?" Edward replies, "You may of course, but you must not use the Godly colours of our realm with any incursions, these foray's must be put down to the reputation of outlaws by perception." Brus replies, "As you wish Sire." Edward continues, "Now my Lord Cressingham, does Lord Butler, De Courtney and squire de Percy still remain in Scotland?" Cressingham replies, "No Sire, they await orders in Carlisle Castle." Edward sighs, "Good, now lord Robert, I will give you sealed orders for their eyes only, they will aid you in getting the Comyn, Graeme and Baliol dogs to bite." Robert Brus is almost lost in his own thoughts of his unexpected elevation to palatine Lord Constable. "Lord Brus?" barks Edward. Brus snaps to attention, "Sire?" Edward enquires, "Who may ally with the you Brus to make the Comyn tribe in particular, set foot across the border to assault our blessed realm?"

"Sire," replies Brus, "my good lord and loyal friend here Cospatrick de Dunbar and his three sons, Patrick the Master of Dunbar, Alexander and John, then there is the high Steward of Scotland, Sir James Stewart and his brother, John Stewart of Jedburgh, Sir Walter Stewart the Earl of Menteith and his two sons, and I may also call upon Sir Richard de Burgh the Earl of Ulster, Thomas de Clare and the Lord of Thomond. The Lord of Islay Aonghas Mòr Mac Domhnaill his son, Alexander Óg of Scatha ..." Edward interrupts, "Nay, no more lord Brus, these men are enough for the moment. I understand that your trust in them is complete. I also know this from their hitherto service to me. Goronwy, I want you to have five thousand Welshmen ready to march to Carlisle as soon as possible. Lay off twenty miles south and await all instructions from my lord Brus, send the rest to Llangybi." Goronwy replies, "My lord."

Edward then turns and focusses on young Robert Brus for a moment, he says; "Do this duty for me Lord Robert, and I shall right a terrible wrong when I strip the tabard from the bones of the treacherous Baliol and his whispering assassins. I give to you the word of an English King, that I shall soon remedy a grave error of judgment made by the assessors during the interregnum, then my lord, the throne of Scotland shall be yours." Again, an audible gasp could be heard as everyone at the table hears Longshanks words. Robert the Bruce looks on in awe, it appears that his grandfather's claim to the throne of Scotland is finally about to be recognized, and his family will soon take their rightfull place as the royal house of Scotland. Edward is amused at the consternation and the look of surprise on everyone's face. He looks at Robert the Bruce, "Did I not say one day you may be the King of Scotland Robert? Now my lords, we must procure more refreshment and deliberate the finer detail of this day's work, for all of you here will surely share in the timeless glories of this England."

Day passes to night, as everyone works feverously refining the strategies of Edward to make all legal in practice, soon the early hours of the morn comes and everything has been detailed in the minutia. All have their royal writs sealed by Edward, confirming their duties and responsibilities. Everyone departs then Edward sits down by the great pavilion Brazier with Edmund Crouchback, Walter of Lanercoste and Bishop Bek. They sit a long time in silence; then Walter speaks, "Sire, I never knew when this day would come, but your wisdom, your foresight, this has truly been a day of revelations. God has surely blessed us." Edward sighs, "I knew the Great Cause would begin some day too Walter, but I could never have thought it would be when the Scotch and the Frenchies declare alliance to resist England's glory. I saw it in your earlier words Walter, as though God himself was speaking to me through your pious wit."

"Meritorious my Lord," says Bek, "An extremely exhilarating day this has been Sire, the honour of being witness, has me with the vigour of a hot bloodied youth, but…"

Glaring at his loyal Bishop, Edward says, "But what Bek, what worms are eating your brains?" Bek replies, "Sire, I do not doubt your wisdom, but to strip Baliol of his crown and place it on another such as Brus, is this not a risk?" Edward grins, "No risk Bek, for Scotland shall never have any other as king but the King of England, Brus will sadly perish in his endeavors, and that of his blood, in the meantime, you must always give them hope." Everyone laughs as Edward continues, "De Courtney, Butler and de Percy are to visit the Comyn and Baliol lands in Scotland in the apparel of Brus' armorial trappings. It will not take long for the Comyn to rage and seek out the Brus. When Comyn finds him and crosses onto English soil with an army of Scots, we shall be waiting near Berwick to prize their jewel away from that shit realm. I intend to leave none there alive, for we shall seize Berwick and supplant it with colonists, then two most important financial ports on these Islands shall be in our grasp." Bek enquires, "And Goronwy's support for the Brus?" Edward replies, "The Welsh will be too busy elsewhere, like the Scotch, I do not trust a single Welsh cur. Goronwy will travel in my entourage, but I will keep a close eye on him. I will use the Welsh and Irish freely in battle, for they are cheaper than slingshot and they may soak up Scotch lance and bolt before I send in my brave English yeomen." Bek ponders, "And if Brus does survive the Comyn attack my lord?" Edward replies, "My dear Bek, no matter, another time will suffice to be rid us of the Brus, we may allow them an empty tabard awhile. I do ask you, what kind of man allows a woman to imprison him till he pledges to marry her?"

Everyone laughs aloud at Edward's reference to the marriage of Robert Brus to Marthoc, the countess of Carrick. Edmund says, "Brother, that I live to witness the day when the Comyn and his army march over the border, thinking they may chastise the Brus for terrible wrongs put upon their people, but instead, they walk into your trap and invite the annihilation of the Scotch, even greater if King John is enticed to accompany Comyn, then all the Scotch mice will be caught in a single trap." Edward says, "We shall make it so Edmund, for I have no doubt De Courtney, de Percy and Lord Butler will leave the Comyn no other course but to attack the Brus, for some of the tactics these men do employ, has made even I to shudder." Everyone laughs again, then Edmund says, "Your brilliance excites me brother, the thought of the Scotch being so full of bluster and a wanting for revenge, in due course will unwittingly deliver to us the fulfillment of Gods plan." Walter says, "It is so my Lord, when the Comyn's, Graeme's and Baliol's do cross the border, they will be seen by every Lord and common man of England as a Scotch army of invasion, all the Barons and church magnates, must then deliver up to us all their retinues and taxation due, and attend to your banners freely in defense of the realm, or they shall face the headsman's axe for treason." Edward smiles, "Then my lords, when the first Scotch boot touches English soil over the border, this will be an act of war forced upon England's sacred realm, and so it finally begins after so many tedious distractions… the Great Cause."

Wolf and Wildcats

A small column of mounted knights and their entourage ride tentatively along the eastern edge of the Wolf and wildcat forest, near Lanark town. They are all extremely cautious while skirting the outer edges of the forest, for it is the home to the feared Gallóbhet, dispossessed men, women, Brigands, cutthroats and outlaws. The entourage bring their horses to a halt adjacent to an obvious entrance that leads deep into the dense woodland. The lead knight, Sir Andrew D'Levingstun, the sheriff of Lanark, shakes his head then he says, "Good Sirs, I shall bid my leave of you here and now, but again I must warn you, if you take any men in there with you, it's most certain that you will all be dead before I've spurred away to a canter. Even veteran English soldiers fear to enter the Wolf and wildcats. Not because they might meet with brigands or outlaws, but for the evil spirits and revenants dwelling within that godforsaken place."

Andrew Moray looks at his friend John, the Red Comyn, then enquires, "Well Comyn, are yie sure this is worth dying for?" Comyn replies, "Well, if you lead the way Moray and you have the heart for it, then this is a Comyn that will fight by your side with honour, and ne'er take a step back." The two knights sit awhile on their horses, gazing at a macabre woodland entrance, festooned and adorned with many dead creatures hanging by hemp strings from spindly branches, with a sundry of smaller rotting animal carcasses arrayed at the base of each tree in some ritualistic ensemble. Moray and Comyn inch their horses a little closer, till they can see all in detail, little headless sparrows hanging by their tiny feet, crows, pigeons, voles, moles and a host of other dead wildlife decorate the entrance. Surrounding trees are also festooned with a kaleidoscope of witch's hair, liverwort and lungwort mosses. The forest floor appears treacherously bog soft, cloaked in a deep thick blanket of moss that clutches to the base of the tree roots. Greyish black dogwort and brown shield lichen creep high into the forest canopy, where the deadly wet glistening specklebelly moss jewels blossom.

Comyn mutters to himself, "Damned sorcery…" Moray turns to his nervous looking troop and says, "There is no need for you men to follow us in there, what needs to be done can be affected by myself and Red Comyn alone. Return to Lanark with the sheriff and we will meet again in three days." Comyn also speaks to his bodyguards. "If we do not return in three days, gather up all my men, make sure all are well-armed and then follow on our tracks as best you can." Grinning, D'Levingstun pulls his horse around then says, "I wish I could do more for you young lords, but it's not possible, you're on your own now, or you may travel with us back to Lanark and then on to Dunbar as fast as your horses will carry you. What's it to be young Sirs, what is your will?"

Moray smiles and turns his horse towards the feared woodland, then he walks-on towards the dark foreboding entrance. As he nears the overhanging canopy of spindly moss-covered branches and ghastly embellishments, his horse begins to shy away, but Moray remains persistent and edges his feisty Arab-cross forward, followed reluctantly by the red Comyn, who gains the same reaction from his own horse. Eventually they urge and spur their horses forward and soon they disappear into the darkened eerie place and out of sight of the sheriff. D'Levingstun speaks to his man-at-arms, "I certainly hope not, but that may be the last we see of those young hotspurs." D'Levingstun spurs his horse away from the ancient forest and rides at speed towards the fortified town of Lanark, hastily followed by his guard and the remainder of Moray and the Comyn's guard. Meanwhile, Moray and the Comyn slowly wind their way along the darkening pathway into the depths of the forest, not really knowing where they are going, but very aware there are hidden mantraps everywhere, with wolf, stag, boar traps and other fantastic killing devices set and prepared to snare those travelling on the footfall of the unwary.

Suddenly the deathly silence is broken by a loud cracking sound... "What's that?" exclaims Comyn. Moray jumps in his saddle; his straining nerves are not much better than that of the red Comyn. Both grip their swords tightly and look around the dark silent woodland, scanning and searching awhile, then, with a sigh of relief, Moray points, "It's just dead branches falling through those trees." Comyn sighs with relief too, he says, "This woodland is like no other I've ever seen nor travelled through before Moray. Look you to the ground where we ride, it would appear as no track nor pathway that we may ever declare a mortal foot or horse's hoof has frequented; yet we seem to be following this route like a well-trodden path? I tell you this Moray, the English may well be right; and we are following a living path to a demonic hell by entering this unnatural forest."

Moray looks down at the path that beckons them ever deeper into the forest. He says, "Comyn, we may as well go forward now, for what choice do we make then if we were to retire accepting failure? And should we step on a mantrap trying to find our way back out, then what purpose would we have served to die of broken legs or worse in this primeval woodland?" Comyn replies, "Ah will tell yie this truly Moray, I've no' got any sense o' direction, and for us to continue following this pathway is pure jangling my nerves to such a degree, I fear that we may no longer go forward nor retire."

Moray smiles then he nudges his horse to walk-on, followed by the nervy Comyn.

Hours pass as they weave their way ever deeper into the dark foreboding woodland; suddenly Comyn pulls his horse to a halt. "I think I hear something?" Moray and Comyn both look around then they notice an obstacle that appears to be a large gauze curtain of hanging moss not far ahead of them. They move their horses forward slowly and very cautiously; then they begin to hear little clinking, jangling noises of many different volumes and pitches. Finally, they reached the source of their curiosity and are bemused, Comyn enquires, "Are those shin bones being used as woodland wind chimes up there?" Pushing his visor back over his helm, Moray studies the gently swaying bones, "I think you're right; it is human shin, ribs and other bone pieces. Feck, I've never seen the likes o' this before."

Comyn pulls taught on his reigns as he leans back in his saddle. "We should get out o' here Moray, this is no' a fuckin' good place to be for God fearing men." Moray laughs then says, "Ach for fuck's sake Comyn, I watched you on the border marches just a few days ago, riding against Brus and de Percy's men so boldly without regard, you were hacking through halberd and spear long before your men were by your side, and still you fought on with naught a care for your flesh. Yet here we are sitting on skittish horses in an old woodland and you're now caking yer breeks?" Comyn replies, "It's just no' the same Moray…" They look around then gaze up towards the dense canopy of the early springtime branches, still blackened and rotting from a harsh winter and constant dampness, then they notice something else unusual when looking further along their impending path. The strange objects of their focus becomes ever more numerous, Comyn exclaims, "What the fuck are those?" Moray replies, "I think its animal carcass, or it's more human bones hanging up there in those branches." Nudging their horses forward, they soon come face to face with one of the curious objects. "Jaezuz," Exclaims Comyn, "It's a human leg with a cracked skull somehow fixed to the knee-knuckle… and there's horse-hair sticking out o' each eye-socket?"

The unusual pieces of human bones sway gently in front of them; then they see more sinister symbols of this strange primeval and macabre woodland art. "It's a Warning," exclaims Moray. Comyn replies, "Fuck Moray, like I need a warning to get out of here? Awe shit, look over there now Moray, to your left… some poor bastard has had his scalp cut from his head and a ram's skull place on top. What the fuck is going on here?" Moray stays silent as they nudge their horses forward, but the bizarre assemblies of human body parts mixed with animal and bird bones becomes, even more frequent, which begins to completely unnerve Comyn.

"This is certainly no' what I expected Moray."

Comyn shudders as he glances at Moray, he feels that the highest woodland boughs and branches are akin to a blackened mass of hellish blood veins, ready to collapse upon their heads and suck their souls and minds away to some evil underworld. Moray says, "Just ignore all the bones and concentrate on staying on this fuckin' path. I've seen this kinda shit before, one moment you're walking on what yie think is soft boggy ground, the next thing is the earth gives way to an ancient bog and yer gone. I've seen whole men and their horses disappear in the blink o' an eye walking on top of one o' these things. Stick to the path..." Comyn says, "And how will we do that Moray, we cannae even see the fuckin' path, these wicked briar thorn patches are as tall as we are on our horses, and as deep as there is no end to it that I can see." Moray says, "Then we'd better be walking with a tender foot and keep on going, for we can't back out now." Comyn looks around and reluctantly agrees with Moray's assessment, they have really no other choice but to keep moving forward on the hidden pathway between the trees and branches, lavishly decorated with human and animal bones or laid out delicately upon luxurious looking green padded boulder mosses.

Cautiously, the two friends ride on towards a destination unknown, to meet with a fate unknown. After following a westward flowing stream awhile, they feel they are making good progress in getting deeper into the forest, then they notice a heavy pungent odour as they come to an opening at the end of the dense track. "For fucks sake," exclaims Comyn, "There are more dead bodies just over there, that's what's stinkin' the place just up ahead of us."

Peering a little distance ahead, they could make out a cluster of five or six bodies, all piled against a sheer face rockwall. The bodies appear as though they are cowering in fear from some evil demon, but they are now long dead and past caring. Moray shakes his head, "It looks like a pile o' dead English soldiers?" Comyn says, "And tortured too by the look o' terror on the remains of their dried-out and rat-chewed faces." The two colleagues search for a route past the putrefying bodies, then they realise they have travelled awhile along a dead-end. "Another wall o' feckn briars." sighs Comyn. Moray replies, "We'll have to follow some other route, or we may finish our journey like those poor bastards did back there." Comyn says, "This whole damned place is the devil's fuckin' trap Moray." They patiently and methodically traverse through the dense undergrowth of the woodland floor, only to be frustrated time after time when greeted with false routes into closed gullies, sheer wall faces, impassable peat bogs or dead-ends, but their persistence keeps them slowly riding west and onwards. Comyn whispers, "Moray, there's something recently dead nearby, can you smell it in the air?" Moray acknowledges Comyn's observation. They slowly pull their swords from their scabbards and lay them across their saddles. Gripping the handle tight, Moray enquires quietly, "What's that hanging in the trees up ahead of us?" Comyn squints his eyes, "I don't know? We should move forward and see though, for waiting here abouts is no' a choice that I wish to make."

Gaining closer to the objects, they observe many human carcasses with recently rotting flesh still attached, with human scalps and hair arranged in some ritualistic symbolic display. As they move on past the makeshift carcass alter, they see hanging from trees along their chosen route, full skeletal remains wearing what appears to be the remnants of English soldier attire. Two carcasses in particular, hang grotesquely in the centre of their path, like bags of human bones, all held together by their own leathery skin torn into binding strips. Comyn looks closely as he passes one of the ghoulish sentinels. "They too wear the garb of the English soldiery." Moray shakes his head, "I suppose if all these bodies that dress this woodland are English; then we may just survive our foolish journey after all." Comyn replies, "Aye, if it be human hands that's placed them so, but if it's the devil spirits or revenants from these woods Moray, then I fear that we are dead men walking."

For many long hours they journey through the sinister woodland, with the darkness of late afternoon magnifying the sinister gloominess of the Wolf and wildcat forest.

Differing scents of rotting woodland and carcass become familiar enough for them to notice the pungent change of scents getting stronger. Moray whispers, "They're on either side of us." Comyn replies, "I know, I reckon they've been following us awhile now and I can hear more behind us." Moray exclaims, "Fuck it…" he pulls his sword tight. Comyn too grips his sword, then he enquires, "Are they human?" Moray replies, "I fuckin' hope so, but I'm starting to think that we should never entered this damned place."

Comyn readies himself, "Follow us if they must, but should one of these creatures show me its face, then I swear to yie, I will sheer it clean from its fucking head."

The erstwhile pair nervously continue to wind their way through the thick woodland as though hypnotically following a path to their own doom; such is the tense atmosphere of their trance-like journey. Suddenly Moray's horse startles and pulls back, "Look… over there," exclaims Comyn. Moray says, "Let's get in there, quick."

They both ride fast towards the glowing edge of a small circular clearing and halt. At first glance the little glade appears to be floored with layers of white chalk and crushed seashells, luminescent and contrasting drastically with the sullen dark brown woodland and grey overhanging sky. Comyn says, "Look Moray, the clearing has about twelve exits to choose from." The dense woods and briar patches surrounding the clearing, makes the throughway channels visually pronounced, akin to natural cloisters in some magnificent cathedral. Moray says, "It looks as though the woodland is now offering us up some options as to which route we may take." Comyn shakes his head, "This is getting fae bad tae worse." Nudging their horses slowly forward, sharp crackling noises underfoot could be heard as the iron shod hooves sink deep into the shell covered floor of the clearing, making the horses even more skittish. They both look down and notice that it isn't marine shells they are walking over, but a thick layer of smashed human and animal skulls, covering an array of rotting bodies underneath, all laid out in unnatural positions, like sacrificial offerings from an ancient tribe. Moray says, "It's obvious that whoever chose these unfortunate individuals, has applied a slow end to the wretche's lives by employing on them every conceivable method of bone-breaking murder known to man." Comyn says, "Aye, restricted only by the limits of imagination."

Moray and Comyn look around in disbelief. Some bodies appear relatively fresh, with their entrails strung out around the clearing, others appear to have been killed a long time ago, with their wind-dried flesh pulling back over bleach-white bones to reveal grinning skulls, now home to green and yellow jelly mosses and industrious insects. Many more bodies hang from the tree boughs with dry gaping throat wounds opened grotesquely to the elements.

"What are we goin' to do now?" enquires Comyn. Before Moray can reply, yells, whistles and hoots come from all around them. Startled, the horses spook into the centre of the clearing, scattering and breaking bones with loud cracking noises, making it even more difficult for Moray and Comyn to control their steeds. Eventually they regain control of their horses, then they see that they are surrounded by near naked teenage boys and girls emerging from the woodland, all armed with makeshift woodland bows, long darts, blackened cudgels and long sharpened sticks. Some of them are dressed in a macabre mix of dank oversized aketon's, with green-brown hemp léine and large leather brats, appearing to be made from human skin as well as animal hide. Many more teenagers emerge, all wearing strange looking head-dresses and human flesh facemasks, with horns and small antler of beast attached to bizarre looking helmets. Their bodies are covered with reddish mud and blue wode. Others have long gnarled hair, hanging like unkempt rat's tails, entwined within, are small finger bones and amber orbs, it appears as though these young warriors have stepped out from the ancient legends of the Aicé. Comyn whispers, "Are these hellish brownies following us to claim our souls?" Moray replies, "Naw, they're Gallóglaigh Ceitherne Comyn."

Moray and Comyn gaze at this encirclement of incredulous looking youngsters. They pull their horses around in circles, but it is obvious there can only be one way out, and that is to fight through these entities that appear half human and half animal, but yet they are not much more than children, who stand motionless, watching them silently, intently. Comyn says, "I have never seen the likes Moray, even when I travelled with my father to the Crusades." Another group begins to emerge throughout the woodland perimeters. Stepping silently from the dense forest into the clearing, these are powerfull looking warriors, walking tall and wearing deep conical helmets, their faces obscured by large beards with black mud packed heavily under their eyes, with finger bones and amber stones tied throughout the beard hair. "Gallóglaigh," whispers Moray.

These fearful looking warriors carry their infamous spartaxe, every second individual is an equally determined looking Gallóbhan, dressed in similar garb of cross-stitched metal studded aketon, but without the chainmail. They carry short horse-bows ready knocked with deadly hunt arrows. Other women of the Gallóbhan hold their hellish ring spears at the ready, while others flash their infamous curved blades, the sgian cuartha. Moray and Comyn sit motionless as the primeval looking warriors silently make their way through the young Ceitherne to the front, then they stand shoulder-to-shoulder, completely enclosing Moray and Comyn in a ring of impenetrable chainmail, steel and a forest of lethal looking weaponry. "Gallóbhet," utters Moray. Comyn replies, "Naw, they're devils ah tell yie."

Comyn grips his sword and bravely spur his horse forward towards a section of warriors that surround them, but the group he rides towards holds stoically firm, aiming their ring spears directly between the eyes of Comyn's horse. Most of the spartaxe men and ring spear women raise their weapon points; while other Gallóglaigh silently raise their axes high, preparing to fell the horse. The Gallóbhan between each Gallóglaigh, aim their fierce hunt arrows at Comyn's heart, and though Comyn's horse is bred from the same exquisite Arab-Andalusian cross stable of warhorse as Moray, and trained well to the sights and sounds of battle, it quickly shies away.

Frustrated, Comyn pulls back over beside Moray and waits. There is a long silence that is soon followed by a low volume snake-like hissing noise, an unnatural and unnerving sound made by the young Ceitherne standing behind the Gallóbhet. As the hissing gains louder, it begins to severely spook the horses of Moray and Comyn. Again, Comyn attempts to break free through the cordon, but he could gain no vantage. Eventually he pulls up his horse beside Moray once more. Comyn exclaims, "This is fuckin' madness ah tell yie…" But Moray doesn't acknowledge Comyn, for he's keenly watching the unmovable Gallóbhet, suddenly Moray calls out, "Who is your chief? We are here on urgent business on behalf of King John of Scotland. We seek only to engage in a peaceful parlay with the Wolf and wildcat chief, Mac Álainn Mòr…" The silence by reply is deafening as Moray's voice echoes round the unnatural theatre. Moray calls out once more,

"I am here to…" but his words are lost when the hissing sound from the Ceitherne begins once more, as though all the snakes of the forest are weaving their way through the dense gathering. Suddenly the cause of the sound bursts through the front ranks of Gallóbhet.

Moray and Comyn look on in amazement as they gaze into the faces of young male and females, all are near-naked, save for large gamebags hanging from their shoulders. Their bodies appear to be covered in layers of red clay, with symbolic ancient knotwork designs in ochre and wode painted on their bodies. Their long unkempt tousled hair hangs down their backs as their Ceitherne brethren. Suddenly a shrill loud whistle pierces the air, then the young Ceitherne immediately step forward; reach into their bags and begin hurling what appears to be small wet mud balls at the two knights of the realm. Upon impact, the mud balls explode when hitting Comyn and Moray, the contents cover them in a layer of flour grit. The few balls that miss, have the young throwers quickly rewarded by a hefty and vicious slap on the back of the head from a nearby Gallóbhet, encouraging greater accuracy for the next throw. Comyn wipes flour-dust from his face… "What the fuck is this?"

"Grit," replies Moray, as he too wipes the flour from his face, relieved, he sighs, "If they had really meant us harm, this should have been quicklime and it would have blinded us." Another piercing whistle is heard and the bombardment of mud balls ends as suddenly as it had begun. The young Ceitherne run back towards the woods, as another group runs through them towards Moray and Comyn, but this time the youngsters carry curved-bows notched with arrows. "Look out…" shouts Moray. But it is hopeless as they are struck by a fusillade of arrows. The horses rear and panic; but have nowhere to escape, as the stinging impact of the small arrows strike both riders and their horses. Another loud whistle is heard and the attack stops immediately. Comyn pulls out an arrow entangled in his long hair and examines it. The arrow is flighted with magpie feathers and has a tiny lead ball instead of an arrowhead at the end of the shaft. He throws it to the ground, raging, "Fight me, you unnatural spawn of devil seed, or let us pass on the King's business." But no reply comes from the surrounding warriors.

Long moments pass till a voice eventually speaks from behind them in a soft southern Irish lilt… "Me lords Moray and Comyn, now what brings such dainty young ladies as yourselves into a place fit only for true warriors?" Moray and Comyn spin their horses round to find who had spoken to them thus, but they face another expressionless part of the encirclement. Moray glances at the grim faces. He queries them, "You know who we are?" the voice replies, "Aye, that we do, for you fuckin' nobles like everyone to know who yie are, by yiez wearing of all those fancy colours and symbols that yiez like to call yer very own?" Moray replies, "Then you must know that we're not here as your enemy, we're here on our King's business…"

A tall Gallóglaigh drops his spartaxe by his side and steps out of the ring of steel, "I heard yee the first time." Moray speaks directly to the Gallóglaigh… "Are you Mac Álainn Mòr?" The giant Gallóglaigh pulls his conical helmet back from his face and laughs, "Me name is Hayde, and hell is me business, though I am a kinsman of Mac Álainn mòr. So you be tellin' me Moray, what's yer business with me chief?" Moray replies, "It is between your chief and I; we are…" Before Moray can finish, Hayde spits on the ground and shouts aloud, "Fuck you, fuck your King and fuck any noble who would dare set an unwanted foot into the Wolf and wildcats. This is our domain, there's only one law here and that is the Breitheamh law, enforced by our Chief and our people." Two virtually unseen Gallóbhan archers step forward, with deadly arrows ready to loose, Hayde raises his hand to pause them. The lead archer speaks quietly, but firmly, "Hayde, if you lay even a breath on my flights ever again, I will slit your fuckin' throat from ear to ear, then I'll use yer family as hog food." Hayde laughs, "Sure now, I wouldn't expect any less from you or any Gallóbhan Faolán." Moray and Comyn hear Hayde's comment, Moray enquires, "Faolán, Is that you?" Faolán doesn't reply, but instead she speaks to Hayde… "Will we stick them dead?" Hayde thinks a moment; "Naw, no' yet, ah'll send word back to Mac Álainn mòr, let him decide the fate of these trespassers."

Hayde turns towards a couple of Ceitherne, whispers to them; then they run off into the woodlands. Hayde scowls at Moray and Comyn, he says, "Time my lords, is all that you have left this day, and we will know how much of that remains for yiez soon enough."

"Faolán…" enquires Moray, "is it really you?" Faolán replies, "Aye, of course it is, fool." Moray says, "Don't yie remember me?" Faolán replies curtly, "Should I?" Moray continues, "Aye, we met at Saint Johns of Dalry when de Brix faced off the Guardian army, we stood together on the same side, we even…" Faolán growls, "There is no *'we'* Moray, nor ever will be, you're a fuckin noble." Hayde spits out these words, "Say nothing more Moray, or we will split yer tongue in half to be sure, then you will have to scrieve down your urgent business on a slate for our Chief. Now uze be sittin' your lardy arse's still on your fuckin' horses, shut your mouths and be awaitin' the pleasure of the Mac Álainn mòr. Make a move that displeases us and we'll cut yer flesh so deep, but no' to be killin' yie mind, for we must keep yie alive long enough to hear yer story." The Ceitherne slowly fade away into the woodland, leaving an impenetrable ring of Gallóbhet surrounding Moray and Comyn in the bizarre theatre of bones. Moray and Comyn look at each other in resignation, having no other choice but wait till word comes back from Mac Álainn mòr, word that will decide their fate... They sit and wait impatiently, searching every inch of their surrounding situation, from the expressionless antiquated warriors surrounding them, to the dried-out entrails and fresh bodies hanging in grotesque positions in the trees around and above them. Moray notices many of the carcasses have remnants of English army tabards hanging in pieces from their bodies, but not all. They soon begin to study the faces of the Gallóbhan, men with their conical helmets and the women with their leather aketon armour and hooded brats. They all appear to have patches of living woodland moss growing on their shoulders, such is the bizarre setting before the eyes of the two 'civilised' nobles. The thick floor of white broken bones and skulls crack occasionally underfoot as the horses move about and fidget.

After a while, with both Moray and Comyn's nerves straining, the noise of a galloping horse could be heard close-by, suddenly a rider breaks through into the clearing, his appearance is a welcome relief from the seemingly hours of waiting, the rider calls out, "Moray, Comyn, follow me." then the rider leans over and whispers something to Hayde and Faolán, who immediately signal at a glance to the ranks of Gallóbhet, who in turn drop their guard and begin chatting freely, curiously they disperse as though they were on a joyous springtime woodland stroll.

The strange rider walks his horse close to Moray and Comyn. As he pulls his horse beside them, the rider grins, leans towards them and says, "Wallace sends his regards and hopes you two were well entertained while you waited."

Moray exclaims, "Wallace… William Wallace?" The rider smiles, "Aye, none other. So let me be introducing me'self, me name is Stephen ua Mac h'Alpine, but uze can call me Stephen of Ireland." Comyn enquires, "The real William Wallace?" Stephen glares at Comyn, "Are yie feckn' deaf man?" Moray enquires once more, "You mean, William Wallace… from glen Afton and ach na Feàrna?" Stephen replies proudly, "None other, he himself, aye, that will be him." Moray and Comyn look at each other in confusion, Moray exclaims, "But I thought Wallace had been killed by the English a few months ago?"

Stephen grins with enthusiasm as he turns Fleetfoot to follow the Gallóbhet, now disappearing into the woodland pathways. Eventually he replies, "Sure now, he was dead." Moray and Comyn look at each other in astonishment. Comyn says, "This cannot be true, everyone knows that William Wallace was executed by the English in Ayr town awhile back." Moray says, "I don't know what's going on here, but if Wallace is alive, this is the best news I've had in months." Comyn looks around to find that they are now alone, he enquires, "Where did they all go?" Stephen saunters away from the clearing, "Will you ladies be making sweet love? Or will yiez be following me?"

Nudging his horse to walk on, Stephen lazily wanders away into the woodland.

Moray and Comyn quickly catch up with the meandering Stephen. Moray frowns then he enquires, "So Wallace really is alive?" Stephen smiles, "Sure now, if I tell you once I would think yee to be a whole wit, if I tell yee twice, are yee a bleedin' half-wit?" Moray glares at Stephen in anger; then quickly relents to amused curiosity. "Stephen, you can surely understand, that by us hearing that Wallace is still alive, it comes as a much welcome surprise, for it was made very public by the English that Wallace had been executed in Ayr town, for the killing of a squire called Selby, numerous English knights and various soldiery, they made much ado declaring his death." Comyn says, "If Wallace is alive, then it's truly a miracle… or he's a revenant." Stephen says with a grin, "Now you fella's, there will be none o' that religious shite talked in here." Moray enquires, "So tell us then Stephen, how did Wallace survive?" Stephen replies, "The English, aye well, they killed him right enough, but our bonnie Wallace is a tough young fella to be sure."

Moray and Comyn look at each other in confusion, and frustration. Comyn demands, "For fuck's sake Stephen, my patience has been sorely tested already, do not fuck with us… tell us, is Wallace alive or is he dead?" Pulling on the reigns of Fleetfoot, Stephen glares and scowls at the two companions; then he turns away again and resumes his lazy meander. "Well," says Stephen, "He was dead, but true Tam, ma'self and a few others refused to believe it, so didn't we hunt all o' Scotland looking for him, it was only when true Tam was in a wee place near the Eildon hills called the Luckenhare, a'trystin' wit' his lover the bonnie Elvin queen, she told true Tam to lay his head upon her bosom then he would see Wallace was alive and where he was…" Comyn interrupts, "Hold your heathen tongue still yie filthy Irish dog, for yie make a mockery of the true faith with your evil…"

Comyn doesn't finish his outburst, as Stephen swiftly pulls out a keen edge dirk from under his aketon and swiftly sticks it against Comyn's throat. "Fuck you," exclaims Stephen in anger, "You fuckin' nobles and your one true God shite, you bastards murder freely all who will not believe in your so-called faith. Then you have the gall to question me about me own faith, a man who wages war on none from another belief or because of it, all except the English of course." Moray sits motionless, such was the speed of events, he says, "Stephen, have a care with Comyn, for he is of the faith of the Céile Aicé too, we have just fought a month-long running battle with the Brus and his Pact, seeking justice for the murder and butchery of his kinfolk." Stephen glares at Comyn, then says, "This noble prick here shows disdain for ma faith, yet faith to us is not the sole property o' one religious cult like you Christian fuckers think it to be." As Stephen and Comyn eye each other bitterly, Moray speaks, "I beseech yie both, these are trying times for all of us, this anger, should we strike each other down, can only benefit our common enemy."

The two adversaries continue to glare at each other, then Comyn raises his hand and grips the dirk blade of Stephen, blood begins to run down the blade as the standoff continues. Comyn speaks, "Slit my throat if you must Irishman, for my faith will nurture me after my death, of this I have no fear, but accept my genuine regret from my harsh and thoughtless words, and more so, any offence that I have caused to you and your faith." Comyn opens his bleeding hand and waits. Stephen looks at Comyn awhile, then slowly his determined glare softens. Suddenly Stephen whips the blade away from Comyn's throat, cleans the blade on his leathers, tucks it away again and grins. "Ach me bonnie Comyn," says Stephen, "what kind of host would I be if I were to slit yer bleedin' throat before ah'v even fed ya?" Stephen happily nudges Fleetfoot on, leaving Moray and Comyn looking at each other bewildered, but very much relieved.

The three erstwhile companions ride on wearily as night begins to fall. More long hours slowly pass till eventually, they find themselves entering another clearing that opens up to a beautiful panoramic late evening vista. Moray and Comyn sigh with relief when they see hearth smoke rising through the thatched roofs of many obhainn's and Clachan's, stretching sporadically the full length of a beautiful glen, with evening fires lighting up the darkening depths of this special place. Moray and Comyn notice the faint sounds of children laughing and music filling the air with mirth and joy, all coming from the inhabitants dwelling in the secretive mystical glen Eden of Mac Álainn Mòr. Stephen leads Moray and Comyn down a dangerously slim pathway towards the glen basin, though the two visitors are completely unaware of Gallóbhet guard eyes watching their every move as they negotiate their way down the brae-side, till they eventually enter the secretive village.

As they wander through a Balloch, they observe the goings-on of the inhabitants. Occasionally someone looks at them and smiles, while others would wave a warm welcome. They ride on farther untill they come to a great central fire, where it appears as though all the glen children and old folk are gathered to hear a clarsach player strumming gently, while a wise old seanachaidh tells of a wondrous and fabulous legend. Passing by the community gathering, Moray points at the seanachaidh and whispers to Comyn, "That's true Tam the mystic, and that's Alan o' Annandale beside him pluckin' away on the strings." Stephen says, "No need to be whispering ladies and aye, that's true Tam of Ercildoune sure enough, and this night he will be telling all those wains the legends of Tristan of Loth and Iseult, the beautiful daughter of Conchobar mac Nessa of Tara, a foin Scotch-Erinach tale if ever there was one to be told." True Tam calls out, "That was last eve's tale Stephen. This eve they will learn o' the ancient warrior, Cundda ap Edern Mannau, Chieftain of the Gwŷr y Gogledd s' y ClachMhanainn (King Cundda of Earn, the men of the North and the Stone of Clackmannan.) True Tam winks then returns to the telling of tall tales with the enchanting accompaniment of Alan o 'Dale's clarsach. Comyn says, "Strange it is Moray, that however savage the doings of these people are and the obscure faith they still believe in, whatever they believe, it lets them smile wie' warm hearts for strangers. Moray, I must surely tell you, I've no' felt such peace nor savoured the harmonic accord of happiness to both my ears and to my heart for many a long year in Scotland, not as I have since entering this wonderous glen." Moray sighs, "Ah do agree with yie there Comyn, a few moments o' sharing the same air as these fine people, it makes me think that it's a long time, even since before the death of Alexander, have I felt such freedom and nurture o' a clan gathering, I feel the same peace coming from all o' them as you do my friend... despite our earlier welcome." They both laugh as they ride slowly through the village, discussing the sights of this secretive place in the heart of the infamous Wolf and wildcat forest, then Comyn notices something...

"I see a characteristic in this place that's long gone in the rest o' Scotland." Says Comyn. Moray enquires, "Aye, and what's that?" Comyn replies, "I see these people are not cowed, nor do they scuttle about in the dark, fearful of mounted knights, nor are they pulling their forelocks in base servitude towards us." Moray smiles, "Maybe the faith they cling to is archaic and not of our world Comyn. But if this is what their faith provides, then perhaps we should be fighting for their right to believe as much as our own right to worship as we deem to be proper." Moray pauses and looks around at all the happy faces of the Balloch as they pass by. "Now I see that at least one man in Scotland knows not just tolerance of different faiths is the route of civilisation, but all faiths uniting as a community makes a truth of the word." Comyn replies, "Aye, and that man you speak o' was good King Alexander. He knew by uniting not just faiths, but different cultures too, and then practicing those faiths freely in a master's home is his own affair. He knew how to enthuse all and suppress the avarices of hotheads to make our realm a true civilisation." Moray enquires, "How the fuck did Alexander ever manage it Comyn?"

Overhearing the conversation, Stephen says, "Faith in the Tuatha de Cruinne cè, Magda mòr and usin' the Breitheamh prescriptives, or what you mainlanders call the Brethlaw. We believe in the divine tri-Goddess, that would be, Mother earth, mother nature and yer own mother to you fellas, aye, nurture those three deities and they will sure look after and nurture you." Moray and Comyn nod in agreement. Moray says, "Aye, you could be right Stephen." Comyn enquires, "Irishman, if you Cruinne cè are so placid, tranquil and owe so much to your so-called freedom of individual thought by living as one with nature, why do employ the ghastly tortured remains of wretches that hang grotesquely in these woods and stirring the very bile of righteous men to do vengeance upon the perpetrators?"

Calmly, Stephen replies, "Those so-called wretches and many men like them Comyn, they're but paid back tenfold for what they have already brought to me and mine. For I have lived and loved in peace, offering malice to none, yet these Sudrons came to my place of sanctuary, where my wife, child and unborn dwelt with the kin of Wallace. Those men, and others like them, cared not for the peace that I provided for my wife and children, the bastards tortured and murdered them in such a manner so vile…" Stephen falters. Comyn, replies, "I'm so sorry Stephen, I didn't know." Recovering his composure, Stephen says, "Sure now fellas. If men of this Christian faith wish to employ such holy conversions upon the people I'm sworn to protect, not only as a man, but as a hereditary Céile Aicé, then it's best and fair that we be warnin' these emissaries of your one true God's army well in advance, o' what they will surely be receiving by way of payment for the doin' o' such pious work… them bein' so ignorant of our faith and all. But me fine inquisitive fellas, as you gain closer to our homesteads, you must have noticed that none o' those Christian wretches grace our inner peace?"

Comyn says, "It's against God's will to play with the mortal remains of the dead." Glaring at Comyn, Stephen says, "Aye, unlike you nobles Comyn, we don't have dungeons nor gibbets and cages to hang these wretches from our castle walls for all to see. We have only our common faith in nature that provides for and protects us. What you see hanging in those trees in all o' your ignorance, is what folks like uze base your haughty conclusions upon, that we are savage and in need of your lord's redemption, I think fuckin' not…" Angered by Stephen, Comyn sneers as he replies, "Then Irishman, you would be expecting me to believe that internal wars of the Irish and Scots didn't happen before Christianity reached our shores?" Stephen laughs, heartily, then says, "You take the Cruathnie moon fella, and you look at it in good faith Comyn, all of us see it, but each of us sees it different from the next man, woman or child, but you Christians insist we must see it only your way or we die?" Comyn thinks awhile on Stephen's answer, he smiles then says, "Perhaps Stephen, it may be so that I've forgotten my own childhood faith."

"Q.E.D?" laughs Stephen, Moray laughs as a puzzled Comyn enquires, "What did he just say?" Moray replies, "Quod Erat Demonstrandum Comyn." Moray laughs again as Stephen enquires with a grin "Who's the ignorant savage now me foin fella?" Stephen looks at Comyn, who smiles then begins to laugh too. The atmosphere between the three young men becomes amiable, and a camradre of sorts begins to bond them. Stephen soon brings Fleetfoot to a halt in front of a large obhainn, much grander and longer than the others nearby and much taller too, with a magnificent carved arched doorway opening onto a raised platform, surrounded by stag, bull, grand ox skulls and long horse tail clutches that adorn lodge poles around the entrance. Moray also notices large Ravens are sitting and cackling on the entire ring of totemic lodge poles surrounding only that particular obhainn mòr. Dismounting, Stephen says, "You fella's just wait here by your horses, and I will be telling Mac Álainn mòr o' yer presence." Moray and Comyn rest easy, as Stephen disappears inside the obhainn mòr.

While they wait patiently, they both become aware of the sinister presence of many Gallóbhet in the nearby shadows, ever watchful of the two visitors, then Moray notices Faolán emerging from the obhainn mòr, followed by other ban-kern warriors, including Stephen and a large powerfull looking Gallóglaigh wearing a hooded brat that obscures his features. The giant warrior enquires, "What's yer business with Mac Álainn mòr, chief of the Wolf and wildcats?" Moray enquires, "Are you Mac Álainn Mòr?" The Gallóglaigh suddenly rages, "Answer the fuckin' question ya pair o' noble bastards."

Without warning, Moray and Comyn are gripped from behind with their arms pinned to their sides, at the same moment, the large Gallóglaigh launches himself from the doorway and grabs them both tightly by the throats, raising them up from the ground, squeezing and crushing their throats, when a voice calls out… "Torrance, will yie please be putting our guests back on the ground?" Torrance glares at Moray and Comyn. The voice commands once more, "Torrance, I asked yie nicely, put them down or by the wrath of Dénnaigh your goodwife, I will be telling her of how you treat our guests, and yie know she will no' be happy." Torrance reluctantly eases up on his grip; Moray and

Comyn drop to their feet, grasping at their throats while coughing and spluttering desperately. "Is that you Andrew Moray o' Avoch?" enquires the commanding voice, Moray looks up and sees another large hooded Gallóglaigh, he thinks that he recognises him. "Wallace?" The Gallóglaigh pulls back his hood.

"WALLACE…" Moray exclaims with joy.

William smiles when he sees it truly is his friends Moray and Comyn. William says with a grin, "Unless I'm a ghost, and by the way Moray, did yie bring some o' that sweet vegetable honey with yie?" Moray laughs, "Naw Wallace, there is a distinct shortage o' privilege abroad in Scotland recently, yie may have noticed?" The three friends embrace, then Comyn says, "Wallace, it's beyond words of expression to know yie are alive and how good it is to be seein' yie so, though I must say, yie are looking a wee bit peaky for a dead man." Comyn continues with a frown. He enquires brusquely, "Then tell us Wallace, for you're obviously not the walkin' dead by the look o' yie, are yie perhaps a revenant by chance? For all the world believes yie to be dead."

"Feck off…" laughs William. "Wallace?" enquires Moray, "then why did the English say you were dead, when it's so obvious you're not?" William grins, "I was." Moray and Comyn look at each other. William sees the consternation in their faces and continues, "Well, not dead exactly, true Tam calls it, 'the dead man's sleep.' I've seen it a few times in ma life, where someone never wakes from a terrible head wound awhile. I'll tell yie this though, I've no' any mind o' what happened. All I remember is being in the Laglan woods just outside Ayr town, the next thing I knew was waking up here with the Marion and true Tam tending to ma wounds." Moray and Comyn are still in awe at seeing their friend alive as William continues, "I've many broken bones yet and deep scars, enough to know that someone for sure wanted me dead." Comyn enquires, "What's that on your leg and arm?" William holds up an arm that appears to be encased in a strange looking cemented garment of sorts, as is his leg, "Ach it's an eel and egg-white poultice stookie, held together with straps of willow to mend my broken bones straight. True Tam brought a chirurgeon with him to help ma recovery, if it hadn't been for Tam's magical elixirs and Marion's breast milk, I sure would be worm food and long since dead by now otherwise."

"Maid Marion…" exclaims Moray, "is she's here?"

"Aye she is, and he's no longer the maid Marion," says William with a grin, "she's now Marion Wallace. We committed to our grand Cruathnie haun-fèis here, then we had at a secret wedding in saint Kentigerns in Lanark town to appease her God-fearing father."

Overjoyed, Moray happily shakes William's hand as Comyn slaps him on the back, instantly making William wince and cry out in pain. William tenderly pulls the brat away from his shoulders, revealing more poultices, now sodden in blood. "The English cut my back deeply then they stabbed me a few times as well. Fuck, but the feckn wounds are taking such a long time to heal though." A female voice nearby says, "Andrew Moray, is that you I see?" Moray looks round as a young woman throws her arms around his neck and hugs him dearly, Moray exclaims, "Brannah…" Barely containing her excitement at seeing Moray, she says, "Oh Andrew, how I have missed you so." Moray and Brannah embrace intimately; their love so strong and unashamed for all to see, then Moray notices another elegant woman appearing through the obhainn door. He exclaims, "Marion, you really are here…" Marion replies, "Andrew Moray, of all the people… I hope that you're not too injured by the welcome from our enthusiastic kinfolk?" Moray laughs, "Aye, it was a welcome to remember, I don't think there's any injuries though, ceptin' maybe ma pride Marion, but I'll check and let yie know later if I am still whole." Marion enquires, "And who is your friend?" Moray replies, "Marion, this here fella is John, known to most as the red Comyn." Comyn courteously introduces himself, "Marion, Brannah, such beauty to be found in this land of evil revenants and brigands." Suddenly the air becomes very tense by the remarks from Comyn. The happy smiles on the Gallóbhet standing nearby disappear. Wallace stands back a little and looks at Comyn in surprise and slightly amused curiosity.

"Naw Comyn," says Torrance, "it is you who have come into our homes from the land o' the evil spirits." Comyn replies, "Friends, please forgive me my base and thoughtless words. And not only those spoken here to your very ears, but also, on our route from the edge of this forest, I spoke so carelessly to Stephen too. But if the people of the Wolf and wildcats intend to instill fearful thoughts upon any stranger who dares to enter this place, then please let it be known, your logic strikes deep into the hearts of the unwary, and it does truly linger a long time deep in the soul. This truth ah tell to you my kind hosts, is also my humble apology. It's a poor excuse, but I hope it explains where those rash and thoughtless words were born..."

The silence continues awhile, then William says, "I couldn't have said it better me'self Comyn, I suppose our initial welcome and hospitality does take a wee bit o' getting used to. C'mon into ma obhainn fellas, for it's getting' a bit chilly standing out here debating the welcome, we mustn't be forgettin' our duty of hospitality to our friends." Stephen looks at William and laughs, "Our woodland decorations, they work right enough then..." Torrance smiles and drapes his arm around the shoulders of the red Comyn and begins brushing him down, much to Comyn's consternation. Marion smiles, "Yes, please do come inside, we've prepared some vittals and a grand fire, and you must be very tired from your long journey. We've known of your approach from Scone for the last five days, though we thought you'd have been here long before now."

"Wallace," says Moray, "I am truly grateful for your warm and generous welcome, but I must be speaking with Mac Álainn mòr, I'm here on desperate business concerning our rightful King, John Baliol, it's with great urgency regarding the state of the realm." Brannah giggles as Marion replies, "Please good knights, come into the chiefs obhainn and you may state your business in there." An enthusiastic Brannah says, "Come Andrew, for you both look almost starved to death." Moray looks at William, still amazed seeing his friend. "Wallace you're alive..." Stephen, exclaims, "For feck's sake Moray, didn't I tell you it was so?"

Brannah clasps Moray by the arm, while Stephen joyfully slaps Moray on the back as they all follow William and Marion into the grand obhainn. Comyn keeps looking at the giant Gallóglaigh Torrance, the very epitome of a gentle red haired but very murderous Ettin, who now holds open the obhainn door for his newfound friend. On entering the obhainn mòr, Comyn, who is unfamiliar with the interior of such places, is flabbergasted as he becomes aware of the interior surrounds. He sees thick lush rugs on the floor, layers of thick padded fleece insulation draping on the sidewalls. Hanging between the ribs of the obhainn, are many weapons and shields, all brightly illuminated by a plethora of candles. He also notices there are large and luxurious looking sleeping cribs and thick padded long-seats. As they walk further along fine oak plank flooring into the depths of the obhainn, they meet a beautiful young woman with long thick brown curled hair tied in chords, breastfeeding a child next to the central peat hearth. "Moray, Comyn…" says William "I would like to introduce you to Mharaidh Morríaghan Wallace." Moray and Comyn hold out their hands towards the young woman, "Ah," exclaims William, "I should have said this fine young woman is Brìghde, milk mother to young Mharaidh." Moray looks at William, then points at the child. He exclaims, "You mean…?" William smiles as Moray grins and continues, "Mharaidh Morríaghan?"

Brìghde stands up and passes the infant to William who then sits down, tentatively stretching out his injured leg beside the hearth, while cooing to the young child. He looks up at Moray and Comyn, "My friends, this is ma bonnie daughter, Mharaidh Morríaghan Wallace, ma very own bonnie wee Aicé." Marion proudly drapes her arms around William's shoulders, then she sits on his lap and says, "Moray, Brannah is preparing an obhainn uisge beg for you both and it'll be ready soon. I've also arranged for some fresh hot vittals that are now being prepared, for it looks as though you have not eaten in a very long time." Grinning, Moray leans over and puts his finger out for little Mharaidh Morríaghan, she grips it firmly and smiles, he clucks as she grins, then he says, "Is she named after Marion?" William replies, "Well aye, though it's also in memory o' wee Maw, Malcolm's Margret, Marion's birth mother and my father's wife Mharaidh." Moray nods thoughtfully upon hearing this and continues to play with Mharaidh's little hand and fingers, then a thought suddenly comes to him, he looks at William…

"Lady Mharaidh and Alain o' glen Afton?" William replies, "Aye…" There is a moment's silence as Moray looks curiously at William. The glance between them then the hint of a smile from William, gives something away, then Moray, in a moment of realisation, blusters, "You're Mac Álainn mòr, aren't yie?" William grins, Moray laughs as Comyn exclaims, "Really Wallace, you're Mac Álainn mòr, the notorious brigand chief?" William laughs, "Aye, the very same." Comyn then laughs too, "Ah don't fuckin' believe it, you're Mac Álainn mòr, of course you are, in the Gaelic… you're the son of great Alain." William waves his hand and says, "Sit down ma friends, you two be takin' the weight of yer armoured hides." Torrance shouts from outside the obhainn, "Wallace, ahm bringin' in some fine padded benches for the delicate dainty arses of those two nobles." Moray and Comyn appear a little annoyed at Torrance's comment; then everyone begins laughing when Torrance and Stephen bring in chairs that appear to have been liberated from some English baggage train, as they were obviously not crafted locally. The chairs are placed around the central hearth, where everyone takes a seat in a circle to talk.

"Fuck," exclaims Moray, "You really are Mac Álainn mòr, we should have known, but we couldn't have, for all think you dead."

"Of course," laughs Comyn, "it all makes sense now." William smiles, "Nobody outside the Gallóbhet can yet find out I'm still alive or the English may try to find me, and the consequences would be too great for the people here and for ma uncle Ranald. When true Tam and Stephen brought me here, everyone thought me dead, but as you see, I'm very much alive. The folks here believe I was saved by Neachneohain, the fairy Queen lover o' true Tam, so the Gallóbhet…" Comyn says, "Whoa, just wait there Wallace, not you too?" William enquires, "What ails yie Comyn, yie look as though yie might o' seen a ghost?" Comyn replies, "Naw, it's this fairy queen nonsense. I can understand it from Stephen, as I do believe it's truly his faith, but not from you,

you being a Christian and talking about being saved by some Elvin' Queen of the underworld?" Marion lifts little Mharaidh to her bosom, William smiles, "I forgot about the sensibilities of the outside world Comyn, but however you may believe it, true Tam found out about ma whereabouts. The English assumed me dead in their dungeons, so they dumped ma body in the castle shit-moat that runs into the river Ayr to carry away all the rotting carcasses. That's where true Tam and Stephen found me."

"Then tell us?" enquires Comyn, "how did true Tam know exactly where to find you?" William replies, "After true Tam spoke…" William pauses and looks at Comyn. Moray shakes his head and smiles. Torrance and Stephen grin, then Stephen laughs and says, "Go on Wallace, tell him again." William exclaims, "Fuck it… here's a Christian version. True Tam was on his way back here from the Eildon hills, he rested awhile at St. Mary's abbey of Fáile near Machlainn, where he met with Eddie óg, who told him that I had left the Laglan with Cormack for Ayr, they all worked it out from there. True Tam dressed up in a monk's outfit and gave some auld spey-wifey a groat to say she was ma milk mother, then he paid the jailers to have ma body given a Christian burial."

"You're one lucky feckr Wallace." quips Moray. William looks at Marion then replies, "I sure know that Moray." Marion stands up with the child, "I'm going to the lower hearth now, for little Mharaidh needs her feeding. Good Sirs, your obhainn uisge beg will be nigh ready, so if you'd like to prepare?" Comyn and Moray stand up as Marion retires to the far end of the obhainn, to breast feed little Mharaidh. William enquires, "So what brings you fella's here at the risk of your lives to ask o' me something, and aye, what the fuck possessed yiez to attack de Brus in Carlisle?" Moray and Comyn look at each other, then Comyn replies, "Wallace, we were attending the call of King John at Scone, he's gathering an army to sweep the English back across the border, but even now we're not sure what really happened next. News came to us that Brus of Carrick and his Pact were attacking our lands in the borders once more. King John excused the Comyn and Graeme's from the muster, for the men were beside themselves thinking of the safety of their loved ones. We immediately made for the borders, there we met Lord Hardy Douglas who was travelling with a force of three thousand loyal Scots, all moving to secure Berwick, for news had also come to king John that Longshanks was mustering a large army at Norham on the tweed. I tell yie this Wallace, when we reached our lands, it was as bad as we had ever seen, the killing and murder was beyond description..."

Comyn falters.

Moray then speaks, "Wallace, they soaked the land with Comyn blood. The Brus pact spared none the sword or headsman's axe, no man, no woman nor any child survived. Then Brus raided the Graeme and Baliol's territories, murdering all who dwelt there..." William replies, "Aye, I've heard this much from the Gallóbhet who followed yiez." Comyn says, "Brus the bastard, when we arrived in force, he retreated across the border and we made chase, but he just kept retreating, leaving the Welsh to fight us, and I am sorry Stephen, but there were Irishmen there fighting against us too. We killed them all, but Brus himself would not fight us. We kept up the chase till we reached Carlisle, it was there that Brus and his men hid in the safety of the castle. We surrounded the place for a month, but the Brus stayed put. We had no fuckin' siege engines so couldn't force them out." William says, "Brus didn't retreat to Carlisle castle, he lured yiez there, for he's the Constable o' Carlisle marches, he's Longshanks' man." Moray and Comyn are stunned to hear this information. "How do you know of this Wallace?" enquires Moray "This is our country too," replies William, "We've spies everywhere, but we were also at a loss as to what was happening in the border marches. I don't know, but I think we Scots have been duped into something. True Tam says that by you all chasing Brus over the border into England, and flying Scotland's royal colours, this gives the English King all the justification he needed to attack Berwick and secure its trading wealth as their own."

Comyn exclaims, "How could true Tam know of this?" William shrugs his shoulders, "Ah don't know how, but that's what he thinks." Stephen sighs, "Naw, that's what he sees." William enquires, "So why did you lift the siege of Carlisle Castle?" Comyn replies, "King John sent out heralds ordering everyone to gather near Dunbar, for he plans to retake Berwick. King John requires all of us who can raise even a pitchfork to stand by his side, that's the reason we were sent here to gain the support of Mac Álainn mòr's Gallóbhet." William replies, "You won't get the support of the Rhinns and Machars Gallóbhet, for they will no longer be involved in your noble's wars, nor will the Gallóbhet of the Wolf and wildcats."

Comyn is surprised to hear this. He says, "We need you and your Gallóbhet Wallace, Scotland needs all the warriors we can muster." Stephen says, "I'll go Wallace, let the Irish Gallóglaigh fight for Moray and Scotland, for here we have found a welcome home amongst yer kin, we will fight, we owe yiez that much." Torrance says, "I'll go too Wallace, for the English killed near all of my clan. I'll stand with Baliol." Faolán steps from the shadows, she says, "This is not our fight Moray, none of you nobles cared a fuck for the life of a Gallóbhan when we were being raped and butchered by the Pact but a few years ago. You noble bastards just stood aside whilst the Christians beat our heads bloody upon their shrines, forcing us to worship your one true God. Yet you turned your faces away from our plight, simply because we are women? Naw Moray, fight yer own war, for the Gallóbhan will remain here to protect our own."

All eyes are now focussed on William, he glances round and sees his love Marion breast-feeding little Mharaidh. Marion looks up with a countenance that chills William to his very soul. He looks again at everyone awaiting his reply. The silence in the obhainn mòr is unusual in the fastness of the Gallóbhet. William studies the faces of his friends, then says, "I am going to…" Suddenly Brannah and Chianna, a single girl of the Balloch, rush into the obhainn, obviously excited and dressed in very flimsy and revealing léine. Brannah appears as beautiful as her older sister Marion, it's apparent both she and Chianna have spent time preening themselves for the visitors.

Brannah walks over to Moray while Chianna makes eyes at the red Comyn. Brannah says, "That's the obhainn uisge beg ready, come my lords for we have everything prepared to wash away all your cares." Moray is surprised seeing Brannah thus; his thoughts are compounded by the intensity of the meeting and is perplexed by William's incomplete reply. Brannah senses something is amiss then Marion stands up from the feeding, she walks over with little Mharaidh in her arms and says, "Moray, Comyn, I think that you should be taking this opportunity to cleanse yourselves and relax from your exertions." She winks at Moray then says, "I'm sure you will both be the better for it." Marion continues, "Stephen, Torrance… I'll be having time with my husband if you please, for we have much to discuss." Everyone looks at each other; then William says, "Aye ma friends, do not dwell on the niceties of court life whilst you're our guests. Take up the homely offer from Brannah and Chianna, and when you are both rested, we'll talk further, for yie cannae be leaving our fastness till first light o' dawn anyways." Everyone leaves William and Marion to have some precious time together. William struggles to stand up as Marion puts little Mharaidh into her crib. When the child is finally asleep; Marion walks over to William where he wraps his arms around her. They sit awhile together on a soft crib near the lower fire, embracing passionately, but saying nothing as they stare thoughtfully into the flames of the fire. After a while, Marion enquires, "My love?" William replies, "Aye ma darlin?" Marion enquires with trepidation, "What is your will upon Moray's request?"

Dunbar Falls

Days turn to weeks, then into months, since the Gallóglaigh had departed from the Wolf and wildcat fastness, in the company of Andrew de Moray and the red Comyn. Their combined forces, numbering over five thousand, rode together as one to join with king John's twenty-three thousand strong army, to fight against the English invasion of Longshanks, who has brought over forty-five thousand barons, knights, cavalry and soldiers into Scotland. Life in the hidden glen at the heart of the Wolf and wildcat forest has become sullen, sombre and subdued, as fleeting news filters in that the Scots army has been slaughtered at the battle of Dunbar.

William and Marion sit in their obhainn mòr with true Tam, who is preparing to remove the resin-honey cast poultice from William's leg and arm, now fully healed from the breaks and fractures suffered at the brutal hands of the English soldiery in Ayr castle dungeons, five months since. "For fuck's sake Wallace," says True Tam, "yie would think I was trying to break yer leg, no' fix it. Feck me man, it's only a wee bit o' hair ahm pullin' and your cryin' like a newborn wain wie a well slapped arse." William winces, "But ma hair has grown back on ma leg since you first put that thing on Tam. Now the hairs are stuck to the feckn honey cast and…" William doesn't finish his sentence but roars instead when a white-hot pain rips through his body, as true Tam rips the cast completely from his leg in one single frenzied attack. Tam falls laughing from his stool as William immediately jumps up and down while holding his leg and screaming in pain. Marion laughs out loud while she nurtures wee Mharaidh Morríaghan. She says, "Och William, stop yer crying yie soft big lump, you're scaring the wain." She shakes her head, "It's a good thing that you men don't have baby's." While William moans and rubs his smooth leg, true Tam says, "There yie go Wallace, that was easy, wasn't it? Now give me your arm and we'll get that done next. Soon yie'll be able to go out and boot a haggis over the Black Craig hill like nothing ever happened to yie."

William naively looks at true Tam with a confused expression, then he tentatively relaxes as true Tam gently grips his arm, while deftly picking at the edges of the solidified honey-resin wrap, preparing the dried poultice for removal. William tenses himself for the impending removal of the arm-stookie, when True Tam glances at Marion and enquires, "Well Marion, have yie told him yet?" Looking at Marion curiously, William is confused by Tam's words. He looks at Marion then enquires, "Have yie told me what?" Marion smiles and pats her stomach, then she pats her stomach once more. William's eyes slowly light up with joy as he realises what she means. He exclaims, "Marion, YA DURTY BASTARD…"

"William," exclaims Marion, "surely you can't mean me?" Marion fakes shocked indignation as she teases him. But William doesn't reply, for True Tam has ripped off the poultice wrap in one mighty stroke, removing all of his arm hair with it. William vigorously rubs his now equally smooth skinned forearm, while glaring down at true Tam, but he quickly relents and grins. "You mean…" enquires William, almost in disbelief. Marion smiles, "Yes my love, I'm quite sure." She chuckles then she says, "I've missed my third moon so far, and that I think is a good sign." True Tam laughs, stands up and then he looks curiously toward the roof of the obhainn mòr. He strains his ear, completely un-noticed by William, who drops to his knees and places a hand on Marion's stomach. Totally elated and overjoyed, he says, "Another wee Wallace already?" Marion smiles, "At least one, Dénnaigh asked me if twins ran in our family and I said aye, both of us have that trait." William exclaims, "Two wains?"

True Tam mutters, "There's somebody comin'"

"I can't hardly believe it." says William. Both he and Marion are too engrossed in each other to notice true Tam's intense distraction. Marion smiles as she looks into the eyes of her Anam chara. Suddenly Brìghde and Brannah come running in, breathless and excited. "Wallace..." shouts Brìghde, "Don't yie hear the hunting horns? Stephen is coming back; he's leading a large force." William looks at Marion, "Do yie think...?" Marion says, "Go and see, I'll tend to little Mharaidh Morríaghan. You go and find out what's happening." William runs to the door, but his excitement is too great, he grins then runs back to Marion, "I don't want to leave yie." Marion laughs, "Och, away yie go William. I'm with child, not falling off a horse." William enquires, "Are yie sure?" Marion clasps William gently by his cheek, smiles then says "Do you see a horse?" she laughs, "I love you Wallace." He clasps her hand tightly, "I love you too... wee maw Wallace."

He jumps up and rushes towards the door, then he stops and glances back at Marion, who waves him away as she turns to nurture wee Mharaidh. William hastily follows true Tam outside, there he sees many of the Glen clan folk are also coming out from their obhainn's or workshops to look toward the eastern side of the glen, where it appears that three bedraggled columns of armed men are approaching. True Tam says, "It doesn't look se' good Wallace, those men look spent." William hears horses thundering up behind him. He turns to see armed Gallóbhan pass by to cover the rear of the incoming columns, two horses pull up beside him. He looks up and sees Faolán and Eochaidh Gunn. Faolán pulls hard on the flighty horse's reigns, then she says, "It's Torrance coming back with the forest guard Wallace. He's bringing in the Gallóglaigh who left to fight with Balliol. But by the look of them, there's no' se' many returning. I fear that the glen will be host to much weeping this night." Faolán and Eochaidh then spur their horses and gallop towards the Gallóglaigh now entering the glen basin.

William searches the front ranks of the approaching warriors as they gain closer, searching each wretched bloody face for friends, then, much to his relief, he sees Stephen with Torrance and Gormlaidh, all walking and leading their horses, with other Gallóglaigh dismounting or following on behind them. Relieved wives and children are greeting some of them, but so it is, the wailing begins, as many other families search for husbands, brothers, sons and daughters, only to be told that they would never be returning. True Tam walks towards the returning warriors, followed by William. Brìghde runs up to Stephen, but he falters and stumbles. Brìghde quickly catches him, but she struggles to support him. "Stephen…" exclaims William.

He rushes towards his friend and could see that most of the Gallóglaigh are all terribly battle-scarred and many are badly wounded, some are barely alive, yet still cling to their horses. The spread of injured men falling off their mounts to the ground behind them, are quickly being tended by the glen folk. William reaches Stephen and supports him with Brìghde. Stephen looks up and grins, "Wallace me foin friend, it's glad I am to be seeing yourself now." William can see that Stephen has been wounded many times and appears gravely ill. "What's happened to yie Stephen, where are the rest of the Gallóglaigh?" Stephen smiles, "Ach Wallace, I'll be tinkin' it didn't all go to plan. It was a much bigger party than we thought, but we sure left many o' the Sudrons toes up, many more than they left of our own fella's. But Wallace, the feckn English just kept coming, I've never seen so many blade-hoppers intent on throwing themselves onto our brands."

Stephen stumbles and falls to his knees; then he rolls onto his back, groaning in pain. Brìghde kneels beside Stephen and cradles his head, He looks up and clasps her long soft braided hair… "Ah me bonnie Brìghde, I've missed yie so much me darlin' girl." William kneels beside them as Stephen continues, "I couldn't not never be coming back Wallace, no' wit such a fine lovin' woman as Brìghde here to be caring for all me aches and pains." William is greatly relieved at his friend's good-spirited demeanor, and the display of tenderness that both Brìghde and Stephen obviously share.

William enquires with a knowing smile, "You and Brìghde then?" Stephen attempts a reply; but closes his eyes and passes out. Brìghde looks at William in despair. He stoops and lifts Stephen up in his arms. He says, "He'll be fine Brìghde, I think it's more that he's exhausted than death pained. We'll take him over to his obhainn, then I need it to be you that's tending his wounds untill true Tam and Dénnaigh can see to him. Will yie run on ahead of us and fix up a wee fire, sort out a fresh thick crib and then get a wee obhainn uisge beg heated to bathe him?" Brìghde strokes the unkempt hair away from Stephen's eyes, then she looks at William despairingly. William says, "He'll be fine Brìghde, I've seen him far worse from a night out on the craitur." Brìghde smiles nervously, lifts her skirts and runs as fast as she can towards

Stephen's obhainn to make preparation and tend to his wounds. Walking slowly behind her, carrying his friend in his arms, William watches Brìghde as she runs towards the obhainn, he looks at Stephen, "Yie kept that spring blossom quiet there me fine Irish brother." Stephen opens his eyes as though waking from a drunken sleep; he smiles and winks at William, then closes his eyes again. William grins with relief upon seeing the humour of his friend, though sorely wounded. Just to have Stephen back alive is enough for William to have faith that all is not lost. He carries Stephen to his obhainn and leaves him in the capable hands of Brìghde.

Upon leaving the obhainn, William watches the remains of the Gallóglaigh rearguard disperse, appearing extremely tired and fatigued, while others are being covered with shawls and brats where they had fallen from their horses… and died. William thinks there will be many pyres before this night is over. His solemn thoughts are broken when a voice nearby calls out, "Wallace?" He turns and is completely surprised when seeing a bedraggled and haggard looking monk, standing a little way just in front of him, wearing a bloodied grey cassock, carelessly open at the neck. Then he notices a bloodied hauberk. The monk pulls back his monastic hood, William instantly recognises him… "Dáibh, mo bràthair mòr." Dáibh is also a walking wounded combatant, but the smile on his face demonstrates he is in better condition than most who have returned, the two friends warmly embrace. William exclaims, "Dáibh what are yie doin' here? And yer still wearing that manky cassock you had on yie up in Dun Dèagh." Dáibh replies, "Ach Wallace, it's a long story, but ah'v found this auld cassock to be useful on occasion."

"What brings you here with the Gallóglaigh?" enquires William. Dáibh replies, "I was with the Moray volunteers, when we met up with Stephen and the Gallóglaigh at Dunbar, after that feckn drave, we backed up Balliol by fighting rearguard for him. Ah tell yie Wallace, the English were so many, they replaced each one we killed with two or three more, it was impossible. After all was lost we dispersed, so I rode to Badenoch with big Rob MacGilchrist as fast as we could, there I found Daun safe and well. Rob heard news that Caisteal na Sròine (Urquhart Castle) at Loch Ness, Inverness town and the docks had all fallen to the English. Now some English fella called Sir William Fitz Warenne is the Constable up there, he's declared big Rob and the loch Sloy and Moray men as fêted outlaws. We had nowhere else to go except here with the Gallóglaigh."

William enquires, "Is big Rob here too?" Dáibh shakes his head, "He is, for big Rob has no family left alive up in Avoch, and with the English hunting for us everywhere, we had to flee for our lives. It seemed that Galloway was the only place we could think to go. We couldn't go northwest, no' with the sons o' Donald of the isles allied with the English and chasing us too. This is bad Wallace, the English have tens of thousands of men sweeping the east coast of Scotland and now they're marching totally unopposed throughout the lands and glens of Moray, Avoch, Badenoch and on through the great Glen, killing and murdering with impunity. We were damned lucky to be escaping and meetin' up with the surviving Gallóglaigh near Lanark, then we came back here with them." Concerned, William enquires, "What about Daun, is she safe?" Dáibh turns and points at a two wheeled cart pulled by an ox, William sees Daun sitting in the back of the cart, tending to injured warriors. He runs over quickly and leans on the edge of the cart, "Daun, ahm so relieved to be seeing you're here safe and well." Daun looks up, but before she could reply, William notices the two men she has been tending in the cart, he recognises one of them instantly,

"MacGilchrist?" Big Rob, his face bloodied and swollen, looks up and a faint smile passes his lips, "Wallace, ahm glad to be seein' you." Suddenly the other wounded man, covered in dried blood, bruised and older than Rob, sits bolt upright, but he doesn't appear badly wounded. William enquires, "Who's this fella?" Rob replies, "This here fella is Máel Álainn MacDhuibh from Mortlach in Banff. He's the bastard brother to the old Mormaer o' Fife, Colbahn, blood kin to the murdered mormaer Duncan MacDuff the Guardian." MacDhuibh holds his hand out, then he speaks...

"By the blood o' the black son of the revered Aicé Queen Gruoch, and by my own birth in sight o' the mighty cross of MacDhuibh, I hereby claim the right of sanctuary and composition, for murder done most foul to my kin." True Tam overhears MacDhuibh's words. William enquires, "What did he just say?" True Tam grins and replies to MacDhuibh, "I'll tell yie this MacDhuibh, advance payment o' nine cows and a heifer for what your planning, will no' really be acceptable to that there English king, nor will it be much to his liking ah reckon."

"What are yiez both talking about?" enquires William, True Tam replies as he helps big Rob and MacDhuibh to the ground. "Ach, MacDhuibh here is from the ancient Cruathnie Mormaers of Moray, Fife and Fothriff. His blood is prominent in the spiritual teachings of the east coast Céile Aicé. I know what he meant when he spoke o' the Gruoch Aicé." True Tam pulls aside MacDhuibh's long black pleated hair and examines the back of his skull, he smiles knowingly... "MacDhuibh has a very big and split lump on the back of his head, but I reckon he will be right enough after some rest." MacDhuibh looks at William and shakes his fist in the air, "William Wallace, know that I, chief of Dhuibh Fothriff, shall bear to arms the Red Lion Rampant of Royal

Scotland, then we will rest the mighty Coronation Crown once more on the King's head seated upon the Lia Fáil. And should our King set battle arms toward his enemies, then I, that same MacDhuibh, shall lead the Vanguard of his host against all the transgressions of this bloody English King. The venerable Aicé will be finding that any deed done by me and mine to protect the crown of Scotland, shall absolve us of any wrong-doing and I will be released from any punishment, protected by the ancient Dhuibh Privilege."

"Ha," laughs True Tam, "now I understand, MacDhuibh here is invoking an ancient law in lieu of a murder he's planning. Anyways Wallace, will yie help me get them both to ma obhainn where ah can tend to their wounds?" William enquires curiously, "Who is MacDhuibh wanting to murder?" True Tam replies "Why, the English of course."

Thinking it best not to ask anymore questions about MacDhuibh, William reaches up to the platform of the wagon, puts his arms around Daun's waist and lifts her to the ground, whereupon she rushes over to Dáibh and they embrace. Daun begins fussing over Dáibh, who is looking very tired, with a grey pallor on his face. William enquires, "Are you well enough ma friend?" Dáibh replies, "I'll be feeling better after some stovies and a good long sleep." Daun smiles then walks back to William where they embrace, she says, "I was so sorry to hear about your family, we all feared that you had been taken from us too, it wasn't till young Moray told us that you were safe and well, but I miss lady Mharaidh, William, I..."

"DAUN..." Everyone turns to see Marion and Brannah rushing over to greet Dáibh and Daun, the women meet first and embrace, while true Tam and Rob help MacDhuibh onto his feet. True Tam says, "We'll go to my obhainn Rob, there's plenty o' room there for both o' yiez to be restin' awhile and get your wounds tended." Just then, Fallon and Eochaidh arrive back. Eochaidh says, "There's nobody that's following the Gallóglaigh into the Wolf and wildcats any longer Wallace. A few English trackers had tried to follow us, we let them in a distance before we captured them." Eochaidh laughs, "They didn't want to be talkin' very much at first, but after some encouragement, they had a much to be telling us before we gifted them their reward." William enquires, "What did they say?" Faolán dismounts and shows an unusually rare hint of a satisfied smile, "The English told us their friends will not be coming in here for a very long time, for they simply fear this great woodland. They be thinking it's cursed and full of demonic spirits. They also told us their masters have more than enough to be doing amongst the chaos abroad in the realm, than waste time looking for a few outlaws and cut-throats in the Wolf and wildcats. Once we gleaned what we believe to be honest answers, what we left of them was hung up to wind dry as a warning to their Sudron fuckin' brothers… should they ever be tempted to follow."

"Aye," exclaims William, "but you said the rest of the realm, what's going on?" Faolán says, "Wallace, we can talk later, for I have many of my own wounded that needs care and must be tended right away." As Faolán and Eochaidh leave, Marion approaches, she says, "William… Daun and Dáibh may share our obhainn till we can have one built for them. Come over when you're ready, for we need to talk about what should be done for the wounded; and those who have passed to a better place than this."

Dénnaigh, the wife of Torrance, a slight framed woman with long and intricately braided blond hair, is especially gifted with the care and nurture of others. Known as the good wife of the glen, she approaches William, "I've all the young women helping me make salves and balms Wallace, but I need more help to organise…" Brannah, who is looking desperately for Moray, arrives and enquires in a state of angst, "Does anyone know what happened to Andrew, is he still alive?" Daun puts her arm round Brannah's shoulders as Dáibh replies, "He's well enough Brannah. Andrew was lightly wounded at Dunbar, but he was taken prisoner by the English, as far as we know, he's still alive." Both tears of sadness and relief begin to well up in Brannah's eyes as Daun comforts her. Dénnaigh holds out her hand as Brannah composes herself, she says, "I'll help you tend the wounded Dénnaigh. Just tell me what you need me to do?"

Shaking his head in dismay, William looks all around the glen basin, for it resembles a bloody battleground, with riderless horses wandering about aimlessly, trailing their reigns. Women and children wail over the bodies of Gallóglaigh who had stayed alive just long enough to see their loved ones one last time, others are being mourned amongst the bloodied rags and detritus of war, all scattered asunder. William turns and looks at Dáibh who is sitting on a small ale barrel. "Fuck," he exclaims, "What's happened Dáibh? I've never seen the Gallóglaigh so hard pressed before, and there are so few returned."

William looks up to see Daun and Marion enter their obhainn mòr a little distance away; then he sees true Tam, Torrance, Dénnaigh and Brannah helping big Rob and MacDhuibh into Tam's obhainn. Dáibh says, "Help me up Wallace, for ahm no' as young as I used to be." William responds by putting out his hands, both grip each other by the wrists; then he pulls Dáibh to his feet. "C'mon wie' me Dáibh," says William, "Let's get into the obhainn mòr and get you fed and settled." As they walk towards the obhainn mòr, William enquires, "Have you any notion where Moray is bein' held prisoner?" Dáibh replies, "Aye, I've heard both him and his father are already in England, Lord Moray is bein' held captive in some place called the tower o' London." William exclaims, "What? Lord Moray's a prisoner too? If he's in the hands o' the English, we really are leaderless now. Is young Andrew with his father and where's the red Comyn... and what's their chiefs doing about it?" Dáibh replies, "We don't know where they all are. I heard that a knight called Sir Hugh de Lacey, has young Andrew imprisoned in the northwest of England somewhere. Someone said it was near a place called Wrexham or Chester castle, but I don't yet know where the red Comyn is, I only know that he's still alive and bein' kept as a ransom prisoner of the fuckin' English."

"What about King John, does he still fight on?" enquires William, Dáibh shakes his head forlorn, "Naw, he was taken prisoner too, I heard that he was sent to that London Tower place in chains." Dáibh, with a grim countenance looks at William, he says, "Scotland is lost Wallace." William doesn't quite understand Daibh's statement, he enquires, "What do yie mean, Scotland is lost?" Dáibh looks down at the ground, "We're finished, fucked Wallace, it's all over..."

William is confused, "Dáibh, I don't understand what yie mean, Scotland is lost, it's over?" Dáibh continues, "Wallace, Balliol is no more, he's now a prisoner in England. The Brus Pact betrayed him and handed him over to Longshanks. The Pact of de Brix upon his death, has been taken over by his son the earl of Carrick, with the support of Cospatrick o' Dunbar, Walter Stewart the Earl of Menteith, Bernard Bruce of Cleveland and James the High Steward, wie Angus Óg and that Aslikkør Ranald fucker, the bastard sons o' Donald, they're all allying with the English." The full realisation of these' words concern William greatly, as Dáibh continues, "Those treacherous fuckers, the confederation that Brus brought onto the field at Dunbar in sworn allegiance to

Longshanks, aye, it was a force of near on twice the size of Baliol's entire army, with almost forty thousand English, Irish, Welsh and Gascons behind Brus, King John and our wee Scots army never stood a chance." Dáibh looks away, then he mutters, "What a fucking jest the Ragemanus rolls treaty was, *'Saving every article for the honour and liberty of Scotland, providing the conditions should involve nothing to which the future ages may be detrimental or prejudicial to the realm and people of Scotland.'* We're fucked now Wallace; simply because our noble bastards betrayed us. More like the Ragemanus should be called the ragman's fuckin' shit roll for all it is worth now." Walking with Dáibh towards the obhainn mòr in silence, William is sickened by what he has heard. On reaching the obhainn, William helps Dáibh up the stairs and inside, to find that Daun has already prepared a comfortable seat and footbath for him.

Marion has a large bowl of stovies and jug of hot whisky prepared on a small table near the fire. William looks at Dáibh and sees the strain on Dáibh's countenance and realises he is pressed to disguise his pain and fatigue. Marion begins fussing. "Dáibh, you get seated over there by the fire, I'll get you a clean léine and a fine fleece brat to be keeping you warm. After we bathe you, we'll get you fed proper too, for there is more than plenty fare to go round us all." Marion nudges William and points to a large cauldron of hot water, "William, bring that cauldron over for Daun, then I want you to go back out and see how everybody else is fairing." William dutifully fetches the cauldron over, much to the amusement of Dáibh. William says, "I'll be back in a wee while Dáibh. I'm going out just now to see true Tam and Dénnaigh and find out if they need any help." At that moment, Dénnaigh enters the obhainn, with her aprons and skirts stained and soaked with swathes of blood. "Wallace," she says, "We need yer help urgently, we desperately need fiongeur for the wounded, there's none in the Glen, and we are almost out of bryony, hemlock, salt and henbane too. If we don't source plenty more soon, many of the wounded will die." William looks to Marion as Dénnaigh continues, "I've sent all the young Ceitherne away to the woods and upper moors to seek out wild-foul eggs, boar and sow bile, red nettle leaves and hollow leek as they can find, but I need the fiongeur in particular, to mix and make duile (Aenasthetic) and sleeping potions, that we may cut the limbs from those poor fella's who will die if we don't. Some of the younger wains are away searchin' all the burns and wee rivers hereabouts to fetch as many eels as they can catch, but we urgently need salt and fiongeur more than anything else, and there is none left hereabouts."

Marion says, "I may have a solution, Brannah and I will go to Lanark first light of the morn, for it's the market day there. I'm going to see my father anyway and then tending to my duties at the Bruin hoose. I'll see what I can source there and bring it back with me. William, if you can send some of the Gallóglaigh to wait at the edge of the Lanark woods, then we'll get as much as we can find and send it out to them, after that they can drive back here with whatever we may find."

Looking at Marion apprehensively, William replies, "Naw Marion, yie cannae go to Lanark on yer own, we don't know what's happening there and it's no' safe, not with the English roaming about looking for those who sided with King John..." Exasperated, Marion exclaims, "Och William, my father's the Lord of Lammington. The English wouldn't dare to cause me harm; and Sherriff D'Levingstun is a good friend, he will make sure that we come to no harm, besides, who would tend to the poor if the Bruin hoose is closed?" William says, "Naw Marion, I won't let you take a risk like that. We'll send someone else to Lanark." Marion gives William the *'Look.'*

William smiles in seeing her expression. She says, "Listen you to me Wallace, there are souls here desperately needing our help and if we tarry hereabouts debating this, many will suffer terribly and many more will likely die. Would you have me hide away and ignore their pain? If you would have me do that, then you have sorely mistaken the grit of the woman you've married. If we cannot give succor to those who sought to defend us, what would you have me do?" William replies, "Then I'll go with you, if yie think that I would wait here and let you go alone, then you have sorely mistaken the will of the man that you've married."

Marion and William stand glaring at each other, caught in an impasse, then they hear a voice nearby saying, "Two sides of the Cruathnie chóinn there ah reckon?" Both look round to see Dáibh smiling; they look at each other and then they laugh. "All right," says Marion, "Away you go and be seeing to big Rob, we can blether about who does what later, have yie got that?" William replies, "Aye ma dear." Dáibh laughs then quips, "Ho Wallace, it'll be the list next." William laughs then looks at Dáibh and mutters, "Feckr…" Marion winks at Daun then enquires, "What did you say to me Wallace?" William exclaims, "No' you darlin' I was talking about Dáibh." Marion smiles, "I love you Wallace."

William's heart melts hearing those words from his beautiful wife. He kisses Marion then walks to the door, where he turns to see all three grinning. William smiles, then he leaves the obhainn mòr. William pauses and looks around the glen, suddenly all the humour he felt moments ago, quickly dissipates. Faolán was correct when she had said that this night would be a night of much weeping in the heart of the Wolf and wildcats. He walks slowly towards true Tam's obhainn, wishing he could close his ears to the terrible wailing coming from many obhainn's near and far.

The bereavement cry of the women unnerves William, for he bitterly remembers the grief he felt in his own life that is now being visited upon others. He feels a wave of emotion, and also futility, for there is nothing he could do about any of it. As he enters true Tam's obhainn, he sees true Tam and Rob talking intently, while MacDhuibh lay sleeping like a baby on a crib of furs, pelts and skins by the fireside, his head roughly bound with one of true Tam's honey craitur potions. "Haw Rob, are yie all right?" enquires William. Rob looks up and smiles... "Aye tá Wallace, a lot better now that I've had some scran and my wounds tended, and of course, fortification from true Tam's fine craitur." William enquires, "Have you been wounded bad?" Rob laughs, "Naw, no' too bad, just a few scratches, but from what ah hear, certainly no' as bad as you were from your time in Ayr dungeons as a guest o' the English."

Laughing, William sits down at the fireside as true Tam fills their bowls with stovies, then he pours them all a large quantity of his new experimental craitur. William looks inside the craitur jug then glances at true Tam, who raises his jug in the air for a toast, he says...

"Ahm still working on it."

William and Rob laugh then they too raise their jugs as true Tam proclaims, "Slàinte mhath." They crack their jugs and all say as one, "He's still working on it." They settle down around the hearth fire, then William enquires, "So what happened at Dunbar?" Rob shakes his head as he stares into the flames, "It's all fucked up Wallace. Both Lord Moray and young Andrew are prisoners o' the English, along with Baliol, red Comyn, Sir William de Sinclair and about ten more barons and at least a hundred more brave knights o' the realm, fuck knows how many quires were caught too. It was a complete disaster, I knew it to be so when the good Sir

Pádraic de Graeme went down, it was fuckin' sinful, but he took a good few o' them with him though." William exclaims, "Pádraic de Graeme... he's dead? Fuck naw, he was a good man, that's bad, for I had a great liking for Pádraic, he'll be sadly missed by many." Everyone nods in solemn agreement, then the obhainn falls to thoughtful silence. After a few moments, William enquires, "So Rob, are yie going to tell me, what happened after Moray and Comyn left the Wolf and wildcats? They said they were going to meet with the main Scottish army at the Caddonlee, then they intended to advance against the English army at Berwick to take back the port into Scottish hands."

"Berwick yie say?" Rob sighs forlorn, "Wallace, the English murdered everyone in Berwick, every man, woman and child were put to the sword, then the English set about building new defenses and moving English traders and their families into the houses o' the folk they had murdered, while their blood was still warm and wet in the streets. We should have nailed them there and then, but our squabbling nobles ruined that opportunity. Then we heard Longshanks was moving his army north to siege Edinburgh, word was afoot that he was going to put all to the sword in his path, so it was decided to cut towards Dunbar castle and make a stand on the Lammermuir's, but the earls of Athol, Mar, Ross and Menteith split Baliol's army in two, then they marched back on towards Carlisle seekin' vengeance on Brus. Fuck, but he wasn't there, he was away with his master Longshanks, marching over the bodies of murdered Scots in Berwick."

William exclaims, "This is so hard to believe or take in, that our own blood would fight against us, for what... a free fuckin' meal in the palace of Westminster and supping with the English King?" Rob continues, "We heard that de Brus and his Pact had sworn another oath to serve Longshanks, this time they solemnly pledged their word on the Gospels and sword of Saint Thomas à Becket, to give absolute unquestioned fuckin' loyalty to Edward Plantagenet, the King of England, Ireland, Wales and now it would seem, Scotland too." Rob spits in the fire in disgust; then he continues, "The English are slaughtering everyone within a twenty-mile arc of their army as it moves north, and they're sparing none. Towns, Balloch's and Clachans are being burned down, they're destroying everything and everyone by fire and sword."

"So tell me then," enquires William, "What happened at Dunbar castle?" Rob replies, "Lady Marjorie Comyn and her retinue, along with the castle guard, were holding the Castle for Balliol…" William exclaims, "Marjorie, Cospatrick's wife, from Comunnach?" Rob nods, "Aye that's her. Fuck, that wee woman can sure organise a braw fight." William enquires, "Is she safe?" Rob shakes his head; "Nobody has seen her since the English took the castle. The warden, Sir Richard Stewart, he betrayed all the Scots who had sought shelter in the castle. The day after the battle, all the Scots were led away shackled in irons and chains. It's known Cospatrick was so enraged by the insult to his name in the face of Longshanks by lady Marjorie's defiance, rumour has it Cospatrick murdered her and her ladies, then hid their bodies away somewhere."

"This is a disaster," says William. He is completely dumbfounded by this news, for lady Marjorie is a close friend to both him and of his family. He remembers how she had consoled and sheltered him when he discovered the massacre of glen Afton. He speaks out with great urgency in his voice, "We must go out and find her." Rob says. "We'll seek her out when everything settles down again Wallace, for this is a realm in great flux, despair and chaos. Fuck, our entire population is fleeing they know not where. But ahm hopin' that Marjorie will be safe, surely even Cospatrick wouldn't slay a woman such as Lady Marjorie, for retribution from her kinfolks that the Comyn's will most surely seek out, would be a terrible vengeance upon him and his supporters. But we don't know the truth of it yet, as she has ne'er been seen since."

"Ah'll tell yie what else happened at Dunbar," continues Rob, "when we arrived several miles to the southwest o' the Lammermuir's, we could see that the English vanguard had brought three large siege engines right up to the castle walls and were preparing to attack, so Baliol initially positioned our army well enough on the high ground o' the Doon hill, when the English saw us, Bishop Bek o' Durham immediately sent his army directly at us. That would have been perfect, but for the red Comyn, he thought he saw his chance and led forward a reckless attack on Bek before he could be stopped. Balliol's war standard was carried into the battle by young Thomas Sinclair, instinctively following the red Comyn, then half our fuckin' army, who all thought it was the signal to attack; they followed Comyn straight into a novice trap. Nobody could fault the red Comyn's courage Wallace, but that elemental mistake o' losing the high ground, it cost us the entire battle." William exclaims, "Comyn left the high ground?"

"He did, aye," replies Rob, "He rode straight at the siege army at the castle, just then we noticed over to the south, another English force was fast approaching, led by Sir John de Warenne the Earl of Surrey. Bek intercepted Comyn's force before they could reach the siege engines at the castle, so Balliol had no other choice then but to attack de Warenne, for it looked to us from the heights, that the English of Surrey had fallen to disorder when they halted on the north side o' the Spott burn, prior to them attacking Comyn, for he was blindsided in the flank. Balliol's only mistake was that he misinterpreted the English deployment as disorder. He ordered the remaining part of our army down off the high ground, thinking to take advantage of what he thought was confusion among the English ranks, but the English were advancing, not disarray nor retreating, and many of them were already hidden out of sight down in the defiles o' the Spott burn and crossing it out of sight of Balliol. The charging Scots led by the Red Comyn ran straight into a trap, then a bloody massacre ensued." Rob falters, weak with pain.

"Eat your scran Rob," says True Tam, "It's gettin' cold, yie can finish the story later." Rob pushes his scran aside, "I cannae eat no more Tam." William, needing to know more, enquires, "So what happened Rob, how did Balliol lose Dunbar castle?"

"Fuck Wallace," exclaims, Rob "If it hadn't been for the discipline of Stephen of Ireland, Torrance and the Gallóglaigh, we would have lost Balliol there and then, for it was the Gallóglaigh who held on to the high ground while everyone else raged into battle, but it was hopeless. We had about a thousand cavalry and fifteen thousand infantry and as many again who didn't know what the fuck they were doin'. De Warenne had near on five thousand Cavalry and about fifteen thousand men and Bek had three thousand cavalry and near on twenty thousand infantry. We were well outnumbered and the English outthought and outfought us at every turn, it's that simple. Balliol got trapped trying to retreat and it was only then that the Gallóglaigh came down from the heights of the Lammermuir. They fought a ferocious rearguard action allowing Balliol to escape, but in the debacle, Lord Moray, young Andrew and many of the nobles and our finest knights got cut off from the rest of us, so they made their way to Dunbar castle and managed to get in, but there must have been at least ten thousand o' our brave Scots lying dead when we all left the field, then the English began killing the wounded and all the prisoners of no account, they cut them to pieces. Fuck, it was like hogs to a butchers slaughter, all exceptin' the nobles for ransom that is."

Pausing for another drink of Tam's craitur, Rob then continues, "After we lost Dunbar castle, Longshanks fleet landed more fresh troops at the harbour, just north o' Berwick and Tantallon, that then gained him unfettered access into the entire lower east of Scotland, from there we've been harried by English cavalry for weeks. Ah heard the English finally caught King John hiding in the dungeons o' Kincardine castle, he was taken to Stracathro where he renounced our alliance with the Norse and French. Finally, ah heard that he was driven in an old dung cart to Montrose, where he was humiliated by being made to hold a white wand and baton, then forced to beg for mercy, resigning himself to the grace of Longshanks by giving up all right's he held in regards to the Kingdom of Scotland. Longshanks' the fucker, he had the Scots Royal Arms ripped from Balliol's tabard by Bishop Bek of Durham, with all his royal ornaments and insignia burned in front of Balliol for the amusement of the English King, his soldiery and those Scots traitors who witnessed the shameful deed, ah'll never forgive them for what they have done."

"How did you manage to escape?" enquires William, Rob replies, "The English made for the north towards Elgin, Aberdeen and Inverness, that's where the remainder o' our nobles surrendered and did homage to Longshanks. They swore fealty to the King of England on their knees. The bastards surrendered all our northern castles and fortified towns. But it appears that Longshanks is more interested in securing all the seaports like Dun Dèagh, Aberdeen and Inverness than anywhere on the west coast, apart from Ayr town. Anyway Wallace, to answer your question, the men of Moray left Edinburgh and we joined the rearguard fighting with the Gallóglaigh, when we reached Forfar, we were told to disband by Balliol's officers, it was every man for himself then. That's when I went north with Dáibh, but there we found that it had already been over-run by the English; and we had all been declared as renegade outlaws."

Rob sups some more of Tam's fine craitur, then he says, "Aye, a big reward has been put out on us for the delivery of all our tongues and ears, as Edward sets about putting an English administration into place all over Scotland. I tell yie Wallace, this plan of Longshanks was well thought out and couldn't have succeeded without the aid of many of our own precious fuckin' noble's collusion. Within days, the wardens of all our castles, towns and all our king's men by ancient custom or hereditary right, swore an oath of fealty to the English King. He allowed some of them to stay in the same position and offices they had formerly served, and those who did not bend to the English king... well, we are all here now with a price on our heads." William exclaims, "So we have no King no more?"

"Naw," Rob shakes his head, "We're finished Wallace, in the place of our King, John de Warenne the earl of Surrey, he has been appointed as vice regent, lord chief justice and Warden of Scotland. Sir Hugh de Cressingham is Longshanks' treasurer at a new exchequer getting built to receive Scots taxes at Berwick-upon-Tweed. Walter de Amundisham, he is the new chancellor, he has declared that no Genoese, Baltan, Fleming, Teuton, Frenchman nor any member of the Hansa, henceforth shall enter Scotland, unless for taxable commerce, and only by Longshanks' approval with a sealed license sought through his office representatives in London. Then there's that bloated bastard Cressingham, he with his bandit sheriffs, sending tax collectors backed by armed sheriff's men into all the minor shires and towns of Scotland, all to collect money to pay the English the expense of taking over our realm and maintaining their army here." William gasps, "How can this be, why can no one stop this English king, what justification does he have to invade a sovereign realm."

"Ach Wallace," sighs True Tam, "It goes back well over a hundred years, when our King William the Lion and the English king Henry were at war with each other. The lion was captured by Henry at the battle of Alnwick and taken prisoner to Henry's castle in Falaise in Normandy. That's when it all really started, for Henry took control of all the Scottish castles and filled them with English constables, Scotland was then heavily taxed to pay for their upkeep. Henry forced our king into signing what they called the *'Treaty of Falaise,'* to allow the Lion to return to Scotland. Part of the treaty was that Scotland would forever be subordinate to the crown of England, but that was all abandoned when the Norman King, Richard the Lionheart, needed money and Scots to fight with him in the Holy Land."

Rob sneers, "No agreement of that kind could ever be held as a bonded oath, for it's an agreement made under duress." William enquires, "And that's the legal justification for this Longshanks fucker to attack Scotland?" True Tam laughs, "Aye well Wallace, it's a wee bit more complicated than that son, but that's the premise from which the English King is makin' his claim. His legal right and basis to do so now, stems from the Comyn clan attacking Brus in England's sovereign territory; that's his claim of right for the invasion, you mark my words." William enquires, "I don't understand. Surely all the nobles of Scotland can't be in the pay of Longshanks? There must be someone who will lead the fight against this… fuck, I don't even know what yie could call it, for it seems like a butchery of our race, and it's the wee folk who are paying the price for all this shyster politics of the nobles." True Tam enquires, "Rob? Do yie know what happened to Lord Douglas after Berwick, is he still alive?" Rob replies, "Aye, but he's another one that's been taken to London as a prisoner, to ensure that his Clan and house keep the peace, Longshanks has confiscated all his English estates, Jaezuz, even the Douglas' infant son Hugh has been taken as a hostage ward by the sheriff of Essex." True Tam exclaims, "What…? That's the Brus estate in England?" Rob replies, "Aye, ah know. Longshanks is playin' one off against the other, for he knows he could depend on the support of Brus the earl of Carrick and his Pact. Even his son, young Robert the Bruce, the next earl of Carrick, he has sworn fealty to Longshanks."

"Fuck." William exclaims, "I knew that this day would come to pass, I remember coming back from Ireland a few years ago on the same Birlinn as young Bruce, we talked of a day like this, and if it ever came down to it, we would have to choose a side, but at this moment I am no' on anyone's side. I just want to be left in peace with my family."

Rob says, "Wallace, you'd better be making your mind up damn quick what side you're on, for there will be no neutrals if there is a fight back against Longshanks. This will no' end here, for the Comyn has more than a personal interest in what's happening, now it's a blood feud between them two families. Sure, isn't Comyn's mother the sister of King John Baliol, and as such, he can make a claim to the throne of Scotland should anything happen to King John's sons, Edward and Henry, and they're already prisoners of Longshanks, which makes a Comyn next in line for the throne, not Brus." Suddenly they are startled when a voice enquires from the floor… "Is this a fuckin' tree trunk wrapped in hemp?" William jumps up and curses. "What the fuck are yie doin'?"

MacDhuibh has gripped William by the leg in order to pull himself upright. MacDhuibh enquires, "Where the fuck am I?" True Tam and big Rob laugh, "It's all right Wallace," says true Tam, "I don't think you have taken the lustfull fancy of MacDhuibh, he's just a wee bitty scattered with his wits right now." MacDhuibh stands up and pulls a milking stool across the floor then thumps himself down and rubs the back of his head. He looks at William, "You're one almighty big feckr aren't yie…?" Before an astonished William can answer, MacDhuibh looks at the half-eaten bowls of stovies then he leans forward and tips them all into one bowl. "Ahm se' fuckin' hungry." Snarls MacDhuibh. William sits back amused. True Tam laughs, then he enquires, "So MacDhuibh, yer back with us in fine fettle again then?"

"Aye, that I am." replies MacDhuibh, "And when ahm finished this scran, am headin' north to raise a fuckin' army." William laughs, for this wild looking bastard of an earl, is not like any nobles that he has ever met before.

MacDhuibh continues, "I heard the end of yer chatter there fella's. I will put my sword in my hand right now as my mark, and I'll stand with Balliol and the Comyn's and every other decent fucker in Scotland. Then I will fight against any bastard that thinks that they can walk into our land and just steal it from us. My men are maybe dispersed, aye, but I will soon put the call out and we'll show these Sudron bastards that they may have won a battle, but they sure haven't won a war. They'll find that out soon enough that they're nuthin' but fuckin' kittens that have just nipped the balls o' this hungry northern mountain lion." William is elated and impressed by the rough cut of this northern noble. He thinks *'Is he mad or a natural leader?'* Before William can say anything, MacDhuibh swipes his bowl clean, wipes his hands on his beard, then he says, "Longshanks stole the Stone of Destiny and broke the great Seal of Scotland, then he sent them to England with the Golden Crown. He's also destroyed our ancient historical records, now the only accounts of our history will be written by Englishmen or those in the pay of Longshanks, and that ma friends, will fuck up the heads of generations of Scots as though we had never existed. I tell yiez this certainty, I'll leave my mark on those bastards, they'll know we existed all right." True Tam says, "Aye, it's surely the fate of the people of this land to be extinguished, unless we resist, and not just by using force, but employing a terror much greater than that which the English have visited upon us. That my friends, is the only way we may have a chance to survive, and not just us, but our children and their children."

"We're far frae finished yet," states MacDhuibh "The Clan of MacDhuibh is fucked if we will lay down to this, our family are as close blood-related to the Welsh royal house of Llewellyn as we are to that o' the house o' Canmòre. Longshanks appears to be bent on killing any feckr that may lay a free and proper claim the crown of the Scots, or the Welsh... namely us. So, come first light, ahm going north to rally ma men and ma kinfolks, then we're going west to link with Morrison mòr's Blue Angel fleet and we're going to attack Donald and his Aslikkør spawn allies in the isles, then..."

"Whoa MacDhuibh," exclaims Rob, "For fuck's sake man, will yie slow down a wee bit." MacDhuibh replies, "Slow fuckin' down? The English are raping and killing their way through our country with those bastards from the isles, and he's employing the Brus and his curs as their hunting dogs too... and you're telling me to slow fuckin' down. Wallace, get me a horse, I'm no' going to sit on my arse here telling stories like you bastards, no' when there are good men still out there fighting back, ahm going to be joining them. Are yie with me

Wallace, or are yie against me? State your place and we can finish this right here and now?" MacDhuibh reaches for his sword but finds only an empty scabbard. He raises his hand to his eyes and begins to sway, "Fuck, I'd better sit down first. Tam, did yie put poison in those stovies?" True Tam replies, "Naw, it's maybe just a bad batch o' ma new craitur."

William is unsure if he should laugh or join MacDhuibh's fantastical crusade, such is the passion burning within the heart of this madman... or patriot, he is not yet quite sure which. Rob says, "Listen MacDhuibh, get a good rest then we'll both leave in the morn, but first we'll go to Bothwell castle near Glasgow and meet with Sir David Moray, young Andrew's uncle, perhaps there we'll find out where young Andrew is. If we can free him from his prison, I believe he's a man to bring all the forces of the north together." Rob looks at William, "So, are you with us Wallace?" William is caught off guard by the extreme burst of energy and fighting talk from these men, he replies "Ah..." big Rob snarls in disgust, "Fuck it Wallace, if you were with us, you would have known it and said aye. Well, I will be thanking you for your hospitality, but we will be leaving your fine safe haven in the morn. Now Wallace, it would suite us best if yie leave us, for me and MacDhuibh have things to talk about."

Rob turns towards true Tam, "And what about you Tam, are you with us?" True Tam replies, "Aye, ahm with yiez, but don't be so hard on young Wallace, he'll be there when the time comes, wont yie Wallace?" William looks deep into the grim faces. They are all hardened men of battle, men of great guile and cunning too, and listening to MacDhuibh has inspired William, and though it sounded like ranting, his conviction struck a chord in William's heart. He says, "I will be leaving you now as yie ask o' me, and when I know that my family are safe and free from hurt or harm, then I'll join the fight with yie and for yie, but I will come out in ma own time, not for you, nor for the English, only I will decide when that time is…" Silence greets William's reply, the three men scrutinise William, then MacDhuibh says, "That's good enough for me Wallace." Rob agrees, "Fair play to yie Wallace, yie've made yer mark and yer word is good enough for me too." True Tam says, "C'mon Wallace, ahl walk yie to the door, for ah know that the bonnie Marion will be thinking it's about time she saw that big face o' yours." William and Tam walk to the obhainn door.

As he makes to leave, William looks back into the gloomy depths of true Tam's obhainn; he could see that Rob and MacDhuibh are already deep in conversation. True Tam says, "Wallace, I've already seen that you will make to strike, and that time to strike will be revealed to you and you alone. But for now, go and be with the bonnie lass, for she needs you." William replies, "I don't want to fight in any fuckin' war Tam, I love ma Marion and ma wee Mharaidh Morríaghan, I don't want to leave them, and now that Marion is being with child once more, the only thing that I want to do is live my life in peace, if it means having to bow and pull my forelock to every English soldier I meet, so be it." True Tam shakes his head then simply closes the door behind him.

As William wonders through the Balloch, he can't escape the feeling of letting everyone down, no matter what he chooses. He lifts his head up and makes his way to Stephen's obhainn and enters quietly; there he sees that Stephen and Brìghde are fast asleep in each other's arms beside a peat fire. He feels good that his friend has found love since the murder of Katriona. The friendship and loyalty he has found with this Irishman, he has found in no other. He leaves them sleeping in peace and makes for the obhainn of Torrance and Dénnaigh, again he finds everyone asleep. As he leaves their obhainn, William pauses for a moment, curiously he observes the surreal quietness that has befallen the glen underneath a beautifull falling night sky; the wailing of the mourners, is now muted to sporadic cries of anguish escaping from many dwellings.

Finally, William walks on towards his own obhainn mòr, feeling very conflicted by his experience and what he has heard and said in true Tam's obhainn. He takes a great intake of fresh air then enters his obhainn, he sees Dáibh fast asleep and snoring on an old chair by the fire, while Daun is by his side, sleeping on a soft, thick crib. Marion sits card weaving and rocking little Mharaidh's cot gently with her foot. She looks up and smiles as he quietly closes the obhainn door behind him. Marion's smile changes to a curiosity, she can see that William is troubled. He sits on the floor beside her where she pulls his head to her bosom and begins stroking his hair. "What ails you my love?" enquires Marion. William replies, "I don't know darlin' I've been with true Tam, big Rob and that mad fella from up north, MacDhuibh. There were long talks, and what I heard is bad news, really bad." Marion replies, "I know, when Dáibh fell asleep, Daun and I spent awhile talking, she told me of terrible things and what has been happening in the rest of Scotland."

William looks into Marion's eyes and she smiles. He cannot resist the beautiful sparkle in her eyes when she smiles, it sweeps away any thoughts other than his love for her and little Mharaidh, he says, "Ma bonnie darlin, your eyes sparkle like a million diamonds in the sky." Marion blushes as William settles and gazes into the little turquoise blue flames now dancing on the glowing peat fire. They both sit quietly, contemplating the situation. William is mesmerised by the ever-changing bluish colours of the hearth fire flame, they remind him of the Dragon of his family coat of arms.

He thinks of his father Alain and wee Maw, reminiscing about the time when he first saw his uncle Malcolm wearing his full suit of armour, cloaked in the Wallace armorial bearings, when he rode out to join the Guardians at Dun Ceann Orran. The next time he saw the blue Dragon in all its glory, was when he was presented with his grandfather's armour in glen Afton and he wore it himself when riding out with his father, as a lead hunter-scout for the guardian army, a force that was meant to come between the Balliol and Bruce factions as peacemakers. His thoughts are lost once more to the mesmeric blue flames, when he hears Marion speak to him quietly, "Do you think we may ever find peace William? Do you think that we can ever stay blessed, when all around us, many suffer such cruel torment of loss?"

Thinking awhile on Marion's sombre question, William eventually answers, "Marion ma love, it doesn't matter if the whole world goes feckn mad, I will never leave your side so long as any harm may come to you in my absence." William looks into the tiny crib and watches bonnie wee Mharaidh Morríaghan. He lifts up her tiny hand with his finger and wags it slightly, she yawns and stretches out her tiny hands then she sneezes… William and Marion look at each other amused, then they both laugh heartily together. "Naw Marion, this is my life now as a husband and father, and I sure do love this feeling. It doesn't matter who's the king of Scotland as long as we are left at peace, and even then ma darlin', I'm going nowhere." Marion grips him gently by the cheek, smiles, looks into his eyes and says, "I love you so much William Wallace." William smiles then pulls her close in a loving embrace then says, "I love you soooo much… Marion Wallace."

The Way of Things

A small wagon train tentatively travels towards Lanark market town, along the eastern fringes of the great Wolf and wildcat forest; reigning the lead wagon is William and Marion, who pause to observe the broad open marches around them. In particular, they scrutinise the area between the northwestern boundary marker stones and an unguarded friar's bridge, that crosses the meandering waters of the river Clyde. The road leading over the bridge and up the steep braes into the royal burgh of the ancient town of Lanark, show no sign of any English *'Peacekeepers.'* In sensing no apparent threat, they drive the wagons forward onto the old drove road, where the tall growing willow coppice plantation, obscures the wary traveller's journey from any prying eyes or marauding English army patrols.

Eventually they halt underneath the broad yawning canopy of an ancient oak grove, surrounded and secluded by cluster of dense briar patches near the river crossing. The relief felt by all in the wagon train is palpable, as the drivers and guards rest easy. From this sheltered vantage point, the group sits silently observing a long and scattered column of drovers and traders crossing the Friars Bridge and laboriously hiking up the steep hill towards Lanark town. "I don't like this," mutters William as he jumps to the ground from the lead wagon. Marion replies, "Perhaps it would be best if you wait here with Hayde and the Gallóglaigh, while Brannah and I travel into Lanark first?" William replies, "Naw Marion, I cannae let you do that, it's too much of a risk." Marion sighs, "Och William, we could already be at my father's house in the Hietoun and sourcing the medicines and vittals we need, besides, what would the English want with me?"

William scrutinises the reaches of the burgh boundaries and steep escarpments that lead up to the formidable Lanark castle. He shakes his head and scratches his chin. "I don't know Marion; the country is swarming with English patrols looking for the remnants of King John's army, it's no' safe, I don't trust the English. Fuck, I cannae trust them, I mean, how can I after what's happened, what I've seen, I just…" Marion interrupts him, "Wallace, it'll only be a few moments after crossing the Friars Bridge there and on up the brae till we are through the west port gates and into my father's town house. Once we're there and know it's safe, I'll send for you." Their gentle dispute is interrupted by a voice hailing to them from across the bridge. Eddie óg, whom William had sent ahead earlier to scout out Lanark town, calls out… "It's all fine and well in Lanark." he then bounds enthusiastically across the old bridge spanning the shallow summer flow of the Clyde. Before long, Eddie óg stands panting beside William, gripping the oxen harness and recovering his breath. William enquires, "So how goes it in Lanark?"

Still trying to regain his breath, Eddie replies, "All the English soldiers are billeted in the castle and surrounding barracks. There's none I saw in the town itself though." William looks up towards Lanark curiously, "So what's all the noise that's coming from the town?" Eddie replies, "It's the new English Governor, as a goodwill gesture appointing a new Sherriff taking over from D'Levingstun, the English have extended the Lanemar fair to celebrate his arrival."

William enquires, "D'Levingstun is leaving his post as sheriff, when did this happen?" Eddie replies, "Aye, just this very morn ah believe, and I'll tell yie this, the Lanemar fair is busier than I've ever seen it before." William turns and glances at Hayde who shakes his head…"Don't go in Wallace, stay here with Marion and ah'll go with some o' me men up into Lanark and scout it out proper first." William smiles as he replies, "Ah don't think so Hayde, no' wie you dressed as fighting Irish Gallóglaigh. Even in a friendly burgh market fair such as in auld Lanark, you fine fellas would not go un-noticed for very long."

Hayde glances around at the wild unkempt Gallóglaigh company, dressed in their battle-worn saffron and green coloured léine, rusty hauberk's helms and beards platted with small talisman objects, and all of them bristling with an array of weaponry. Hayde looks back at William and laughs, "You're dressed no' se very different in your green léine, layered brat and fighting vambrace Wallace?" William grins, "Hunters vambrace if yie please."

The two friends laugh then Hayde continues, "Aye well Wallace, it may be so that we don't appear much like traders or even aspiring townie worthies, maybe we could pass as humble hunters though, if you count our trade in ten English pelts for each of our own." William laughs, "Ah don't think so Hayde, for I heard all the hunters are to be arrested on sight, their noses split and right-hand fingers cut off, our way of life has been outlawed by the English, sayin' that the forests belong to King Edward, no' us." He looks at the Gallóglaigh who have a penchant for collecting English archer finger bones for their beard weaves. "And it's especially so when it's their own fuckin' soldiers that are being hunted." Hayde laughs and throws his hands up in the air, "Awe fuck me Wallace, maybe we had better stop huntin' and a' trappin' English soldiers and join the English army to beg for our daily vittals, since they no longer permit us to hunt?" William smiles then he questions Eddie óg, "You say there are no English soldiers on guard at the port gates, nor any English mixing with the common folk o' the fair?"

"Naw," replies Eddie óg, "maybe there's some of ther' women folk that are grabbin' vittals from the markets, but the English soldiers are all congregatin' about the castle for the high moor horse racin' fair, or they're drinking ale and betting at the horse racing on the southeast moor." William is perplexed by this news regarding the relaxed attitude of the English soldiery, and the fact they had brought women with them from England, seems very peculiar too. Eddie óg continues, "I heard too that the new English Sherriff is going to completely take over running the shire from D'Levingstun real soon uncle, and that he and an English lord called De Percy have given all the traders an extended Lanemar till the end o' the month, and he'll no' be taking gang-rents nor any taxes for the privilege."

William hears the name de Percy but shows no reaction in front of Marion. Hayde says, "This is strange behaviour from the English, I don't understand, the first thing the English usually do is secure its army perimeters with rings of guards and patrols, then they relieve all unfortunates caught in their net of all vittals, stock and chattel." William agrees, "Aye, and if it's a De Percy cock who crows over this roost, I need to be knowing which one it is?" Eddie óg looks up and says enthusiastically, "Wallace, this De Percy seems to be an awfy peaceable fella for an Englishman, he has shown a disposition to the local folks that greatly meets with the toun grandee's approval. The market is fair jumpin' wie folk too, all trading and bartering happily for all sorts of goods that have no' been seen in Scotland for such a long time.

The English don't seem to be too much fussed neither, for they've brought with them their own wagons full of dried fish and vittals." William, enquires, "What are you talking about, dried fish?" Eddie replies, "Ah watched awhile as their wagon trains kept rolling up from the southern roads to the castle, then they unloaded them into the barns nearest the castle kitchens." Hayde exclaims, "Wagons full o' dried fish?" William says, "Ah, it's a religious thing with the English Hayde, like the church folks here, they reckon if they eat plenty o' fish, it makes them more Christian and prepares them better for the afterlife." Hayde smiles then replies, "Well ah hope they are eatin' plenty o' fish suppers Wallace, for if I get even half a chance, then any English I come across will be visiting their notion o' the afterlife sooner than they might have expected."

"At least we know they've came to Scotland well prepared." laughs William, Marion is far from amused, she exclaims, "William…" Suddenly a cry could be heard from the back of the wagon. William quickly pulls back the wagon-hap to see Brìghde dry-nursing a hungry little Mharaidh. Marion takes the child to nurse at her breast. "I should go now," says Marion, "It sounds to me like the English are not bothering anyone. And from what Eddie óg tells us, it appears the town is busy with the fair and market trading, besides, I want to get little Mharaidh settled soon, for it's been a long journey and my father will be yearning to see his grand-daughter." William frowns, "I still don't like it Marion." She gives him the 'Look.' William grimaces, then reluctantly he acquiesces, "Ach Marion, what are yie like?"

"I'm liking to be away up into the town now," replies Marion with a smile, "and that's the last I'll hear about it, for I could be pulling into my fathers stockyards by now, but I'm stuck here with you fussing about. You do know how urgent it is to be getting any medicines we can find back to the Wolf and wildcats without wasting any more precious time?" William shrugs his shoulders, "Fair enough darlin' but I'll follow and keepin' close eye contact between us. Ah'll hike up through the hawthorn brags o' the Cartlan footpath near the wagon if you need me." Turning to Hayde, William says, "Follow me Hayde, you keep the same distance off me as I am from Marion's wagon. And string out the men in spars, with crossbows to the front, longbows at the rear, that way the last man will rally to the first by line of sight should they be required, will yie make it so?" Hayde replies, "Aye, that ah will Wallace."

Hayde relays the orders to his men as William jumps on the hub of the wagon wheel. He reaches out and puts his arm affectionately round Marion's shoulders and pulls her close, they gaze lovingly into each other's eyes, "I love you wee Maw Wallace… you take care and I'll meet you at your father's stockyards in a wee while." Marion and William kiss passionately; then he kisses little Mharaidh on the forehead then steps down to the ground, it's then William notices Brannah crossing from the wagon backwell and senses her sad demeanor as she sits down quietly beside Marion. He quickly jumps onto the wheel hub, reaches over and clasps Brannah gently by the hand, he says, "Fear not for Andrew Brannah, if it's true he's a prisoner o' the English, it'll be a ransom they'll be getting for his return, ah reckon he'll likely be home soon enough, for the Moray's are no' short o' a groat."

Pulling Brannah close; William gently embraces her, then he steps back to the ground. Marion smiles and winks impishly at her tall handsome husband, she says, "Soon my love, soon." William grins then calls out to Eddie óg, "You walk alongside Marion's wagon, and keep a good eye on me too, if you see anything at all that would endanger her, you let me know, do yie understand?" Eddie replies, "Aye." William steps away as Brannah drives the wagon forward onto the Friar's ford bridge, followed in train by the other wagons. He watches with uncertainty as the little train makes its way across the old creaking bridge. Hayde says, "You've a hell o' a serious concern etched on your face there Wallace?" William replies, "Ah just don't like the feeling o' this." Hayde says, "Don't be worrying so Wallace, they'll be fine, and mind, we'll be keeping close-by with our arrows tight-nocked and taught on the pull, should it be otherwise." William is nervous, he says, "Fuck Hayde, I'll never do this again, it's too risky. I've let Marion and the wee one go in there together. I should never o' agreed to let them go up into Lanark alone." Hayde nods, "I hear yie Wallace, but she will be sound enough. You can see the crow gables of her father's town house from here; and with us se' close behind yie, nuthin' can happen that we cannae fix. Wallace, ah wouldn't want to cross Marion's path in anger, never mind what would follow should she show any distress and give us the nod, would you?"

Smiling a little at Hayde's words, William replies without taking his keen focus away from Marion's wagon. "I just don't understand why the English would have no guards out or any patrols combing these old roads and fords Hayde, there's something very wrong here, I just know there is…" Hayde replies, "Aye, I admit that I can feel it too Wallace, for we've sure been taught harsh and vital lessons these last few years by the English and their cronies, both here in Scotland and back in me auld Ireland. Like yourself, many of my own blood and kin folks are now singing songs in the otherworld because of English justice." William nods in empathy with Hayde as they watch the wagon train clamber off the bridge and onto the west bank, then they slowly begin to pull up the steep brae towards Lanark. "I swear," says Hayde 'I'll never forgive the English for what they've done to me and mine, nor will I ever trust an Englishman's oath, should they ever live long enough for me to hear it." William, still watching the wagons, says, "Ah'm going across the bridge now Hayde. Ahl follow Marion closely as she pulls up the Falls brae, you follow me once I'm over that bridge. We can easy mingle with the traders and travellers, once we are at the west port, wait for me outside the gatehouse."

Securing his short-sword under his brat, William thumps his hand down on the pommel of his grandfather's dirk then he glances at Hayde, the two shake hands, then he walks briskly across the bridge, taking only moments to catch up with the slow-moving wagons just as Marion pops her head round the side of the wagon to see her handsome lover walking close-by. Their eyes catch for a brief moment, time enough to share the love and intimate passion of two souls being as one that sparkles between them. Marion smiles and holds little Mharaidh's hand aloft to wave to her father as he false stumbles over a gorse bush, much to the amusement of Marion and Eddie óg. William glances round to see a grinning Hayde close by, with the Gallóglaigh well-paced out behind him.

Their journey is short and uneventful and soon they are at the west port entrance to Lanark. William moves closer as Marion's wagon passes through the unmanned gatehouse into an exceptionally busy market square. The noise of the fair crowds and thick heavy cooking aroma's filling the air, is carried along on a heavy blue haze from a variety of different meats cooking on charcoal spits and roast irons, making William's mouth salivates as he observes the obvious gaiety in the busy market town. Pausing for a moment to look around the grand market in amazement, he can see hundreds of noisy traders and buyers haggling for trade goods, with troupes of entertainers playing their music, dancing and singing, while others are acting out impromptu theatrical shows, all vying for the attention and coin from the crowds.

"Wallace…" growls a loud voice nearby that startles him. William immediately spins round, gripping his longsword tight, he exclaims, "Hector Buidhe… Sean Cinneidigh, what are you two doing here?" Hector replies, "We've brought our horse teams over for trading up and racing…" Before Hector could finish his sentence, a hand grips William and pulls him around. "Uncle Ranald…" gasps William. "What are yie doin' here boy?" enquires Ranald, he continues. "Yie know it's far too dangerous for you to be roaming freely since your wee incident in Ayr." William scowls, "A wee incident uncle? The bastards murdered Cormack in front of me for no reason other than for their pleasure; then they tried their best to kill me too…" Ranald replies, "Ah know it's so, but ahm just fearing that it's too soon for you to be recognised by the English, before we can get you a renewed pardon to move about freely." William glares at his uncle, then he spits out the words…

"A fuckin' pardon, from the English, to be walking our own land without malice, a fuckin' pardon from the English, to be hunting our own land? Where is this famed English justice in seeking out those who murdered our family Ranald, where?" Gripping William tightly by the brat, Ranald says firmly, "Calm yourself down Wallace, or your hot blood will be the end of us all. Do yie not think that I too would wish the perpetrators and murderers of our family be brought to justice and answer before us for their evil deeds? Do you think it's just you alone who feels that hunger for justice after all that has passed under this tyrannical English yolk?" William shakes his head, for he loves Ranald dearly, and he knows his uncle cares for him like a son. "Ahm so sorry uncle, I didn't mean to be so feckn angry with yie…" Ranald interrupts; "Never be sorry Wallace, just be cautious, then all will come to us in time, you mark my words." Ranald pauses seeing the fire in William's eyes, then he continues, "Otherwise you'll not be reaching such a fine age as me by being se' hot blooded. Naw William, heed ma words ma boy, cold is the blood that warms to the sweet song of vengeance and retribution." Curious at his uncle's choice of words; William looks to see where Marion's wagon has progressed. Ranald enquires, "What brings you to Lanark anyways? You must have a good reason to be travelling from your lair to this place. Yie do know that Mac Álainn mòr has a price on his head, don't yie? And with so many English spies and collaborators abroad, it won't take them long to find out that you're the Mac Álainn mòr they seek, if they don't already know."

William replies, "The reason I'm here is that many of the Galloway and Carrick Gallóglaigh from the Wolf and wildcats, went to fight for King John at Dunbar, and o' the few who did return, most are badly wounded. We desperately need any remedies and compounds we can find to take back with us. True Tam gave me a list of vittals to procure, or we may lose many a good man that we could otherwise save." Ranald enquires, "So what do yiez need?" William replies, "We need starthistle, dovesfoot and flower-grit. We're also to bring back bags o' oatmeal, blocks of cìr-mheala (Honeycomb) and slabs o' churn-fat bealtaine ìm. (Maybutter) Most important is that we get as much fiongeur as we can get a hold o'."

Ranald says "Listen William, you'll be able to get most o' that here, but not the fiongeur, the English have requisitioned all there is in the shire, but if you move swiftly to Ayr, you may take what you need from my cellars in the Ayr castle's cookhouse. I'll give you a Sherriff's messenger pass, that should suffice, but don't you be goin' to Ayr in the event you're recognised, send trusted men from your camp in your stead, do yie hear me Wallace, are yie listenin' to me boy?"

"Fuck," exclaims William, "even leaving now, it'll be the early hours of morn before I get anyone to Ayr." Ranald says, "Walk with me, I'll fix your port pass, then leave as soon as the seal is healed. But mind son, send some o' the other fellas into the castle, don't go in on your own, do yie hear me, for ah know what yie are like." They continue talking as they walk towards the stockyards, when Ranald notices William walking with a slight limp, "When did yie take off your stookies?" William replies, "Yesterday…"

Exasperated, Ranald exclaims, "Ya eejit Wallace, you should have kept them on to be healing proper, that's way too soon for broken bones to mend." William shrugs his shoulders as they walk into the stockyards. Ranald says, "I'll write out the pass at the auctioneers and fix the seal you'll need, I just want to make sure that whoever you send, goes straight to the kitchens of Ayr castle, and he is to speak only with Douglas Bain MacAnnah, he is my master cook, he'll see to all o' your needs regarding the fiongeur, but you must make haste and be quick about it, as most o' De Percy's garrison is here today for the racin', but they'll be in Ayr easy by the morrow's eve." Ranald pauses briefly, then he enquires, "Who is it that you have in mind for this pass?"

William thinks a moment, then smiles as he replies, "There's a chieftain I know o' the Dregern (Dreghorn) Gallóglaigh. They're no' settled with us in camp, but they protect the Ayr and Carrick borders of the Wolf and wildcats up near the Laglan woods." Hector, standing nearby at the corrals, overhears the conversation, he exclaims, "Naw, Wallace, are yie talking about the Gallóglaigh chief, Sean mòr MacDhuibhsídhe, the mad bastard from the Machars o' Galloway?" William laughs, "Aye, that would be him." Sean sighs, "Don't yie really mean... he of the dark and peaceful clan who takes no feckn prisoners?" Hector exclaims, "For fuck's sake Wallace, ah'v never known the bandit Sean mòr to ever be peaceful about anything, even when good king Alexander sat on our throne. And now that the English have killed most of his clan in the Machars, we've heard it so that no English guest has ever left his company alive."

Curious, Ranald enquires, "I thought what remains of Sean mòr's clan, had all sailed with Morrison mòr to settle the ancient fort of Dun Eibhinn in the isle o' Colonsay?"

"He did," replies Hector, "But Sean mòr brought his fighting Gallóbhet back down again, once his kinfolk were safe from English persecution, now he wages his own personal war against the English." Sean says, "Fella's, much as ah like yiez, me and Hector here need to get our horses up to the fair or our journey here will have been wasted." Hector agrees, "Aye, we need to be leaving yiez, but if there's anything we can do to help yie Wallace, you know that yie just have to ask." William smiles as the two chiefs bid farewell to continue their business. He glances round to see Marion's wagon halt at the door of her father's townhouse, then he sees Sir Hugh and her brother Brian exit their town house to warmly greet everyone, then they begin fussing fondly over little Mharaidh Morríaghan. "She's a bonnie lass," says Ranald. William grins, "Aye, she is all o' that uncle," then William enquires, "So why are you here in Lanark?"

Ranald looks up at the battlements of Lanark castle, "Many of the west coast sheriffs and church leaders have been ordered to attend the new Governor, Sir Henry de Percy's council, in Lanark castle. We've been in here for two days now, listening to all the detail of the new order and what the English are demanding from us by way of regime changes and tax collections." William enquires, "Have you met the new Sherriff yet?" Ranald mutters, "De Hazelrigg," He looks into William's eyes, "Aye, he's vermin in the hide of a man, you need to be watching out for this man William, for he's no fool, and there's something really bad about him…" William interrupts with conviction, "I'll tell yie uncle, I think that I've met this man once before if it's the same Hazelrigg. He wanted to hang me up near Ach na Feàrna, and he would have done so but for the intervention of Bishop Wishart and Gilbert de Grimsby." Both then solemnly look up at the Lanark castle battlements, now flying the three leopards flag of Longshanks.

"Uncle," sighs William, "Ahm tellin' yie, I don't really give a fuck who rules the realm, for it appears to me that all the nobles are related anyway, and they just use us all as sword fodder to settle their disputes. For me, it's just the same shit coming down on our heads no matter who lords over us. Marion and I just want to be left at peace in the Wolf and wildcats and we'll bother none by return." Ranald looks into William's eyes and smiles. William enquires, "Why are you smiling like that?" Ranald replies, "Ach William, yer so like your father, he was the same lovable aggressive rogue as you are now, whenever he spoke with such conviction. But I tell yie this, there will be no hiding place anywhere soon from this English king, for he is a master architect o' tyranny. You must either be in service to him… or dead."

William looks towards Lord Braidfuite and can see the joy in his face as he holds little Mharaidh in his arms. "C'mon William," says Ranald, "let's be meeting with Sir Hugh, I'll write yie the pass in his house to requisition the fiongeur from our stocks in Ayr Castle. But not your name on this pass, naw, yie must tell me who you would trust that travels to Ayr under this writ, but not you, and definitely not Sean mòr." William laughs, "Naw, you have my word, I'll send a mild refined fella called Alan o' dale, he's a minstrel and good trusted friend. I'll send him and a fine Irish Gallóglaigh chieftain called Paul au Hayde." Just at that moment, Sir Hugh approaches them, "Ranald, Wallace…" exclaims Sir Hugh, "My it's fine to be seeing you both here, c'mon into the townhouse and share some fresh vittals with us."

The small group chatter together as they make their way into the townhouse, but William hangs back a little, he calls out to Ranald, "I'll be there in a wee while, then he walks over to the wagon where Marion waits patiently. She enquires, "What's wrong William, I can see there's something bothering you?" William puts his arms around Marion and holds her close to embrace her love. He whispers, "I love you so much me darlin', I never want to let you go nor leave your side again, nor that of wee Mharaidh Morríaghan and the wee one you now nurture, you're all that ah love and all that ah live for." Marion pushes William back slightly and looks into his eyes, "What ails you Wallace, for I know you only too well? I know that when there's something amiss or you're not telling me, you're most affectionate?" William gazes into Marion's eyes, "Ach darlin, a moment ago Ranald spoke o' ma father, then I thought o' lady Mharaidh and all the good folk who have passed, then I saw all their faces and thought, had it not been for the English murdering them, they would still be with us and what could have been…" Marion cries, "Oh William, I love you so much, but we must do whatever we must do to survive this time of upheaval. Even if it means that I take to the fields and till the soil with my bare hands for our new English lords." William smiles as he turns over Marion's hands to look at her tender palms…

"Ma darlin' if the English stole our oxen, I would pull the plough for you to broadcast the seed in every oxgang and arrachor in Scotland, if it meant we could just live in peace.

For I have no wish to be fightin' anyone, nor going to some foreign war. But the fact you would say such a thing, shows how low we have become in our expectations, compared to just a few years ago." At that moment, Ranald returns with writs of pass in his hand, "Here Wallace, I've the port pass made ready for you. If you're in need of the fiongeur urgently, you must be leaving now." While William examines the port pass, Marion looks at him with a confused expression evident, she enquires, "What do you need a port pass for?" William replies, "Ranald's given me a pass to collect fiongeur from Ayr castle, for there is none to be found here." Marion exclaims in a panic, "No, not Ayr William, you can't go back there..." Ranald says, "I need to speak with Sir Hugh William, come see me before you depart."

Ranald walks back into Sir Hugh's house as William again puts his arms around Marion, "It's all right me darlin' I wont be going into Ayr castle myself, but I must be getting back to the camp as soon as possible with Hayde, then send men to Ayr to collect the fiongeur. You'll be safe enough here with your father and uncle Ranald," Marion gives William the "Look" then she says, "It's not me that I'm worried about."

Grinning, William pulls Marion close to the blind-side of the wagon, there they take a precious few moments to embrace and kiss passionately. He pulls back a little, then he says, "I'll meet you and little Mharaidh the morrow eve back at the camp ma bonnie darlin'. I've given young Eddie instructions to pass to all the drivers. Ranald said that he'd help you to get everything else we need here in Lanark. I've also instructed Hayde's men to wait for you at the other side of the Friars bridge and I'll inform true Tam that everything he needs will be coming shortly." Ranald returns appearing concerned, "William, you'd best be making speed now and get your men to Ayr. Sir Hugh has confirmed to me that by mid-day on the morn, de Percy's soldiers will move out of Lanark to garrison Ayr town, so you must be leaving now and be in Ayr by first light o' the morn. Get there before the fair markets starts to be welcoming the new governor De Percy. Heed me, you need to be in and gone before the English train reaches Ayr town boundaries." William secures the port pass securely in his satchel, then holds Marion in his arms, "I must leave now ma bonnie anam chara." She leans her head against his chest, "I love you so much Wallace." She looks up into his eyes, William smiles then says, "I love you too... wee maw Wallace."

* * *

On the battlements of Lanark castle, Sherriff Andrew D'Levingstun has been surveying the arrival of over five hundred English troops into the barracks and billets. He clutches at a satchel of writs, handed personally to all Sherriffs of Scotland by King Edward at Ratho castle sheriff's council. D'Levingstun shudders as he ponders over the radical changes now taking place throughout Scotland. He senses the chilling reality of English rule now descending upon him personally. "D'Levingstun..." The Sherriff sets his satchel down and turns to see Bishop Wishart and Sir John Stewart of Bonkyll, approaching him. Wishart says, "The meeting this morning, that was a rough wooing by the English." D'Levingstun replies, "Aye, it's a harsh regime they intend to employ." Wishart enquires, "What will you be doing when you retire from your post?" D'Levingstun replies, "I'll go back to the family seat Wishart, it would appear there is no longer any need for real experience or knowledge with this new English Sherriff's appointment. De Percy informs me that Hazelrigg will shadow me awhile though, till he is knowledgeable regarding every detail of this shire, which I doubt, then, well... it'll be back to the east coast for me." Stewart enquires, "I thought you were supposed to assist the new Sherriff of Drumry after you leave here?" D'Levingstun replies, "The Drumry appointment has not yet been confirmed, for Hazelrigg intends to be observing and recording everything meticulously, only then will I conclude my affairs here." D'Levingstun grasps the satchel of writs and looks at Wishart, "I have one last duty to perform that spoils my tongue with bile." Wishart enquires, "What ails yie so?" D'Levingstun replies, "I have been issued with lists for the procurement of all young men of Lanark shire. They're to report here immediately for martial duties."

Holding up the satchel, D'Levingstun says, "The lists in here are on writs of compliance and procurement I received from Longshanks himself, at the council o' Ratho." D'Levingstun turns and leans on the battlements, then gazes down into the township below, he says, "I don't like this at all Wishart. These writs make demands under the most severe of penalties for non-compliance, that all young men within the shire boundaries, from Thane's sons to the sons of oxgang ploughmen, to provide forensic service within the English army. Then they're to be marched to London to board Edwards ships bound for France, aye, to fight for the English against the armies of King Philip."

D'Levingstun looks at Wishart, almost in despair, "Anyway Wishart, how was your own council with de Percy and Hazelrigg?" Wishart gazes down on the busy market town, then he shakes his head in dismay, "Not good, the English have almost complete control of Scotland, and now install a governor general, to rule over what they call their Northern Province. I believe they will not just stop there though, especially after the debacle of Dunbar." D'Levingstun enquires, "How so?" Wishart replies, "Oddly enough, the English are insistent the Church of Scotland shall remain independent of English clerical domination, but they've destroyed almost everything of literary antiquity from our records. They continue to falsify accounts of our noble lineage for future purposes, that I know not yet their intent."

Wishart frowns and points down into the town towards the west port gates, "Isn't that Braidfuite's daughter the Maid Marion, in his stockyard, look, down there with the former Sherriff from Ayr, lord Crauford?" D'Levingstun realises to whom Wishart has referred, "Hush Wishart, Hazelrigg stands but a few feet away from us. If he overhears your comments, he may take a particular interest in the maid's presence." Wishart and Stewart glance curiously at D'Levingstun. Stewart enquires, "What interest would Hazelrigg have in the maid?" D'Levingstun replies, "De Percy is insisting the maid be wed to Hazelrigg's son. He wants to establish a union of families, elevating Hazelrigg to a position of standing nobility in Scotland." Wishart enquires, "And this is not good news?" D'Levingstun replies, "Hazelrigg is merely a vassal, from De Percy's County in Northumberland. Apparently though, he has shown remarkable service and diligence to the house of de Percy, but he would never see his just reward in England, because of his low-born caste status. By wedding his son to a lord's daughter here in Scotland, it will serve De Percy well to have his own men ruling vast tracts of territory, on both sides of the border marches. It would also elevate De Percy to a position of a paladin noble of England."

Wishart sighs, "Aye, this is what the Normans did when they first came to our country, when many could find no station in England, they soon found it here, by marrying a local chieftain or lord's daughter for inheritance and to their vantage. Some good, like Sir John Stewart here as I may testify to, but others not so good." D'Levingstun says "But not the maid Wishart. She cannot wed the son of Hazelrigg." Stewart enquires, "Why do you say that, she's free to be wed is she not?" Wishart suddenly exclaims, "D'Levingstun, do my eyes deceive me?" he urgently points down at the stockyard, "I think I recognise that young man beside Marion, but it can't be... he's supposed to be dead? Stewart look, isn't that young Wallace of glen Afton?" D'Levingstun quickly pulls Wishart's hand down and glares at him with a grievous countenance, "Quiet your voice Wishart, do not say the name Wallace aloud, for that man there is Mac Álainn mòr, the maids ghillie."

Wishart gazes at D'Levingstun, then he glances back at the tall young man standing beside the maid. Looking curiously at D'Levingstun; Wishart says, "No, that is young Wallace D'Levingstun, for I know him well enough, and his family too. What goes on here, for I had heard that young Wallace was executed by the English, many months ago in Ayr town?" Stewart exclaims, "That is Wallace, I know him from his visits to his uncle's lands near Auchencruive, he has often collected my father's horses and taken them to the Ayr and Lanark fairs." Wishart smiles, then he looks at D'Levingstun, "Tell me, what trickery is this D'Levingstun... and don't be telling us that's not William Wallace, for I recognise his gait and have known him since he was but a child."

D'Levingstun holds up his hands to silence Wishart, he looks around to see that they are not being overheard. "It is young Wallace." utters D'Levingstun. Wishart and Stewart look at each other in amazement, as D'Levingstun continues, "He's been living in the Wolf and wildcats with a small army of Gallóbhet and dispossessed men, but they cause me no trouble Wishart, and I will be keeping it that way." Wishart says, "You may not keep it that way for much longer methinks D'Levingstun, what will happen when you retire, and Hazelrigg assumes your position as the Sherriff of this shire?" D'Levingstun replies, "I don't know the answer to that, but Wallace is not the only problem you may have with Hazelrigg Wishart." Stewart enquires, "Then what say you?" D'Levingstun looks cautiously around the vicinity; then replies, "Wallace and the maid, they are already wed by the faith and oath of the Cruathnie prescriptives."

Wishart and Stewart are completely astonished upon hearing this news; then the seriousness of the situation becomes even more apparent as D'Levingstun continues, "Marion and Wallace have a newborn daughter, and I am also well informed that she is again with child." Stewart gasps, "That's sure going to be a real problem for Sir Hugh, if de Percy is insistent the maid is to wed Hazelrigg's son." Wishart enquires, "What about the other Daughter of Lammington, Brannah, isn't that her name, is she not of an age to be wed?" D'Levingstun replies, "Aye, it's Brannah, but she's already betrothed to Andrew Moray of Petty and Avoch." Stewart ponders, "Wasn't he taken prisoner by the English, along with his father after the battle of Dunbar?" Wishart scratches his chin, "It matters not Stewart. If de Percy is set on the maid Marion being wed to the son of Hazelrigg, then this may be a grievous situation indeed, for this is a political maneuver de Percy requires and is not merely a gesture of union. De Percy is a favourite of Longshanks, particularly from when the English slaughtered Berwick's towns-people."

Stewart sighs, "Wasn't it Sir Henry de Percy who was awarded the knight's garland by Longshanks, for his part in ensuring all the folk of Berwick were put to the sword?" Wishart replies, "Aye, ah'v heard it so." he continues, "Longshanks has also granted de Percy the Baronies and rent gangs from the counties of Lanarkshire, Galloway, Ayrshire, Westmorland and Northumberland. He has also been given the task of governing all north and west, from Grey Rock castle in Glasgow, making him one of the most powerfull barons in the two realms." Stewart sneers, "Don't you mean the one realm Wishart? now that we're merely a province of England?" Wishart ponders awhile, then he says, "D'Levingstun, send a man down there to Lord Braidfuite's yards and fetch Wallace back here to me, for I would wish to have words with him." D'Levingstun replies, "It's not possible Wishart, I'm sure that he's still a branded outlaw, he would be arrested if he were to be brought here and then recognised by the English or their spies."

Wishart ignores D'Levingstun's plea… "If memory serves me right, Wallace is already in possession of a pardon, and though it's obvious he is not dead, I will approach De Percy, tentatively of course, about possibly renewing his pardon, he's not sought as a villain or outlaw since his, eh… execution, is he?" D'Levingstun replies, "As Wallace, he is not wanted that I'm aware off, but as Mac Álainn mòr, he is most definitely wanted by the English, for murder and sedition."

"Mac Álainn mòr is it now?" laughs Wishart, "Young Wallace there is the son of his father Alain right enough. D'Levingstun, send a trusted man and bring Wallace to meet me in your private apartments. I understand of your concerns D'Levingstun, but the greater good calls for greater urgency." D'Levingstun replies. "As you wish." As the Sherriff leaves to send a trusted man to bring Wallace back to his quarters, Stewart leans against the battlements and looks at the curious expression on Wishart's face, "What plans are you brewing in that head of yours Wishart? And what service do you really see young Wallace fulfilling? This is not a magnanimous gesture that you seek on his behalf, but a move politic I'll be thinking." Wishart laughs as he watches William enter the house of Lord Braidfuite with Marion. "There are many dispossessed and landless men in this country Stewart, none more so concentrated than those that languish in the great forests of the Wolf and wildcats, Ettrick and Laglan. If the English garrisons are to be kept busy chasing brazen outlaws in the southwest, then this may gain us valuable time to consolidate all good men to our cause. If Wallace truly is regarded by these wild savages of Galloway as their chief, then perhaps there's a way we may regain our realm through mischief." Stewart ponders, "But what of the English army now flooding into Scotland?" Wishart replies, "Not as it would appear Stewart. Longshanks is in England preparing for a campaign, as a war between England and France is inevitable. Longshanks needs every Lord and vassal at his disposal, for he also faces dissent from his powerful Barons, regarding his right to demand military service and his levy of punitive taxes. He must also negotiate with his Barons, a new Magna Carta, which means that only a sparse garrison force remains here in Scotland."

"Then this may be our opportunity," says Stewart. "If we foster enough discontent in Scotland with brigands and outlaws, while the English King is busy in England or Flanders, then we may yet grasp victory from this English usurper." Wishart says, "My thoughts exactly." Stewart continues, "I ask yie Wishart, what good is mere discontent going to do? Even if we do push the English out of Scotland, wouldn't Longshanks simply invade once more after he has dealt with Philip, and with vengeance and retribution upon his return from France? For we will be standing alone with no allies." Wishart replies, "We may join the Hanseatica federation, long before Longshanks has warmed his boney arse in France." Curious, Stewart enquires, "The Hanseatica?" Wishart watches the crowds below as he replies, "Free trade Stewart, free trade in Europe, that's where Scotland's destiny will be fulfilled, as full members of a European league of peoples, where all members do flourish and individual religious beliefs are respected and loved as a source of solace, inspiration and enlightenment, not feared as an oppressive self-denying source of misery. Think about it Stewart, life without tyranny from inbred rulers and feudal lords who only see trade as a means of taxing the poor. This is where our future is Stewart, a future for Scotland that is within this great European union of the Hansa, this was Alexander's dream, and what he died for I fear. With Wallace and youngblood like him, we may yet achieve this." Stewart enquires, "Explain more to me of Alexanders dream Wishart, for I hear the wheels of intrigue grinding in your head, you see something more, don't you?" Wishart replies, "Have you really any idea as to why Longshanks desperately needs Scotland?" Stewart replies, "No, not really, though I do know you will put forward a plausible account."

"A plausible account?" laughs Wishart, "I shall tell you then Stewart, King Alexander and I had been negotiating with the principle cities of the Baltic Hanseatic federation, for membership of Rosbroch, Berwick, Leith, Perth, Dundee and Inverness to join the league. After the death of Alexander, we were still committed, but just a month from concluding our membership with the Hansa, Longshanks used de Brus to foster a false war by coaxing Comyn and Graeme to invade England and attack Brus in Carlisle. It's under this pretext that England, a Christian kingdom, could invade Scotland with the blessing of the Holy See." Wishart continues, "Longshanks' real intention was to thwart Scotland from joining the Hanseatic federation, for the Hansa is the most radical and wealthiest trading alliance in all of Christendom. Now with the Pope calling for another crusade and Longshanks making war on Philip, this opportune moment may be the last opportunity we have to push the English back over the border and reclaim our time-honoured sovereign destiny." Stewart exclaims, "But... most of our loyal nobles are either dead, imprisoned in England, dispossessed, or in the pay of the English treasury. Who is there to raise an army in Scotland? Certainly not Wallace, not even if there were ten thousand of him. According to D'Levingstun, Wallace and his men won't fight for Scotland, so what force is strong enough that could protect us from another English invasion, once their war with the French is over?"

Wishart replies, "The Hanseatic federation has a strength of great political cohesion. Nigh on a hundred great and wealthy cities are sworn on oath to protect its collective interests, and that of each individual member from interfering monarchs, piracy and rival traders. Already the Hansa has built a more powerful fleet than any King of Christendom ever could, and while these incestuous Kings, Dukes, princes and Margraves of Christendom squabble amongst themselves, the Hansa establishes itself as the way of the future Stewart. When Longshanks attacked Berwick, the Hansa deputies were already establishing a Kontor there, unfortunately they were in Lübeck when the English attacked, or Longshanks would now be facing a wonderous fleet and army, that would even put the Templars to shame."

"Stewart." says Wishart, "The Hansa is a shrewd body of peoples, it really is the future. All they require is that all its members do support any singular conflict involving another member against any aggressor, be he a rightfull prince, a king of that territory or otherwise. Collectively the Hansa provides monies and resources for the hire of a large mercenary army and navy. The Hansa collective has the common wealth to out-finance any known ruler in Christendom, including the Pope and any Phoenician banking conglomerates." Stewart says, "I see now what you are saying, If we achieve the wishes and dreams of Alexander and become a European member of the Hansa, Longshanks couldn't risk ever threatening Scotland again..." Wishart says, "And should we achieve membership before Longshanks can muster another army to attack us, then Scotland will be within a European brotherhood of sworn allies, free of English imperial aggression, unless the English want a war with all members of the Hansa. We must be free of English rule Stewart, but the Hansa will not accept us while we are in a state of flux. If we push the English out and reclaim our sovereignty, we must be ready to conclude the Hansa contracts." Stewart enquires, "Would that not mean a war of annihilation with England though?" Wishart replies, "Aye, but it's a war the English could not possibly win. In fact, had Longshanks not struck at Scotland when he did, then perhaps he saved the sanctity of England, for his realm is nigh on bankrupt."

"Then you're correct." replies Stewart, "If Scotland is to recover our sovereignty, perhaps even to save our very existence, then we must act now. But how can we do this without a standing army at the ready?" Wishart replies, "We can do this Stewart, If Wallace is indeed one of the chosen leaders of the Gallóbhet, then we must formulate a plan that will sting his senses into action, and duly force him to lead his people into a guerrilla war of attrition against the English. We need Wallace and other young bucks like him throughout all of Scotland, to bite and nip at the heels of the English, but only as outlaws and brigands, never as a cohesive army, nor as an outright uprising, just mere outlawry, for this would not distract Edward and force his return here, but it will surely weaken his garrisons and gain us time to bring many of our imprisoned nobles back home. Men like Lord Moray and his son Andrew; then we will strike the English and strike them hard, we just need a little time to resurrect the guardian army in secret. I know Lord Moray has already set up the principle leaders, which includes young Wallace there, and when that time is right, and the English are stretched to their limits chasing outlaws and brigands, we will strike at all their garrisons throughout the realm with such a merciless ferocity, we'll drive them out of Scotland, never for them to return." Stewart enquires enthusiastically. "What would you have me do?" Wishart replies, "Visby on the island of Gotland. Lübeck, Cologne and Russo Novgorodians Stewart, they are the principles of the Hansa. I require you to gather all the remaining trusted officers of the Garda Rìoghail, while I will assemble the great council and other imminent clergy for a secret parliament. From there, we can pick up the finer detail of the previous Hansa agreement and familiarize everyone with the contents therein. I will then send secret ambassadorial deputations to the Hansa fathers and also I will plead openly with Rome to reject Longshanks claim of sovereignty over Scotland."

Stewart says, "Good Bishop, you have lifted my spirits up, when I thought them sadly resigned in base servitude to this English usurper king, Longshanks."

"Well Stewart," replies Wishart, "If we can finally secure an alliance with the Hansa federation, we will remove forever the threat of England's yolk that's strangling our realm by this so-called bloody union. With this one opportunity, we now have two choices to make instead of none." Stewart enquires, "Two choices?" Wishart replies, "With hotheads like young Wallace prodded enough, we may stir up this Sudron cuckoo that's settled in a wasp's nest, then we shall seize this opportunity to be free, or we can stay subjugated under English oppression and feudalism. Hear me well Stewart, it's not only the Scots church and our common faith that shall be destroyed if we do nothing, for the English will bring a feudalism to this country the likes of which has ne'er been seen before. Scotland will be enslaved into bonded service to England's crown for a thousand years, and our realm will forever be indebted and enslaved as a backwater province."

Stewart sighs, "Then tell me Wishart, how do we initiate this grand scheme of yours?"

Before Wishart can reply, D'Levingstun returns with some news… "Wishart, my man was too late." Wishart enquires, "How so?" D'Levingstun replies, "Young Wallace has already taken leave of Lanark and has returned to the Wolf and wildcats." Wishart replies, "Then more is the pity, as I've something in mind that may bring him back into the peace of the English.", D'Levingstun says, "You must forgive me Wishart, but De Percy requires my attendance, we shall meet later this eve." D'Levingstun bids his leave, then Wishart speaks with Stewart. "This may be an even greater opportunity than I thought."

"Explain yourself?" enquires Stewart.

Wishart replies, "I'm privy to where young Moray is being held prisoner in England, and the cost of his ransom bond. If I were to assist the Moray's to secure Andrew's return, then I may also have a solution to ferment unrest in the north. I'll send young Wallace, Moray's friend and future kinsman, with the ransom payment to get him out of the way awhile, then I shall prepare their reason to bite at the English upon their return. Both Moray and Wallace may be our only hope to provide the distraction we need, to bring the guardian army to arms in secret." Stewart enquires, "Why do you choose young Moray, and not his father?" replies Wishart, "Impetuosity of youth Stewart, young people believe the world can change or that they can change it, then we must give them this hope, for we are well placed this very day to manufacture an opportunity. Both Wallace and Moray foster strong loins that ache for both the daughters of lord Braidfuite. While we send young Wallace away on noble service for his friend Moray, I will nurture the next part of my plan." Wishart looks across the battlements and notices that Hazelrigg and his son are very much deep in conversation... "This is a shit ridden country," says Hazelrigg to his son "These Scotch rats that scurry beneath our feet, are created only to serve us. I want you to remember this Arthur, for the Scotch are savages, should I witness you granting them anything more than the privilege of licking your boots and bowing in our presence, I will thrash you well, do you hear me boy?" Arthur replies, "Yes my lord." Just then, Wishart calls out, "Hazelrigg, may I speak with you, there is important detail I believe, that may be of great value to you." Hazelrigg looks at Wishart with suspicion, for he neither trusts nor likes any Scot.

Sneering, Hazelrigg says, "It's not about the monies extracted from your congregation is it Wishart, for you know I have nothing to say on this matter?" Wishart smiles as he approaches Hazelrigg, "No, no, quite the opposite in fact, I am aware your white-knuckle bean counters watch every single pelt and grain of salt traded here by these joyous simpletons in Lanark. In that, you may later recover a true and accurate account of the resources in this shire, for your own larders in Northumberland." Hazelrigg exclaims, "What say you so brazenly..." Wishart interrupts, "Hazelrigg, if you please, calm your spurs and hear me out. For it is of a more eh, delicate matter that I broach you upon. I would speak with you in regard to your proposal of marriage with your son to the maid Marion, daughter of Sir Hugh Braidfuite of Lammington." Hazelrigg smiles cautiously, "You're a shrewd fellow Wishart, what is it then you would you want from me by way of repayment if you were to bestow the marriage blessings upon my house?" Wishart replies,

"No payment Hazelrigg, just a gesture of good faith in our Lord King Edward's appointment of you as Sherriff, and of course, aiding my good friend, Sir Henry De Percy." Wishart continues, "Will you walk with me?"

"Only if I must." replies Hazelrigg, Wishart puts his arm around Hazelrigg's shoulder and guides him towards the stairwell. Hazelrigg enquires as Wishart winks at Stewart, "And what may you do my lord Bishop, that would lend itself to this union, that I could not take for myself?" Wishart replies, "I will make a proper sanctioned introduction to Lord Braidfuite on your behalf Hazelrigg, for the sooner we bring a union between your son and the maid, the better it will be in establishing your ascendancy de facto in the eyes of Lord de Percy." Displaying great delight upon hearing Wishart's words, Hazelrigg replies, "A favourable thought my lord Bishop, what do you suggest?"

"I would suggest," replies Wishart with a smile, "that we visit upon Lord Braidfuite now, for he is a dear friend and I shall make a proper introduction, and I may add Hazelrigg, politically it will be well received by all concerned, if your sons wooing and betrothal to the maid has the blessing of the Church of Scotland. This may be the right time for you Hazelrigg, as the maid is in residence at this very moment in lord Braidfuite's townhouse." An excited Arthur exclaims, "Father, she is here; can we do as the bishop advises?" Thinking about the Bishop's offer for a moment, Hazelrigg finally turns to Wishart and says, "I think it so Wishart, shall we go?" Wishart grins, "Can you think of a better time?" Hazelrigg scrutinises Wishart closely, "I know that you are up to something Wishart; and I wonder... anyhoo, let us not delay." They make their way down the stairwell and through the busy market streets towards the townhouse of lord Braidfuite, where Marion, Brannah, Brian and Eddie óg are watching the last of the Wolf and wildcat wagons laden with medicines and vittals, exiting the west port, Marion smiles, knowing that urgent medicine is now on its way back to the wounded in the heart of the Wolf and wildcats.

"Well Brannah and my dearest little brother," says Marion, "Shall we be picking fine herbs and vittals for tonight's supper?" Brian coughs, splutters, then says, "I'm away up to the fair, for I have to see a man about a dog." Marion and Brannah laugh as Brian disappears into the milling crowds. "Marion, Brannah..." calls out Sir Hugh. Both sisters turn to see their father beckoning. Marion replies, "Aye father, what is it?" Sir Hugh continues, "Come to the house, we have very important and imminent guests, and they wish to talk sincerely in your presence."

Marion waits till the last wagon is out of sight, then she and Brannah walk into the townhouse. As they enter the main chamber, they see a group of men standing near the fire, and are warmly greeted by Bishop Wishart... "Ah, my dearest Marion, Brannah, good to see you both," Marion looks around the chamber, acknowledging Wishart, Stewart and her father, but she does not know the knightly company standing to polite attention beside them. She says, "My Lords, Bishop Wishart, Lord Stewart." Sir Hugh says, "Marion, Brannah, sit by me that I may introduce to you the new Sherriff of Lanark, Sir William de Hazelrigg, and this fine lad here is his son, Arthur."

Hazelrigg bows and kisses the hands of both Marion and Brannah, while Arthur stands dumbfounded and flushed. Marion and Brannah sit on either side of Sir Hugh. He says, "Be seated my lords." He continues, "Now, what brings you to my humble abode on such a beautiful day as this?" Hazelrigg brazenly announces his purpose. He says, "Braidfuite, I shall waste no time upon frivolities, Wishart has told me that you are pragmatic and understand the way of things, and most certainly, the way of things that shall be from now on." Sir Hugh is astonished at Hazelrigg's arrogance, as he continues, "I have no need to be telling you that Scotland is finished as a realm, so you heed me well my lord of Lammington, many Scotch nobles will fall by the wayside, in particular, those who are not in the service of King Edward. Simply put, there are two lists, and your name is yet to be placed on one or t'other…"

Sir Hugh sits with a thunderous expression as Marion begins to tremble in anger; she reaches out beneath the tabletop and firmly grips her father's hand. Both Wishart and Stewart are angered too, but Wishart discreetly stalls Stewart's reaction, to say nothing and watch the scene play out. Hazelrigg boldly continues, "I can see potential machinations of protest my lord Braidfuite, but please, you must be at ease, for I bring deliverance to you and your household, a future of great prosperity by virtue of my good will." Sir Hugh demands clarity, "Explain yourself Sir…"

Hazelrigg sits back in his chair and throws his chainmail gloves haphazardly across the table.

"Really lord Braidfuite, I see that perhaps your wit is not as sharp as the good Bishop here would have me believe. Therefore, I must put my requirement to you very simply, should you wish to be favoured and see your lineage prosper… or wither, the choice is now yours to make." Hazelrigg sits forward in his seat and looks firmly into the eyes of Sir Hugh, he continues, "Arthur here is my eldest son, he will wed your daughter the maid Marion in a union of our two blessed families. The purpose is for the breeding of your family into fine English bloodstock, this will ensure that the future of your entire household survives, I trust that you understand that any alternative would bring an ignoble end to your line."

There is an audible gasp in the room from all, other than Hazelrigg and his son. Even Wishart could not have predicted such a blunt delivery. Marion looks at Sir Hugh and pleads, "Father..."

Sundrum Falls

William, Stephen of Ireland, Alan O'Dale and Hayde, ride fast with a troop of twenty Gallóglaigh towards Ayr town, on an urgent mission to procure medicinal fiongeur for the wounded survivors from the battle of Dunbar, and all others who sought refuge in the safety of the notorious Wolf and wildcat forest. Upon reaching the vicinity of the Laglan woodland several miles southeast of the town, the Gallóglaigh bring their horses and packhorses to a halt near the Boarstone of Culton, there they dismount and rest awhile. Hayde takes some oatmeal biscuits and cheese from his backpack, while William pulls out a whisky bladder, some oats, sour bread and wind-dried meat from his saddlebags. They all sit or lay down on the grass to rest awhile and take in some much-needed nourishment.

Stephen comments as he munchies his scran, "Would you be looking at that bleedin' sunset, that's the biggest reddest bleedin' sunset I have ever been and seen in me whole life." William laughs, "The condition you were in a yesterday, I wasn't sure you were going to see another sunset, or sunrise, either that or you'd seen your last." Stephen smiles, "Ah, yie know me Wallace, it'll take more than a rovin' English army to be putting me down." Hayde quips, "Aye, that may be so Stephen, but credit to bonnie Brìghde, for it didn't take her long to get yee fit n' and back yer feet again." Stephen replies,

"Ha, healthy enough to make sure you fancy feckrs don't start a blade party without me." The friends all laugh as they watch a glorious sun setting far beyond the horizon across the wide bay of Ayr, the Ynches of Argyle and Northern Ireland. Alan O'Dale suddenly raises his hand, motioning for them all to be quiet…

Everyone grips their swords and looks around; Alan O'Dale lifts his head, as though listening to a voice in the distance. He motions for the others to be still; after a moment, he points towards the back side of the great Boarstone, a large boulder as tall as ten men, as long as six shire horses and as broad as any hay cart, so finely balanced on two great pivotal boulders, a gentle breeze from the beating wings of a Corbie chick can make the great stone sway precariously. Alan O'Dale cocks his crossbow as the other Gallóglaigh begin to encircle the Boarstone, when Stephen hears a slight scuffling noise coming from what appears to be a tiny hollow, barely noticeable, at the base of a pivot stone, he motions for everyone to hush, then he pushes back the dense long hairgrass that conceals a tiny entrance, revealing a small natural cavernous space, where wild goats would shelter and gain safety from hunter wolves.

Stephen reaches deep inside and drags out a frightened young boy about eight years of age, who kicks and screams wildly. "What the fuck?" exclaims William. Stephen grips the boy firmly and raises his hand to slap him about the head, "Why were yee hiding in there boy, are yie spying on us ya durty little feckr?" Hayde calls out, "There's another one in here." he reaches into the hollow, "Wait, it's a wee girl." William calls out, "Hold on there Stephen, that wee fella looks starved, would yie look at them, they're filthy and stink o' piss, and those rags for clothes they're wearing barely covers them." Hayde brings the girl over. She appears a little younger than the boy. Suddenly she wriggles free of Hayde's grasp then runs and clings desperately to the scrawny boy, who quickly pushes her behind him, he then pulls out an antler knife from behind his back and stabs at Stephen and Hayde. William and the Gallóglaigh admire the tenacity of the young boy, defending what appears to be his sister. Alan O'Dale and Hayde offer the two youngsters some oatmeal biscuits and cheese to perhaps calm them down.

For a few moments the children recoil, but the girl eventually reaches out, then she quickly snatches the food from their hands. The two starving youngsters huddle below the Boarstone and ravenously eat the food. Stephen looks at William and smiles, "Hungry wee mite's those two." William squats near the two children, studying them. "Aye, and starved near to death by the look o' them." Everyone returns to eat their vittals, but William remains near the children, with more food offered in his outstretched hand. Although distrustful of William, they gaze at him with wide, dark, sunken eyes, then the young girl smiles. William smiles back by return, but he feels the hairs on the back of his neck prickle. He ignores the sensation, then he notices the boy's smile turn into a grin. William grins, instinctively he turns to catch the flash of a blade bearing down on his head. Immediately he moves to the side as the flat of a sword-blade glances off the side of his skull. Simultaneously and despite the pain, he throws his arm over the assailant's sword arm, forcing it upwards and back, causing the assailant to drop the sword as William grips him by the throat with his other hand.

Everyone in the camp rushes over with swords and axes at the ready, while William holds the assailant high and tight against the rocking stone, helpless and unable to finish his attack. "Kerlie…" exclaims William. He looks into the familiar face of the assailant, who stares back at him through severely bruised and blackened eyes; his bloody face almost hidden by long tousled blood-knotted hair. William lowers the injured Kerlie to the ground and calls out, "Quick, fetch me some craitur," then he speaks to his would-be assailant. "What's happened to yie Kerlie, and what are you doing so far north, and why did yie feckn attack me?" Kerlie sits against the Boarstone and groans in pain from apparent flesh wounds. Alan O'Dale brings over some whisky and food, "Wallace," croaks Kerlie, "Is it really you?" William replies, "Aye Kerlie, but tell me, what the fuck's happened to you and these two wains?" Kerlie replies, "I was with ma father Wallace, we were visitin' your kinsman at the Sundrum fortalice when the English arrived behind us and surrounded the place, they said to us they were searching for runaways from Baliol's broken army."

"Sundrum?" exclaims William, "Fuck, what's happened at Sundrum, is everyone all right over there, what o' chief Duncan...?" Kerlie sits up and wipes the long and matted tresses of hair away from his face, as everyone come over to hear his words, "Ahm sorry Wallace, but I think everyone down in Sundrum is dead." William gasps, "Naw, how can you know they're all dead, I mean, what the fuck's happened?" Kerlie explains, "Me and ma father brought a herd of horses across from lower Kilmaurs, heading for Lanark horse fair. We stopped at your kinsman's fortalice for a rest and to feed the horses, we'd just arrived when a troop of English cavalry came in behind us. They were peaceable enough at first and your kinsman Duncan met them offering hospitality, but once the English were all inside the fortalice, they drew their swords and attacked everyone they saw, men, women, wains... everyone, the folk never had a chance to defend themselves." Kerlie's head sinks as William urgently enquires, "What about Duncan and his family, did they escape?" Kerlie shakes his head, "Naw, I don't think so, I was near the fortalice cludgie when it all started, standing just above the cludgie run-off grill, yie know, the one that runs underneath Sundrum and comes out near the falls... Fuck, the English slaughtered everyone Wallace; I've never seen anything like it. I thought that they would catch me too when ah tried hidin' these two wains, for they both started screamin' when seeing all o' the killin'... it was pure carnage." Kerlie drops his face into his hands in a futile bid to blind himself from what he had witnessed.

"The screams Wallace, I've never heard anything like it." William shakes Kerlie roughly, "Tell us what yie know?" Kerlie continues, "I feared we would be caught too, so I dropped down into the cludgie trap with the two wains. We made our way through the underground caverns till we came out down near the falls o' Coyle. There were two English soldiers guarding horses that I didn't hear nor see at first and I walked straight into them. Luckily, I caught them by surprise and launched straight at them with flail and blade before they could draw their weapons... ah managed to beat them down dead, then made ma escape with the wains." William demands, "Tell me, did yie see if Duncan and his family escaped?"

Kerlie replies, "Wallace, I just don't know for sure. Ah hid with the wains in the briar patches on the slopes near Sundrum, it was there we watched as those who were not killed in the first onslaught, taken out to the trystin' thorn. Everyone there was forced to kneel and then they were bound with their hands behind their backs. Some bastard knight who was in charge, ordered his younger soldiers to dash everyone's brains out with maces and clubs... Wallace, I couldn't do a thing to save any o' them. The knight then commanded his archers to use surviving wains as targets, he let others run for their lives, but the archers had sport with them too, then the cavalry trampled the bodies, be they alive or dead..." There is a loud sorrowful groan emits from everyone gathered around Kerlie. "Did yie hear the name of the knight at all?" enquires William. "Aye," replies Kerlie, "his name is de Percy."

"Fuck," exclaims William, "It can't be the same de Percy who's residing in Lanark, it couldn't be?" Kerlie says, "This Percy is awfy young for wearing the mantle o' a knight, but he appears to have an authority that has his men obey him without question." Hayde enquires, "When did this happen?" Kerlie replies, "It was about two or three days ago." Stephen curses, "Jaezuz, that's your kinfolks down there Wallace. We've got to be going there fast to see if there are any survivors." Kerlie continues, "We met some folk from the Clachan o' Joppa and Taighlam. The say the English had come from Ruther's glen castle and were scouring the countryside for vittals, killing without mercy nor any pity. When we came through Joppa making our escape, there were none of the folk there left alive. The only ones we saw had met with a cruel and merciless end."

William exclaims, "Joppa... that's where Gilbert de Grimsby hails from, his father is the blacksmith there." Hayde enquires, "Did any others escape Joppa?" Kerlie replies, "Ah don't think so, it was just another slaughter, I had to keep goin' and look after these two wains. I thought to get to the Laglan woods, then deep into the Wolf and wildcats, but as far as I know, any of the surrounding village folks who managed to evade the English, made to hide up at the Martnam loch Ynches. Some of the others were going on up to the old crannog beds at loch Fergus, but ah thought it best to make my own way, ahm glad ah did, for not long after, I watched troops of English soldiers followin' the villager's route wie' huntin' dogs." Hayde calls, "Get mounted." Stephen speaks with William, "What is it you want to be doin' about this Wallace? Kerlie here says de Percy's responsible." Thinking a moment, William replies, "We'll mount up and get down to Sundrum fast to see if auld Duncan or anyone else has survived, before we go chasing after some knight because of his name. Fuck Stephen, I thought that after Dunbar that this madness would have ended. I thought there would be peace now that Baliol is imprisoned and the warring seemed to be over, ah mean, look at the Lanark fair earlier this day..."

Laughingly, Kerlie spits out the words, "Over... Fuckin' over, where have you been Wallace, it's only just beginning? The English have been stripping the country of all resources, food and vittals they can find, and killing any and all with impunity. I heard it said the entire east coast is under severe martial law and the English are pressing all the young men there into their army, then their bein' taken away to fight in some foreign fuckin' war. The country folk are starving, eatin' summer fruits, roots and worms. Where have you been Wallace not to be knowin' all o' this? When my father..."

Kerlie hesitates, "What is it Kerlie," enquires William. "Where's Fearghal?" Kerlie bows his head and digs the nails of both hands into his scalp, dragging them forward as though to cause a pain of repentance. William kneels beside Kerlie, "Is your father...?" Staring at William, Kerlie replies with great angst in his voice, "I don't know where he is Wallace, that's why I still linger hereabouts. It all happened so fast, so quick, now I'm shamed to my very soul that I didn't stay by his side," William says, "Kerlie, you MacFhearghail's (MacKerrels) have blood o' the finest mettle, you're here with us now only because of circumstance and no other reason, do yie hear me, so don't be fretting. Auld Fearghal will be safe and hiding out somewhere down about Sundrum, maybe he's reached Auchencruive? Kerlie, you don't know what's happened yet, so yie don't need to be feeling shame. Fearghal's a tough auld fella." Kerlie stands up and shouts at William…

"Fuck Wallace, I've scouted around the outskirts of Sundrum without getting caught for nigh on two days. I tell yie, there were none in the vicinity of the place that I could find, other than the dead. The English are running bloodhounds everywhere, hunting our folk down like animals… ahm telling yie, none has been left alive at Sundrum." William says, "Maybe he's a prisoner of the English?"

Kerlie walks in circles like a deranged caged animal, then he snaps, "Fuck you Wallace and your fucking maybe's, look at yie all in your fake war garb. Do yiez know o' anyone taken prisoner by the English and lived, other than a precious fuckin' noble? Fuck you and your kind Wallace, for yiez hide away like rats in the fuckin' woods. You think it's safe for you and yours to be robbin' honest traders and travellers, then hoping that all of this will just go away. Yiez skulk and cower in the forests, dreaming that someone else will deal with the English, but you Gallóglaigh bastards know nothing of what's going on in the real world. You Gallóglaigh cunts make me fuckin' sick…"

Suddenly William thrusts his hand forward, catching Kerlie by the throat, ruthlessly forcing him against the Boarstone; then he backhands him hard across the mouth. Kerlie vainly struggles, but his efforts are futile trying to free himself from the iron grip of William's hand around his throat. Stephen rushes over and grabs William, but he is shoved unceremoniously to the ground. Alan O'Dale speaks calmly, "Give Kerlie grace Wallace, his wit is gone." Meanwhile, Stephen lay curled up on the ground, groaning in agony. He curses, "What the fuck are yie doin Wallace? Ma wounds have opened up again, ya arrogant big fuck." William glares into the face of Kerlie, who is helpless to resist William's brute strength. Stephen shouts at him, "Lay Kerlie down Wallace ya fuckin' idiot, for he may not be so far wrong in what he thinks and what he says to us, striking him down will no' be changing any o' that." William ignores Stephen and spits his words out with venom, "You don't know us Kerlie, nor can you know what has happened to me and mine to speak this way." William's anger is broken upon hearing Hayde call out his name. "WALLACE..." William drops Kerlie to the ground and glances at Stephen, who is pained and holding his side, then he notices blood is seeping through Stephen's léine. Alan O'Dale quickly rushes to his aid.

"Wallace?" enquires Hayde, "that's us ready to leave, so what's your plan?" William looks deeply into Hayde's eyes, "What do yie mean, what's ma plan? I'm not your fuckin' chief." Hayde snarls back, "Stop fuckin' about Wallace, what do you want us to do? Do we ride for Ayr, loch Fergus or Sundrum?" William looks at Stephen who grins back at him, though obviously he is still in much pain. Stephen shrugs his shoulders and smiles at William's apparent discomfort, and the obvious natural leadership mantle he carries, but so often denies...

Stephen says to Kerlie, "How many English were at Sundrum fella?" Kerlie shakes his head, "Ahm no' sure, I reckon maybe about a hundred or so horse troops and about the same in soldiers, with wagon crews in attendance too for collecting vittals and everything else they can steal." William enquires, "Are they still in Sundrum?" Kerlie replies, "Aye, there's a small garrison left down there. I heard that English knight order his men to follow any survivors towards Loch Fergus, then he commanded the rest to move out and continue collecting taxes and vittals. I think their main force might be away over by the old Coyle forts at Drongan and Auchencloich by now, maybe even they're at the Comunnach barracks." Irritated by William's apparent indecision, Hayde demands, "Wallace, what's your feckn orders?" William curses, "Fuck it Hayde, take a dozen men and head for Martnam Ynches, see if there are any survivors there. I'll go to Sundrum with Kerlie, Torrance, Gormlaidh and the other Gallóglaigh. Meet us at Sundrum falls by daybreak if we haven't sent riders for each other before then." Hayde replies, "We'll head to the old caput at Marroks mote first, if we haven't found anyone there, it'll mean likely there no' any survivors at all."

William acknowledges Hayde, who nudges his horse to walk-on, then he canters off with the rest of the Gallóglaigh. William turns away and squats beside Stephen, now sitting upright with a big grin, though still in obvious discomfort. William says "Ahm so sorry Stephen, ah don't know what I was thinking, and my apologies to you too Kerlie…" Stephen replies, "Ah sure now Wallace, I know what you were thinking, didn't you just feel shame by way of Kerlie's honest words? Mind that ah know yie well, I know you wouldn't be hiding away if yie didn't have bonnie Marion, the family and all those disparate folks to be protectin'. Naw Wallace, you'd be out there hunting and stripping the land o' this Norman fuckin' pestilence that's taken ma bonnie Katriona, me wains, your own kinfolks and so many other good folks too. Now isn't that the truth of it all, and so it'll be the root o' yer real anger wit' Kerlie there?"

The worldly opinion of Stephen strikes a true chord with William. He knows Stephen's observation is part reason for his anger and frustration. Not that Kerlie was completely wrong, but the fact he was mostly right. William turns to Kerlie, "Will yie take ma hand and accept my apologies."

Kerlie looks at William for a moment, then he wipes his bloody mouth as he leans against the Boarstone. He glares at William, then replies, "Aye, but only if you give me your bond that my words are passed and no longer can they bring shame upon us, nor anger between us. Fuck we're hunters Wallace, never were we born to be the fuckin' hunted." Stephen watches Kerlie and William talking, then he speaks quietly with Alan O'Dale, "Who's that Kerlie fella? He's a wee feckr, but he has the sinews o' a chieftain o' the hunt sure enough." Alan O'Dale replies, "He is one of the old Aicé Devorguilla's lead huntsmen from a place called loch Maben in Galloway. He and the Wallace go way back in their history together. I think they're both distant kinsmen to each other through Wallace's kinfolk the Crauford's."

"Ach now," says Stephen, "It would appear that me brother Wallace there has a much bigger family cluster than ah ever considered." Alan O'Dale laughs and points, "Everything you see westward and everything north, is Wallace and Stewart country Stephen. Below us and to the east is Crauford land, all who live there and beyond are kinfolks to each other. That's why the English are having so much more difficulty here and in the southwest, than anywhere else in Scotland. Everyone hereabouts is close tight related and the Gallóbhet sure love blood feudin' so much, it makes them more than fit for fighting the English one on one, or even ten to one against." Stephen smiles, "Blood feudin'? I thought Ireland was an un-natural inbred feudin' haven, but you Scots could maybe show us a thing or two about that by the sounds of it." William calls out, "Stephen, you stay here with these two wains, while ah go down to Sundrum with Kerlie and the other Gallóglaigh, we're goin' to scout the place out. And before yie object, it's a good thing that I did shove yie on yer boney arse, for you're no' in any fit state to be fightin anything off, including sleep." Stephen protests, "Fuck off..." but William continues, "Watch the three o' them Alan O'Dale. If we're no' back here by sun-up, you're to go on and get as much fiongeur as you can carry on the packhorses from Ayr Castle, then get back fast to the Wolf and Wildcats. And you Stephen, it's your mission to get the two wains back to the safety of our camp."

Alan O'Dale nods in compliance. Stephen makes to stand up, but the opened wound forces him to sit back down again. He shouts, "Who the fuck are you to be giving me feckn orders Wallace?" William smiles as he walks over to Warrior and grips the horn of his saddle. He looks at Stephen, then replies, "Ahm that chief yie wanted so badly, ya contrary Irish feckr." Pulling himself up and into the saddle, William laughs as the other remaining Gallóglaigh mount. Stephen replies, "Sure now, isn't that' delightful news to be hearin', and so much more like your auld good self there Wallace. It's a fine thing when working with another who humbly knows his station in life. I just needed to be hearing yee say it, that's all." William laughs and gives Stephen the "Look" Stephen laughs too, then William says, "Kerlie, you take Fleetfoot, for he's the only horse that could keep up with Warrior should yie be needing fast heels." Alan O'Dale and Stephen watch as William and the Gallóglaigh. canter off in the direction of Sundrum.

After riding only little while, they soon gain near to Sundrum fortalice grounds. William raises his head and his heart sinks, for the faint but familiar scent of death is in the air. Memories come flooding back from the many other horrendous sights he has witnessed. He thinks long and hard about the massacre of Glen Afton, but quickly regains his senses and raises his hand to halt the others. He glances at Kerlie and is momentarily startled in the dim evening light. For just one brief moment, he thought Kerlie was Coinach. He studies Kerlie and notices how close in physique and stature they both are, curiously, the same tension emanates from both in similar circumstance. William nods at the Gallóglaigh and everyone dismounts and quickly hobble all their horses, then they move to observe the Westport of Sundrum.

"Look, over there…" whispers Kerlie, "There's two guards at the gate sitting beside a brazier, they don't appear to be expecting anyone by the look o' them." William signals two Gallóglaigh, who immediately make their way stealthily towards the two gate-guards. After a few moments, the two guards appear to be enveloped by shadows and pulled silently away into the failing light by monsters from another world. Kerlie says, "We should follow the cludgie passage up and into Sundrum, its small, but there will be no guards there." William replies, "Wait till the Gallóglaigh get back Kerlie, they'll have good information for us, then we can decide how best we broach Sundrum."

It is only a few moments till the two Gallóglaigh are back beside William and Kerlie. Torrance appears contented as he wipes blood from his dirk and reports his findings.

"There's only a dozen Sudrons in the fortalice Wallace… well ten now. A Sudron told me that the English are doing a territorial sweep for food and taxes as far as the Wolf and wildcat borders, then going to Ayr town with whatever they can find. The other Sudron told me before his departure, they're expecting a full garrison troop for Sundrum within the week." William enquires, "Did you find out anything else?" Gormlaidh, watching the port gate of Sundrum, replies, "Naw," William instructs Torrance and Gormlaidh to take the other Gallóglaigh to flank the fortalice perimeters and make their way into Sundrum, while he and Kerlie will enter through Sundrum' underground passage. Both William and

Kerlie make their way cautiously towards the falls of Coyle as the sun finally sets. Approaching the falls, they are halted in their tracks by a horrific scene. "Naw…" exclaims Kerlie as he drops to a squat and stares at the falls. William stands in silence, observing the bodies of men, women and children bobbing up and down in the shallows of the falls basin. Others are tumbling, sinking and re-appearing in the drop of the falls, like autumn flotsam trapped in the churning waters. "C'mon Kerlie," William grips Kerlie by the neck of his léine and pulls him roughly to his feet.

They both walk along the muddy path, avoiding stepping or stumbling on bloated bodies all scattered asunder on the route along rivers edge. They traverse the bodies and terrain till they eventually make near to the falls and enter a nearby secretive passage leading up to the Sundrum fortalice. William and Kerlie agonisingly feel their way along the small dark cavernous tunnel. The horrific stench of death, human excrement and the burning sensations from urine ammonia, cause them both to stop and wretch.

They struggle forward, continually stumbling over corpses and sliding about on bloody human remains, till finally; they reach the heavy iron trap that will allow them to enter Sundrum and free them from their ordeal. Raising the trap grill slightly, they both gasp and fill their lungs with precious, clean air, freeing them from the nauseous confines of the tunnel. Quickly familiarising their eyes to the low evening light and brazier glow, they begin to understand what they are seeing. Without warning Kerlie shouts, "Dá…" Before William can react, Kerlie brutally clambers over him and scrambles out of the cludgie and runs at speed towards the far end of the Sundrum courtyard. William curses as he climbs out of the cludgie and runs after Kerlie. Drawing his sword, he crouches, watching for any English soldiers to show themselves and then make for the reckless Kerlie, who is now pulling at a body sitting against the wall of Sundrum tower. Two characters move towards Kerlie from the shadows, William instantly recognises them as two of his Gallóglaigh. "Wallace…" William spins round to see the sombre face of Torrance standing behind him, "There was only ten of them here right enough, we've got what's left of them over in the far side of the yard." William looks across the courtyard at Kerlie, crouched with what appears to be his father cradled in his arms. William says, "Hold them fast Torrance, till I see to Kerlie."

Walking across the courtyard, William instinctively knows what type of scene will greet him as he approaches Kerlie, who sits rocking back and forth, grief stricken while holding his fathers head in his lap, William notices the back of old Fearghal's skull is crushed and caved in and his throat has been violently cut. Kerlie looks up at William and then hides his face away while pulling his father even tighter to him, as though trying to protect him from any further violence. William knows there is nothing he can say or do and begins walking back to find out what Torrance and the Gallóglaigh have discovered. As William walks back across the courtyard of Sundrum, he gazes up at a polar blue and cloudless night sky, the beauty of the midsummer's night allows him to take his eyes and mind away from the earthly sights and scents of bloody carnage, so savagely brought upon another peaceful Scots community in Sundrum.

Gazing up at the mesmerising beauty of a honey-coloured moon, blissfully surrounded by stars twinkling in the soft heavenly canopy, reminds William when as a child, he enjoyed the happy atmosphere at Sundrum, when visiting with both his uncle Malcolm and his brother wee John. He thinks of his teenage years and the respect he gained as a

Sundrum Falls

Cappalmaraich (Horse-Wrangler) for old Duncan of Sundrum. He affords a little smile, reminiscing of the times he watched wee John wrangle horses and getting bucked through corral fences, against trees or into any variety of solid objects when they spent long summer days of their youth there, taming the wild moorland and forest horses for the old chiefs. He remembers too when taking the unshod horses and meeting with their childhood friend Gilbert De Grimsby, at his father's smithy in Joppa, then they would all gang the horses together to take to the markets around the south and west of Scotland. But now, Sundrum, like so many other places of his youth, is nothing more than a fading memory from a different time... just one more devastated ruin whose community has been shown no mercy, be it a high-born noble, clan chief, man, woman or child, from this foreign army of occupation, who's increasing visitation of brutality upon all his kith and kin, seems endless.

Suddenly William hears a noise that brings his senses back to the hellish reality of Sundrum. He quickly follows the sound that has distracted his solace. Rounding a corner, he sees seven bodies lying prostrate, they differ from all the other bodies by the way they are laid at the feet of the grim-faced Gallóglaigh. As he gains closer, it becomes obvious they are English soldiers that have been killed. The Gallóglaigh quickly get busy stripping the bodies of all armour and weaponry. Then he notices two Englishmen are still alive at the feet of Gallóglaigh guards, who stand with one foot firmly placed on their faces, with the tip of their spartaxe pressed hard into their backs. "Who's this?" enquires William when noticing an elderly English knight sitting nearby shivering against a stone water trough, dressed only in a flaxen nightshift that drops down his bony white spindly legs, his demeanor is completely disconnected from the reality of William and his Gallóglaigh's world. Torrance says, "We found this old bastard in the chambers o' Duncan." William walks up to the English knight and looks him in the eyes... "Are you responsible for all o' this?" Torrance steps forward, spits on the ground and scowls at the English knight. "When we entered Duncan's quarters, we found this durty scum bastard defiling two young boys maybe no older than six summers. We wanted to skin the fucker alive there and then, but we thought you might be wantin' to be givin' him the question before we splay him tenfold by return."

Torrance steps back as William puts his thumb and knuckle to his own eyes and rubs hard, trying to stop his mind from losing self-control. He refrains from killing the knight and forces himself to ask a question, "I'll ask you just the once Englishman..." Before William finishes his question, a scream comes from one of the English soldiers behind them. Turning quickly, William sees a Gallóglaigh pulling the soldier up by the hair, while another grips him tightly, pulls his head back, then Kerlie brutally saws through the soldier's throat with a skinning knife. The soldier's screams are quickly replaced by the audible flapping of blood running into lungs, trying desperately to breath in air as the head is being hacked from the body.

William has no care for this savage revenge, but he has no care to stop it either. He knows each man deals with grief in these circumstances differently from the next. He turns and looks at the old knight who believes this example of brutal execution is meant for him to talk, and talk he does. He falls to his knees and grabs William by the hand then tries to kiss it. William pulls his hand away and the old knight falls forward, trying vainly to kiss William's feet. The old knight lifts his head up and pleads for his life, but he freezes when he sees the Gallóglaigh cutting the fingers from the hands of the headless corpses. "Wallace," says Torrance, "We're gonnae be throwing all the English dead down into the cludgie run-offs. When their friends come to find them, they'll find no trace, and be thinking the demons o' the Wolf and wildcats has taken them away to the underworld, for those English don't look se' much different from us in death, do they." William nods, then he turns his attention back to the old knight, "I will ask you again…" the old knight cries out, "I plead mercy my lord, I am just a poor scribe, memorialising all of the provisions we can find while scouring for food. I beg of you; I had no part in this butchery by hand nor by design." Torrance snarls, "He fuckin' lies Wallace, no fuckin' knight was ever a scribe to another, let me send him on to a better place… real fuckin' slowly." William replies, "Have patience Torrance, let the auld fella have his say first."

He kneels down and looks into the eyes of the old knight. Suddenly the old knight blurts out "Marmaduke de Percy…" William stands erect and exclaims, "Marmaduke de Percy?" the old knight replies, "Yes my lord, he is on a mission here to root out and eliminate all sedition connected to the bloodline of certain houses and clans in Scotland. De Percy has a list, and like so many others, he acts out-with the accepted rules of chivalry. When I heard your man say your name, I knew I must tell you…" William enquires, "Tell me what?"

The old knight clasps his hands, as though kneeling at the altar of the faithfull, "Your name good Sir, if I heard that beast address you correctly." William enquires, "What's the name that you think you heard old man?" The old knight gazes around for a moment; then he looks up at William, "Wallace my lord… Wallace is one of the names high on the list, for they are blood of the Scotch royal Guard commanders, and also, most of the Wallace family ne'er signed the Ragemanus, as was required by our king." A shrill cold feeling sweeps through William's head, upon hearing this conformation of the death lists from the mouth of a ranking English knight. William turns and walks away a pace, he has to think, he already knows of these lists, but... Suddenly he hears a gut-wrenching scream, then Kerlie comes rushing out of the shadows and bull charges the old knight to the ground, before anyone can stop him. Kerlie grapples the old knight, grabbing him from behind by the throat and trapping him by the legs in a wrestling grip. In an instant, Kerlie stabs at the gut and genitals of the old Englishman with a skinning knife. "KERLIE…" roars William.

But Kerlie doesn't hear William, nor any of the Gallóglaigh screaming at him, such is his frenzied state of mind as he repeatedly stabs the old knight about the heart. Kerlie grips the old knight's forelock, pulls his head back and rips at his throat with the ferocity of a fighting wildcat's claws. "KERLIE…" shouts William once again, the wild staring eyes of Kerlie and those of the old knight, still in shock in his death throes, gaze up despairingly at him. Kerlie kicks the Englishman's shaking body away and scurries backwards along the ground, resting up against the stone trough.

William glances despairingly at Torrance, who simply and unemotionally shrugs his shoulders. William stares at Kerlie, who now reminds him even more so of Coinach. He says, "I needed that old bastard to talk …" Kerlie glares at William like a trapped beast… Moments pass as both young men glare at each other. Kerlie then stands up and brushes at his filthy léine while trying to compose himself… "I'm with yie Wallace… I'll lay down my life to fight by your side, this is my oath to you by the blood o' ma father." Exasperated, William replies, "If and when you ever fight under my command Kerlie, if you ever disobey me just once in war, I will cut your fuckin' head off myself…" He glances at the gathering

Gallóglaigh, who are all listening intently. "And that applies to any man here who is thinking to be calling me his Chief…"

William recalls the consequences of Coinach's understandable but rash actions on the Duibh hill of Invergarvane. Ultimately it was his own indecision that cost the lives of his boyhood friends and many of his kinfolk. If his own instincts are now forcing him to be this so-called *'Brigand Chief,'* and leading them all into battle, then it will be to bring more back alive than otherwise would under the command of another. He knows that his instinct and his commands must be pure of heart, which also means, being completely devoid of any pity and having total confidence and precision of judgment in himself, knowing that when he issues orders, they must all be carried out precisely, no deviations. If only Kerlie knew the implications of what he has just said to him, and what he himself said about killing him if he disobeys a crucial order. William knows what must be done without favour for the greater good, for the survival of everyone, he knows the Gallóbhet need to believe that he actually will carry out the threat of execution if given, for ruthlessness of leadership and abiding by that eternal truth, is their only hope of winning this seemingly unwinnable situation.

Looking around at all the tough Gallóglaigh, William reflects on their camp in the Wolf and wildcats, where many landless, broken and disparate men surround him. Killers, murderers and freemen alike, all looking to him to command and lead them. Despite his own doubts, William understands the principles of trust, honour and good faith, so well taught to him by wee Maw, Malcolm and his father, this eternal code will keep good order amongst them all, perhaps may even provide for their very survival in these tempestuous times. He also knows this could only be maintained by the certainty of the most severe punishment for any transgressions within this outlawed community. "Wallace..." says Gormlaidh, "We've found the remains of old Duncan and his family." It is then that William notices Kerlie has stood awhile gesturing out his hand in friendship. Kerlie looks at William through tear-stained and bruised eyes. William accepts his hand. Kerlie says, "I'm yours Wallace. I understand and see that your way is the only way. I give you my word here and now, my honour and obedience is yours in all our endeavors by the blood of my father and as a witness to my commitment to our cause." William understands Kerlie's words, and the heart pain he is going through, but commitment to a cause? He thinks, *'What fuckin' cause... survival?'*

Maybe another time he would set Kerlie straight about causes, but first, there are more pressing needs. "Kerlie," says William, "you be taking care of your father and we'll have a pyre for the many..." William looks around at the human detritus where each body had fallen. Some appear to be sleeping peacefully beside the body of another, who could easily have been mercilessly torn asunder by the hounds of hell, such is the law of indiscriminate slaughter, but there are so many bodies in Sundrum and surrounding area. William walks with the Gallóglaigh to witness the defiled remains of Duncan Wallace and the ancient family of Sundrum.

The sombre group have only walked a short distance, when the Gallóglaigh ahead of them slowly opens up the two large oak doors to enter the lodge of old Duncan. William stops dead in his tracks, for he has witnessed this barbaric scene once before. "Ahm sorry to be the one showin' yie this Wallace." says Torrance, William stands emotionless as the wild Gallóglaigh gather and scrutinise him for his reaction, then they all turn to observe the macabre scene where old Duncan, his wife and children have been skinned, deboned and their hides pinned with horseshoe nails to the inside of the great oak doors. William senses the Gallóglaigh are watching and waiting for his reaction, but he has no care for what they want, nor has he any emotions or feelings to hide or show them. He simply says, "It would appear this particular de Percy has it in his mind that the Wallace folks are to be skinned and hung out to dry, but by destroying my family in this way, he has made me lesser in my feelings when I see this death perpetrated upon the bodies of others, even though they be kin of mine." Torrance says, "We weren't sure what to be doin' Wallace, take them down or leave them up. We thought it best that you make that decision over the remains of your kinfolks." William replies, "Torrance, send some o' our men out to look for Hayde, then prepare pyres to be lit at daybreak for all the good folks you can find. When Hayde gets back, I need you and Alan O'Dale to take a crew through to Ayr for the fiongeur, send Kerlie back to the Wolf and wildcats with Stephen and the two wains, for his body is no' fit for any other mission..." Gormlaidh says, "There's the other youngsters here too Wallace, the ones the old English bastard defiled." William replies, "Send them up to the Boarstone and make sure they get back to our camp with Stephen and the others. Tell Stephen to beseech the fresh widows to tend to all o' those youngsters needs."

Torrance enquires, "So where is it your goin' Wallace?" William replies, "I'm going to ride ahead and see my kinfolks over at Auchencruive and warn them of what I've heard from that English knight, then I'll ride over to Yardside and meet another kinsman of mine, Simon Wallace, and warn him too. I just need to know if they are all aware of these death-lists that old knight mentioned, for I've heard this said before from Lord Moray, that there are many assassination squads abroad and killing off many o' our native Scots families. I'd already known that the name of Wallace is definitely one of many bloodlines the English wish to have culled or extinguished." Suddenly a loud scream pierces the air, startling everyone, they immediately look towards the courtyard. Torrance exclaims, "MacKie... he was left guarding that last English soldier."

They all run at speed towards the courtyard, there they see Kerlie kneeling beside MacKie. Kerlie points to the port gate and shouts, "He ran that way..." the Gallóglaigh give chase while William and Torrance stop beside Mackie, who lay in great pain holding his bleeding groin. MacKie tries to explain, "Ahm sorry Wallace, I took my attention away for just a moment and the bastard pulled out a hidden dagger and stabbed me between the legs, I'm sorry... I..." William replies, "Don't fret MacKie, we need to get yie sorted." He looks at his friend and says, "Kerlie, you tend to his wounds while we try and catch that fuck, before he makes contact with any English patrols out there."

William and Torrance run to join the Gallóglaigh hunters to help search and apprehend the fleeing soldier. But after many long hours of fruitless searching in the dark woodland and briar fields around Sundrum, it was impossible to find the soldier. Eventually, everyone gathers back in the courtyard of Sundrum. William bids all to circle, then says, "We can't wait here for more English to be coming in on us now. Gormlaidh... Torch the place and everyone in it as fast as yie can. This will have to suffice as a funerary pyre, for there is nothing more we can do for those already dead and gone." He continues, "And you Gormlaidh, after you've torched the place, get everybody else back to the Boarstone and wait there for Hayde, I'm going to leave immediately to warn all ma kinfolks about the Death list. All things being well, I'll meet with yie all at the Castle corrals in Ayr by early-morn." William walks over to Kerlie, who is helping the wounded

Mackie to his feet. "Will yie live?" enquires William. MacKie replies, "I think so, ah feckn hope so. That fucker took out a wad o' skin, but thankfully missed ma vitals." William looks at Kerlie, "And what about you?" Kerlie replies, "I'll be taking my father home to the lands of Maben. I have the strength to do it, and I must as a duty to my father and my clan."

William nods then walks over to the oak doors and pays his own silent respect to his kinsman, auld Duncan Wallace and his family. For a while, he sits on the steps of the lodge, thinking of how he first met with the same scene so cruelly inflicted upon his Father Alain, lady Mharaidh, his half-sister Caoilfhinn and the folk of Glen Afton. His mind begins to rage in turmoil and doubt, for he had given his word to his beloved Marion that he would stay away from trouble, but how could or can he explain to her that anyone carrying the name Wallace, is being sought out and murdered in such a barbarous way as this. It is now a situation of kill or be killed. How is he going to rationalise to Marion what he must do? His thoughts are interrupted when he hears a horse behind him, he looks round and sees Torrance.

"I've brought yie Warrior," says Torrance, "but we should wait till Hayde gets back and we'll all go into Ayr together at first light." William is about to respond, when something benign catches his eye, then realises he has been staring at the object, all the while his thoughts of his kinfolk had his full attention. He walks towards the object laying at the side of the oak door and picks it up…"A knight's five-point flanged mace." says Torrance. Holding the mace high, William senses the awesome destructive injuries that such an innocuous looking weapon would inflict upon an opponent. He hangs the ornate mace on his saddle-rings when Torrance enquires, "Where to now Wallace?" William queries Torrance, "What would you have me do? I've other kin I should be warning who are only a short ride away from here. Should I no' be going to them and making sure that they have this knowledge of the death lists? What is it you would have me do?" Torrance shakes his head, "Yer right Wallace, I would be doing as you intend, so I cannae be faulting yie there. But why no' ride to Auchencruive as you've planned, and ah'll go to warn Simon? We can meet up with you in the Laglan later and ride into Ayr together as we planned?"

Pulling on the horn of his saddle, William mounts Warrior. Gripping the reigns, he says, "Naw, I ride to warn ma uncle James at Auchencruive, then goin' on to Simon at Yardside." Torrance replies, "Then ahm coming with yie." William looks at the tall muscular battle-hardened redhead, relieved to have such a staunch loyal friend. He says, "My orders are to make sure Alan O'Dale is in Ayr by mornin' and waiting by the corral's, I know that you will make sure that is exactly what will happen." Torrance acknowledges William's order, "It'll be done Wallace, you take care."

Nudging Warrior to walk-on through the port gates of Sundrum and into the dark of the midsummer's night, William's eyes soon become accustomed to the darkness. He can easily see that the drove road leading towards Auchencruive, is well illuminated under a moonlit cloudless night sky. He rides along the drover's road when a sudden wave of emotion engulfs him and his eyes fill with tears. The pain of loss almost overwhelms him. He sees Marion in his mind's eye and little Mharaidh Morríaghan laughing and giggling. The feeling of love for his family becomes magnified in his heart, for he knows that his duty is to live, to serve and to protect them. He shakes his head to try and dissipate this near overwhelming moment. As he meanders along the road, he thinks maybe that his emotions are rampant because he saw the carnage on his kinfolk at Sundrum. He can't rationalise what is making him feel this way, all he knows is that he doesn't want to fight anyone; he just wants to love and be loved. But the awful relentless evil that follows him, is tearing at his heart, the frustration he feels knowing that better men than he, are waiting for him to take the lead, for it gives them hope. He knows he has that gift within him to orchestrate and give that hope, but he doesn't want this responsibility. His mind is conflicted. *'Why me?'* he thinks to himself. Then he hears a horse whinnying not far ahead of him…

"You there, Scotchman…"

"Fuck…" he mutters when hearing the English accent. He quickly wipes the tears from his face and focuses, only to see two tough looking English yeomen standing not far in front of him, behind them he sees an English knight, sitting upon a large Destrier warhorse. William slowly reaches for the mace with his left hand while pulling his sword ajar with the other, dispelling all thought for self-preservation. In this moment, he finally accepts the instinct that's telling him there is no more negotiating with the English. He calmly dismounts, his conviction in his given duty feels comfortably cold and bereft of any emotions or feelings. He knows that his given mission, is to offer up his own life to tear the hearts from these English soldiers right out of their chests. For he also knows that if they have him… then he most definitely has them. The two English yeomen affix their lethal bill points directly at William's chest.

The leading yeoman commands, "On your knees Scotchman and kiss the ground before our lord Longcastle." William stands defiant and motionless as the yeoman commands… "Drop your weapons you Scotch cunt." Almost casually, William assesses the two Englishmen holding their lethal sharp bill point's mere inches from his heart. Apparently Ignoring the command, he begins walking slowly forward, directly into the deadly bill-points. The yeomen are momentarily startled by this movement, when a voice beside Longcastle screams, "That's him my lord, that's the Wallace... he's the Brigand Chief." William recognises the wretch who fled Sundrum. The two yeomen give no ground as they hold firm against William's pressure, waiting on the order from their knight to skewer him with their bills. As they press deeper against William's chest, Longcastle smiles, then casually enquires, "So you are the wanted felon known as the Wallace are you?"

But there is no reply from William as he stares at Longcastle. The knight laughs, "You're but a youth; you cannot be this notorious brigand chief I've heard so much about?" Suddenly William slaps the blades of the billhooks together, causing the needlepoint tips to rip along his chest. He pushes them hard to the side, far enough for him to quickly move down the inside of the polearms before the yeomen could retract them. William knows that once past the lethal points and inside the shaft length, the notorious English bill is rendered useless. Closing on the first yeoman, William easily cleaves the yeoman through the neck and down into his chest. He shoves the falling yeoman's bill high in the air, causing the other yeoman's bill to rise up, leaving a slight gap. William rushes forward and smashes the mace down on the helmet of the second yeoman, momentarily stunning him, simultaneously William swings his sword from ground level with such a velocity, it takes the yeoman's head clean off at the neck.

A combined explosion of a white-hot pain and a blinding light, flashes through William's head, causing him to fall to the ground..."Kill him." screams a voice. William has just felt the awesome dynamic power of the flailing hooves of a warhorse that's been trained to stamp down and crush their enemies, but the great iron-shod hoof misses full contact with William's head by a fraction of an inch, he deftly rolls away and jumps to his feet. Longcastle immediately pulls his horse around, causing it to rear and then kick forward, the monstrous hooves brush past William's face, he quickly moves down the horse's flank as the swish of the knight's blade flashes across his eyeline. Now seeing an opportunity, William stabs his own blade high towards the stomach of the knight, but it deflects harmlessly off his armour. The knight rears the horse high on its hind legs and raises his sword to strike, but William quickly brings the mace down hard against the side of the knight's knee with every ounce of his strength, smashing the knee-joint to pieces.

Longcastle screams and inadvertently pulls down hard on the reigns, the startled warhorse, confused by this signal, kicks back and smashes the iron hooves into the skull of the soldier who had escaped from Sundrum earlier. William moves at speed while the horse is off-balance, he grabs the reigns and jerks them back, toppling the mighty destroyer and throwing Longcastle to the ground. William ignores the powerfull flailing hooves of the great warhorse, grabs the knight and smashes the heavy mace against his helmet, stunning the knight momentarily. William, now in a complete bloodlust frenzy, rips the knight's visor open and mercilessly brings the mace down with manic ferocity and pulverises the gaping face, completely obliterating the head inside the ornately protective helmet. William doesn't stop, he cannot stop, he keeps on hammering at the head of the now dead Longcastle, landing blow after vicious blow. Knocking the helmet off the remains of the head, does not stop William's frenzy as he beats the skull to a bloody pulp.

"WALLACE…" growls a voice, "WALLACE…" Commands the voice once more. William is completely oblivious to the call and keeps pounding the skull remnants in a manic rage, till blood and brain spatter residue from the knight, causes the mace to slip from of William's hand. He raises his head and looks up to see Hayde, Torrance, Alan O'Dale and the rest of the Gallóglaigh, staring at him in awe from their horses. William rolls over, completely exhausted and dazed. Torrance says nonchalantly…

"Ah see that yie have found a use for yer new plaything…" Wiping his mouth, so parched from his frenzy, William stands up and steps away from the corpse of Longcastle, but he staggers then falls on his backside, where he eases himself down to lay in the grass, there he gazes almost hypnotically at one solitary early morning star. It is then that he realises a new day sun has begun to rise. He also notices the birds are singing their morning chorus, making him laugh at the madness of his own thoughts. Throughout the chaos of his thinking, William senses a calmness return to his soul, regardless of the hideous moments in his life and senseless brutality of man, then he notices that his trivial thoughts hold no interest for nature or the birds and bees who greet the morning sun with birdsong and flight and so full joy, welcoming a new days feasting upon worms or gathering nectar.

"Yie really are a mad bastard Wallace," says Torrance, "Ahm sure glad we're on the same side. Yie just fucked up three Englishmen and a knight on his horse." Hayde notices William's senses return. He says, "C'mon Wallace." William looks up at Hayde and Torrance who are towering over him, they lean forward with outstretched hands and grab William by the wrists and pull him to his feet. Hayde hands him back the bloodied mace, Torrance says, "Here, have a drink o' some water." William takes the leather flask and gulps down the entire contents. Torrance continues, "Wallace, go over to the wee burn there and wash yourself down, for yie are covered in a muckin' mess o' blood and brains." William dutifully walks over to a small burn beside the drove road, washes himself down; then uses his léine sleeves to dry himself, he looks around curiously, then he enquires, "Where is he?" Hayde enquires, "Where's who?" William, replies, "The other Englishman, the one who escaped us from Sundrum?" Hayde laughs then replies, "He's lyin' face down in the bog just a wee bit back the way, that big horse near kicked his head clean off." William calls out to nearby Gallóglaigh, "Strip those bastards and collect all their armour and weapons… let them lay naked where they've fallen for the wolves, corbie and rats, they can feast on their carcasses this day."

"C'mon Wallace," says Hayde, "Let's be gettin' on for Ayr." Torrance says, "Will ah send one o' the Gallóglaigh back wie that big horse for Stephen and the wains."

"Aye, do that Torrance." replies William, who is now returning to some state of normality, he enquires, "Hayde, did yiez find any survivors at all?" Hayde shakes his head negatively, "Naw, we went up to Martnam then across to loch Fergus and then up to Marroks mote, but the English had caught up with everyone along the way, none were left alive." Torrance comes over with the knight's chainmail haubergeon and hands it to William, "Put this on yie Wallace, for yie need body protection o' some description and there are no' se' many your size to be se' choosey. If we get into a scrap in Ayr town, you've nothing on yer body to be protectin' yie."

Dutifully, William puts on the haubergeon that reaches to his knees, he shrugs his arms and the chainmail haubergeon falls into place, as though crafted for him personally. He affixes his sword-belt, dirk and Anam Crios, then he mounts Warrior. "Where are we goin' now?" enquires Hayde.

William nudges Warrior forward, then he replies, "Auchencruive." Hayde swiftly grips the reigns of Warrior and holds fast. He says, "I sent men on ahead to both Auchencruive and Yardside when we first left yie, Auchencruive has been ransacked and burnt to the ground. Wallace, there were none there left alive. We don't yet know of what's happened up at Yardside." William lowers his head and closes his eyes as Hayde continues, "We should be going to Ayr Wallace, there are many men dying every moment we tarry about here, there's nothing more we can do for those already dead." William, appearing very sullen and tired, looks across to the grand bay of Ayr; then he enquires of his men who are gathering around him…

"Answer me this question, all o' you Gallóglaigh, would you give up warning your kinsfolk that their names are on a death list, for the sake of many wounded and dying men that you don't know? Most of whom you've never spoken with, nor would they look your way in any other circumstance?" The Gallóglaigh all look at each other, certain their collective reply would be to favour their kinfolk. William pulls his reigns away from the grasp of Hayde and nudges Warrior forward, he walks a few paces, then he halts and speaks without looking back, "Hayde, send another two men to Yardside, we ride on for Ayr castle…" Hayde replies, "Wallace, it sounds as though there will be a hell o' a lot of English in Ayr already, and likely that de Percy fella and his men too?" William replies, "Ah know, it's time to write our own Death lists… in blood. We ride for Ayr Town."

Sundrum Falls

Dregern Gallóglaigh

Morning cocks crow boisterously, as the Wolf and wildcat Gallóglaigh meander along the old town drove route on the banks of the river Ayr. The roads are already busy with traders and others rushing in for the fair, anyone seeing the Gallóglaigh give them a wide berth, for these men can't hide their wild warlike features nor given natural air of intimidation as they ride on recklessly with a carefree abandon. Eventually they wander up beside the market's horse corrals and stockyards, a place safely screened from view by the myriad of tents, stalls, bunting and many large haystacks situated behind the busy market-place, near to Ayr castle. The Gallóglaigh lazily pull their horses into the most sheltered corral and tether them. "This is fucked up," says Hayde. "We've just ridden into the midst o' madness. The country folks are all starvin' and slaughter runs every glen red with rivers o' blood, yet here in this fair as it was in Lanark, it's as though Scotland is the garden o' fuckin' Eden." William says, "It's the folks Hayde, they're all bein' fooled into thinkin' it's English generosity, but they're really being tested by the Sudrons to see what's available for them to steal or tax later. The trader folks don't seem to be realising that in their thirst for profit, they will sure pay dearly later on, for them bein' se' blind..." Scanning the busy market, William leans against a corral post, then he stares awhile at the ground around his feet. Alan O'Dale speaks quietly, "What ails yie Wallace? You've said nuthin' since we left Sundrum, well, nothing much since we found Jop's auld maw, hanging by the neck in the old forge o' Joppa." William looks at the handsome character of Alan O'Dale; obviously he is not a man of violence by any description, yet William feels his presence is as reassuring as that of any of his trusted Gallóglaigh. Alan O'Dale enquires once more, "Wallace, talk to me, at least give to me the port pass that I may gain entry to the castle and secure the fiongeur." Alan O'Dale pauses and looks closely at William, who appears morose.

"What humours yie so ill-tempered Wallace?"

Looking away for a moment, William then replies, "I stand where the English beheaded my friend Cormack in front of me just a few months ago. The hell and torture those bastards put me through, before throwing ma broken body into that stinking fuckin' shit pit used by the English soldiery, that's partly what ails me O'Dale. I've also given precedence to the wounded over the safety of ma own kinfolk, this ails me very badly." Alan O'Dale nods in understanding… "I too have suffered greatly Wallace. When de Brix drew the line in the first civil war for the crown of Scotland, I lost all o' my family to marauding bands o' English mercenaries away down in the Annan dale. Not one single member o' ma family, kith, kin or clan survived those times, not my wife, not my two sons nor my bonnie wee girl with her beautiful long brown curly tresses, they're all now gone to a better place."

Surprised to hear this, William hadn't contemplated for a moment, not with O'Dale's gentle demeanor, that he too had suffered such barbarity as a son, a father, a husband and as a man. Perhaps he had suffered more than most if that were humanly possible, for he has neither any family nor any kin left alive, yet he still has the wit and optimistic spirit of an untainted soul. William bows his head in respect to this man of nature's peace, for O'Dale has never shown anything other than a love of life and a passion for his music.

"Here Wallace," says Hayde, "Shove these feckn rags on yie, for we should be making some attempt at a local disguise if we're to get into Ayr castle and steal their fiongeur." William and Alan O'Dale grin when seeing that Hayde and Torrance are also wearing filthy, ragged clothing, then they notice that all the Gallóglaigh have donned similar decrepit rags by way of a fairly useless disguise, doing nothing to hide away their powerfull frames and the barbarous character of these untamed wild men. "You're feckn jesting me?" laughs William, "For fucks sake Torrance, yiez are awe stinkin' o' fish... and would yie be looking at yourselves Hayde, uze two would o' been better putting on women's skirts to be less conspicuous, and yiez want me to be wearing that shit too?" Torrance laughs, "Ho Wallace, it was the best we could buy from yon poor fisher folk down at the wharfs, but we saved the sweetest smelling rags just for you."

The motley gathering of Gallóglaigh all laugh as they look at each other, realising they had mistakenly convinced themselves they could blend in with any townie population, no matter what they wore. "Here, give me that shit over here," says William, "If I'm going to die stealing fiongeur from Ayr castle, then I may as well look as fucked up as you lot." Alan O'Dale laughs heartily; he says, "I don't know how the fuck we'll be able to pull this off?" The fierce Gallóglaigh go deathly silent to a man, glaring at Alan O'Dale, he begins to panic, "What is it, why are yie all starin' at me?" William puts his arm round O'Dale's shoulders, "This must be an extremely serious situation O'Dale, for we've never heard you curse before." The group all laugh heartily once more, some of the burly Gallóglaigh slap the lightly framed O'Dale affectionately on the back. "C'mon" Says William, "Let's move to the corner o' that corral nearest the stockyards and get some shelter behind those hay stooks and trader bays. There we can work out how we're going to get into the castle, then get back out again without attracting the English garrison's attention, too much."

"Too much?" repeats Torrance curiously.

"Aye, too much," replies William nonchalantly. Torrance laughs and shakes his head as the Gallóglaigh wander through the corrals and stockyards then up behind the stooks. Once there, William hands over to Alan O'Dale the port pass from Ranald. O'Dale opens the pass and reads it, he says, "So my not-so-noble subjects, I'm the honourable Sheriff of Ayr's gangmaster am I?" Hayde laughs, "No rags an' smellin' o' rottin' fish or pish for you then good Sir." Alan O'Dale replies in a haughty voice...

"Methinks not ya manky Scotch scruffians."

The humour continues between the Gallóglaigh, bringing much needed relief from the tension and horrendous experience of the previous night. Weary and exhausted, they each begin looking around the stooks for a place to rest in relative safety, they spread out then lay down, gratefully resting their tired bones on a large pile of hay, at the foot of a large stook in particular. Hayde nods towards two Gallóglaigh, who immediately move to position themselves on lookout nearby, while the others discuss methods of entering the castle. For a while they think of all possible scenarios and what they might do in the event of something going wrong, suddenly the two Gallóglaigh guards come rushing back around the stook, dragging a semi-conscious English soldier behind them. "Northumbrian by his tabard." remarks Torrance. "Aye," agrees William "that's the arms o' Hazelrigg's household." One of the Gallóglaigh guards offers an explanation, "We tried to hide when we noticed this feckr approachin' us, but then he took his feckn prick out for a piss and wandered right into us, so we fucked him on the head with a rock a couple o' times and brought him back here." Hayde says, "Watch out, it looks like the bastard's coming round."

The dazed young Northumbrian recovers with a start when he sees the fearsome Gallóglaigh looking down on him. Torrance immediately grabs him by the throat and begins throttling him, while another two hold fast his arms and legs, to stop him flailing about in his death throes. William watches the scene, seemingly unconcerned as the youth's face turns blackish purple and his eyes begin popping out from his head. William touches Torrance lightly on the arm; then Torrance momentarily releases his choking grip on the young Englishman. William speaks in a low voice to the youngster... "Talk to me..." But before the gasping Englishman can reply, Torrance puts his hand across the youngster's mouth and nose, then he begins to suffocate the unfortunate youth, timing it to perfection before releasing his hand, allowing the youngster to gasp into his lungs, vital amounts of fresh, life-giving air.

William continues, "Now that you've gained a wee sense o' the pain you will surely endure before death Englishman, heed me well... if you fail to answer ma questions truthfully, yer a dead man, then ma wee Sudron boy, we'll simply find another who would wish to live in exchange for that same wee bit o' information we need. Would yie not be agreeing with ma logic Englishman?" The petrified young Northumbrian nods frantically in the positive. "How many English troops are up in the castle?" enquires William. The young soldier replies instantly, "No more than one hundred my lord, and there are four knights awaiting the train and garrison troops of lord Henry de Percy from Lanark to arrive." William continues, "How many are out on patrol?" The young soldier nervously replies; "There are about twenty or so down at the harbour and some retainers at the castle gate with a knight, but none out on patrol. I... I think that is all." Torrance proceeds once more to put his hand across the young soldier's nose and mouth to suffocate him, "Can ah kill him now Wallace?" William replies, "Aye all right, but keep it quiet, naw wait, cut his nuts off and let him bleed out, that'll be more entertaining to watch."

Torrance and the other two Gallóglaigh hold the petrified young soldier firmly, while another yanks up his tabard, revealing his chausses laced to his braies. Torrance rips them all down around the horrified young soldier's ankles, revealing his genitals. The young soldier screams insanely into the closed hand of Torrance, but he could barely be heard. The Gallóglaigh laugh when Torrance innocently quips, "Now ah understand the Sudron's problems, that wee thing down there between his legs is the real reason why these fuckin' Englishmen are so fuckin' angry all the time." The humour is quickly quelled when William nods to a Gallóglaigh beside Torrance, he roughly grips hold of the unfortunate Northumbrian's manhood, then crudely shoves a razor-sharp knife under the youngster's genitals, nicking them carelessly as he prepares to cut everything off.

The young soldier involuntarily arches his back at the sensational touch of the blade; then William notices a tear rolling down the youngster's cheeks. William winks at Torrance, who slowly lifts his hand away from the youngster's face. "Please..." whispers the youngster. William leans closer and enquires, "You haven't been lyin' to me have yie boy?" the young soldier stammers, "Na... no..." William looks at Torrance who nods back at him in response to his unspoken eyeline command. The Gallóglaigh immediately release the young Northumbrian, who falls back in absolute relief; then he quickly pulls up his braies and chausses to hide his embarrassment. Just John, the dark stocky Gallóglaigh with the cutting knife, binds the young soldier's wrists and legs with twine, preparing to bury him deep in a nearby hay stook. Torrance violently grabs the youngster by the jaw, then he says, "Don't you be worrying boy, for if yie have been telling us the truth, we'll come back and free yie. But if yie haven't told us the truth, then we will come back here and cut yer fuckin' prick and yer nuts off, if that's all right by you?" The young soldier is so relieved that he is being left alive and still in one piece, replies, "Yes, why yes my lord, that would be most kind of you."

Disappointed not to be killing his enemy, Just John and two other Gallóglaigh roughly gag the youngster then they carry him away for temporary burial, securely out of sight from any wandering English soldiery, while William, Alan O'Dale, Torrance and Hayde talk quietly about their objective. Torrance says, "It's a good thing most o' the English soldiery are in the castle, save those down at the harbour." Hayde frowns, "It's a bad thing too, for it means that every fuckin' one o' them up at the castle, will be milling around the kitchens grubbin' for food." Torrance replies with an extremely serious expression on his face, "Naw, it's well known they will be in their cribs shaggin' each other, for that's what the English do, bugger themselves in the barracks?"

"Buggered in the barracks... ach for fuck's sake Torrance?" says Hayde. Everyone laughs heartily. Then William says, "Now listen up, when we get into the castle..." Hayde interrupts, "Naw Wallace, you're no' goin' in there." O'Dale says, "Aye, we gave Marion our word on oath that you wouldn't be going into the castle." Hayde says, "O'Dale's right Wallace, we need you out here for a good back-up...

yie know, in case o' trouble, so pick the men to stay with yie. Trouble with the English is one thing, but I don't want any trouble from Marion because you wouldn't listen to us and yie get fuckin' killed on our watch." O'Dale agrees, "Nor me." as do all the nearby Gallóglaigh.

Suddenly Gormlaidh, who has been scouting the busy fair, comes rushing round the stook, he silently points towards the castle road and beckons them to follow quickly. They soon catch up with Gormlaidh, who is now pressed hard against a stook, observing a scene close-by. He points at a large dray wagon with a broken axle that has tipped four enormous ale barrels onto the market road. Two dray drivers stand idly by, simply looking at the gigantic ale barrels and wondering what to do, while four English soldiers struggle to push just one of the large barrels up towards the castle gates. O'Dale whispers, "Perfect timing, this could be our opportunity to get into the castle."

"You're right." agrees William, "Hayde, you get yer Gallóglaigh and go with Alan O'Dale as his menial tacksman, bordars and cottars. That might help explain your awful fuckin' disguise, and the smell. Just John and McGowan will ready the horses and packers for when yiez get back out." Torrance says, "Me n' Gormlaidh will wait here with yie Wallace." Alan O'Dale laughs, "Then it's your responsibility Torrance to keep trouble away from Wallace, or you and Gormlaidh will sure face the wrath o' Marion if he gets killed." Gormlaidh sighs, "Thanks O'Dale." William curses, "Look, there's a knight with two yeomen talking to the dray drivers." Turning to O'Dale and Hayde, William says, "Are yiez all ready now?" Both nod affirmative. William continues, "Now mind this O'Dale, the man you're looking for is Douglas Bain MacAnnah, he's Ranald's master o' the kitchens. He'll give you all the fiongeur that we need or all that he can spare."

Hayde commands his men, "Lets get movin'. Alan O'Dale looks nervously at William, "Wish me luck then Wallace." William smiles, "You'll be fine, just you get in and get out as best yie can and we'll be waiting out here for yiez."

O'Dale nods to Hayde, then both of them and their men boldly walk out from behind the stooks and into the main market square near the dray-wagon. William watches keenly as O'Dale approaches the knight, the tension for the next few moments is almost unbearable as O'Dale speaks with the knight, who appears to be in charge, then William sees O'Dale beckon his "servants," and puts them to work, pushing the oversized barrels towards the castle. Relieved, he watches the knight and O'Dale walking away together, chatting.

"Thank fuck for that," exclaims William. Torrance says, "I thought for a moment that O'Dale was goin' tae fuck it up, but it looks as though he has the wee English knight eatin' out o' his hand." Gormlaidh laughs, "Would yie look at those poor bastards humpin' those great barrels o' ale. Feck, ahm glad yie choose me to stay behind as rearguard with yie." Torrance comments, "Wallace didn't choose yie Gormlaidh, he's fuckin' stuck with yie." Gormlaidh sighs, "Fine then, you take the first watch, you bein' se' feckn sharp and all o' that Torrance." William smiles, for in all of the years he has known these two particular Gallóglaigh, their resolve and consistent stoic determination, has been more reliable than all the men he has ever met, also, their humour is one major constant in his life, always giving him a personal sense of wellbeing when away from his beloved Marion. William yawns then lies back on a pile of hay, utterly exhausted, he basks contented in the warm morning sun.

After a few disturbing moments of restlessness, William raises his head and looks up at the post then down at the ground where Cormack's brutal slaying took place at the hands of the English. He covers his eyes and lay back down again as a sadness engulfs him, thinking of Cormack, then of his own experience at the hands of the English jailers in the same castle just a few months back, thoughts that still cause him great torment. Then he reflects of the gruesome discovery at Sundrum... "Wallace, wake up..." William feels a hand roughly shaking him. He jumps up, grabbing at his sword and mace, then he sees Gormlaidh pointing towards the castle gates on the rump of a small hill. William peers up at the gates and sees Alan O'Dale with Hayde and ten Gallóglaigh carrying two small barrels under each arm, waiting to leave the castle, but two English guards are interrogating them. "Shit," exclaims Torrance, "There are about a dozen English soldiers supping ale just below the castle gates, and those two gate guards are giving O'Dale grief."

Torrance and Gormlaidh keep up a dialogue, relaying the tense developments, when William unexpectedly walks past them with his brat hood pulled up over his head and rough rags covering his haubergeon and weapons.

"What the fuck?" exclaims Gormlaidh. Torrance and Gormlaidh look at each other, totally bewildered by Williams brazen move. Torrance glances and nods towards just John and McGowan, who have already prepared their horses and packers ready to leave. They both quickly knock their bows with lethal barbed hunt arrows. Torrance looks at Gormlaidh then both quickly walk out behind William. Gormlaidh shakes his head and mutters, "Awe fuck, here we go again into the un-fuckin'-known." Torrance urgently enquires, "What's the deal Wallace?" William replies, "Do yie see that bunch of English soldiers sittin' drinkin' no' far below the castle gates?" Torrance replies, "Aye, so what about them?" Gormlaidh catches up and enquires, "Where are we goin'?" Torrance replies, "Over towards that group o' English soldiers." Gormlaidh replies as he loosens his sword and dirk ready to pull. "Stupid fuckin' question ah suppose." They begin moving at a fast pace, weaving their way through the market crowds towards their goal. William says, "Gormlaidh, you keep your eye on O'Dale up at the gates, for we might be needin' to create a distraction to free them from those guards to let them get away." Gormlaidh replies, "Ahm already on it Wallace, one o' those feckn guards is talking with a knight and both are questioning O'Dale as we speak."

William and his two friends arrive near to where the English soldiers are cavorting about, drinking and challenging locals to an unusual sport. William is stopped in his tracks, astonished to see the biggest man he has ever seen in his life, stripped to the waist and holding a large wooden cudgel in his hand. The giant Englishman bellows, "Who among you Scotch bastards dares to break this cudgel over my back and floor me." His challenge is met with absolute silence from the crowd. The giant laughs again, then he calls out, "Where are all those brave Scotchmen we've heard so much about? Should any of you fell me, I'll pay you five groats, but first, it will cost you a single groat to strike me, and should you fail to down me, I will have one strike at you with my bare hand." The giant Englishman, goaded on by his amused colleagues, beats his chest then he pulls a scrawny old Scot from the crowd and offers him the cudgel to strike his back.

The nervous old man trembles, "Where is my groat Scotchman?" Before the Scot could reply, the Englishman stoops, grabs him by the ankles and holds him upside down with one hand. The giant Englishman then ransacks the unfortunate man's bags, takes out all his money and throws it to his friends, who are all in a great humour at the antics of their colleague. The giant drops the Scot to the ground

DREGERN GALLÓGLAIGH

and demands that he strike, now that he has paid for it. The trembling Scot hesitates as the giant Englishman shouts in his face, "Come on you old Scotch beggar, think of all the ills that you blame us English for, break this cudgel across my back and ground me, then my five groats shall be yours," The giant Englishman bends and rests his great hands on his knees. "Strike me damn you." The petrified old Scot raises the cudgel half-heartedly; then brings it down on the giants back, but to no affect. The giant Englishman stands erect and laughs, suddenly he strikes the Scot in the face with his giant fist, breaking the man's jaw and sending him rolling into the crowd, injured and unconscious. The Englishman and his friends roar with laughter as the giant turns and raises his fists like valiant gladiator of the Roman Coliseum, which draws an even greater crowd, who begin to shout abuse at the giant Englishman.

Throughout the noise, Gormlaidh whispers, "I think O'Dale and Hayde are in trouble Wallace, that knight up there has sent one of his men into the castle damn quick, but ah see the other guard is distracted by this scene down here." Meanwhile, the giant Englishman is parading around with his fists held aloft, William wastes no more time, he steps into the makeshift arena and stands behind the giant. A great cheer arises from the thronging crowd when they see William. The giant turns and looks at him and laughs. William holds out his hand, "I'll give you ten groats Englishman... if yie have the courage to let me break your cudgel and ground you. But if I fail, then you may keep my herd of horses that's being held secure in the stockyards back there, by way of a debt payment. The giant Englishman hesitates, for none has ever voluntarily accepted his challenge. He looks at his colleagues who urge him to accept. The giant scrutinises William, then he hands William the cudgel, "Do your worst

Scotchman, let's see if you can ground me." The crowd goes silent as the giant Englishman rests his hands on his knees. William runs his fingers over the shaft of the cudgel and feels a discreet saw-cut, he knows instantly a forced strike of any merit will break the cudgel and cause the giant oaf no great pain. William looks towards O'Dale and sees the English guard and knight are both distracted watching the scene. William also notices a concerned glance from Hayde. William must act now or never. He stands side-on to the Englishman, puts a finger on the nape of the Englishman's neck and then rests the cudgel between his shoulder blades. Curiously, William notices the Englishman's skin twitching at the gentle touch, seemingly agitating the giant. William raises the baton high to strike…

The silence in the ever-growing crowd is palpable, then unexpectedly and without warning, William begins twirling the cudgel in his fingers and whistling a tune as he walks around the giant Englishman, much to the amusement of the crowd, who all begin to laugh and cheer, then someone recognises William and begins chanting his name, as does the crowd… "WALLACE, WALLACE, WALLACE…"

Nervously, the giant calls out, "Strike me now, you Scotch cunt." William smiles, then he places a finger lightly upon the Englishman's neck and rests the cudgel on the skin, just above the spine. He glances up at O'Dale and sees the English knight at the castle gate suddenly grab Hayde by the throat. William catches a brief glimpse of two slivering white flashes from hunt arrows, shot by just John and McGowan from over a hundred yards away. The first arrow buries itself deep into the knight's shoulder. The second pierces the back of the knight's head, exiting through his face. As the knight falls forward, Hayde catches him and stabs him repeatedly in the heart. Another Gallóglaigh grabs the guard distracted by the scene below. He pulls the guard's head back and cuts his throat. In an instant, both knight and guard are unceremoniously thrown down into the shit pit at the base of the castle walls and quickly sink out of sight. Immediately the Gallóglaigh come rushing out of the castle gates, each carrying two small barrels of the vital fiongeur.

Meanwhile, the chant of "WALLACE… WALLACE…" is reaching a crescendo. William waves in response to gain a little more time and attention, when suddenly he recognises the awesome sight of the notorious brigand Chief, Sean mòr MacDhuibhsídhe, and a group of his Dregern Gallóglaigh, barging their way to the front of the human arena. Sean mòr, though in his fiftieth years, is tall, extremely muscular and has as definitive a physique as the English giant. He grins when he sees the spectacle. His dark piercing eyes smile at William, transmitting an understanding, that whatever is about to happen, he and his men are more than ready to join in.

Agitated and impatient, the giant Englishman growls, "Strike me now you Scotch cunt or I'll…" William slowly raises, then he gently rests the cudgel between the Englishman's shoulder blades, at the same time, he deftly reaches inside his brat and pulls out the ten-pound six-point flanged mace, then, using it's dead weight with absolute precision and all the strength he can muster, he swings it into a wide vicious missile arc then strikes the giant Englishman savagely on the base of his neck, snapping the spine in two like a summer-dry twig. A horrific sound of cracking bone and an un-natural hissing noise, escapes the giants gasping mouth as he falls instantly, floundering about like a slaughtered bull, nail-hammered in the brain. The crowd is stunned into silence as the giant's nerves keep his body flailing about on the ground. Momentarily, time freezes for everyone. William looks directly over at the Englishman's friends, who are absolutely dumbstruck by what they have just witnessed. William quickly pulls out his sword and runs directly at them before they can gather their wits. One Englishman pulls his sword and makes to run straight for William, but he is cut down at the knee by a vicious sword strike from Torrance.

Gormlaidh mercilessly hacks the soldier deep in the forehead then William crushes the same man's skull with the mace. A great roar erupts from the crowd as the other English soldiers regain their wits and composure, they quickly draw their swords to avenge the killing of their friends. The English soldiers charge as one at the three companions and a vicious no mercy hand-to-hand bloody skirmish ensues and although outnumbered, the three friends ply their honed warrior skills to brutal effect upon the English soldiers, taking advantage of their own small number being attacked in such a confined space by an overwhelming English force of men. The rapidity of slashing and piercing strikes from the Scots, soon takes its toll on the English.

More soldiers begin exiting the castle to join the affray, but they are stalled momentarily by the precision archery of just John and McGowan. Two English soldiers rush at William, he catches one by the sword arm then brings his mace crashing down on the head of the other; in the struggle, they all fall to the ground. William scrambles back onto his feet, when he sees another Englishman raising his sword to bring it down on his head, suddenly a spartaxe blade smashes the English soldier full on the mouth and cuts deep into his head. William looks up to see a grinning Sean mòr and his Dregern Gallóglaigh bodyguard, cutting mercilessly through the English ranks with their lethal spartaxes. Bolstered by the fighting of Wallace and Sean mòr's Gallóglaigh, the townspeople of Ayr now attack the English soldiers, who only know that their enemy is anyone who is not wearing the three leopards of Longshanks or lord de Percy's Northumbrian coat of arms. William pauses for a brief moment with Torrance and Gormlaidh by his side.

They watch intensely as fighting breaks out all over the markets, then William notices Sean mòr and his Dregern Gallóglaigh approaching. Sean mor says, "It would seem to me young Wallace, that you're all o' that after all."

"Sean mòr," says William "We've got we came for, now we must leave this place... and fast."

William breaks and runs at speed towards the corrals, followed by Torrance and Gormlaidh. Just John and McGowan hold their horses for them, while the others make their escape along the banks of Ayr River drove road. William grabs the reigns from just John and mounts Warrior. Looking back to where he had stood with Sean mòr, William sees the Dregern Gallóglaigh are still fighting and now surrounded by English soldiers in the midst of the riot. William spurs Warrior into action, jumps the corral fence and rides straight for the centre of the fighting, using his mace and sword to deadly effect, cutting his way through English ranks, who are now in total disarray. Hayde, Torrance, Gormlaidh, just John and McGowan soon arrive to fight by his side till they clear a space to give Sean mòr and his men respite and a way out.

William shouts above the screams of the enflamed rioters, "Where's your horses?" Sean mòr points over to the corrals. Torrance urgently calls out, "Here they come again Wallace..." William shouts over to Sean mòr, "Go to your horses and meet us at the south end mouth of the Laglan woods, we'll keep those bastards busy here." But Sean mòr ignores William, for he sees more oncoming English soldiers. Sean mòr, rather than run, licks his thumb and runs it across the keen edge of his spartaxe and grins. William calls out at the top of his voice, "Fuckin' move Sean mòr, move now..." Scowling at the terse command from William, Sean mòr reluctantly orders his Dregern Gallóglaigh to make a strategic withdrawal to the corral.

Amidst the chaotic melee and seeing Sean mòr's Gallóglaigh retreating, the English soldiers move in to attack Wallace and his men with a renewed vigour and regained sense of valour, for they now know who their real enemies are. Suddenly Warrior rears up and kicks forward, his mighty hoof completely disappearing inside the face of a very brave but very unfortunate Englishman. Hayde, Torrance. Gormlaidh, just John, McGowan and William fight a fierce rearguard action, allowing Sean mòr and his Gallóglaigh time to escape. William pulls Warrior around and calls out to retreat, soon, when they are clear of the rioting townspeople. William clicks his tongue, signalling Warrior to gallop at a fast pace towards the corrals.

Once there, Warrior launches himself high to clear the top rail of the corral. William quickly brings Warrior to a sliding halt as they land. He turns to see Sean mòr and his Dregern Gallóglaigh gather and mount their horses. As they all race towards the Ayr River drove road, the English continue to pursue them on foot, but William simply clicks his tongue and Warrior breaks into a full gallop. Before long, they are all reaching the outer port gates of Ayr town, and after a short while, all of the Gallóglaigh rest safely in a secluded glade at the southern gateway to the Laglan forest.

The exhausted Gallóglaigh all dismount and sit down or lay back in a general circle, tending their wounds or slating copious amounts of water and craitur, replenishing the dehydration from their exertions and nigh-on two sleepless days and nights.

"Well young Wallace," says Sean mòr, "It's good to be meeting with yie at long last." William replies, "Aye, it's good to be meeting yourself too Sean mòr. So what took you into the festivities this fine day?" Sean mòr replies, "My scouts told me what happened at Sundrum, Joppa and Auchencruive, so we rode out to meet with yiez and see what was all goin' on, but we missed yiez. Another scout told me of your movement towards Ayr Castle, so I brought a couple dozen o' ma bonnie scoundrel sons and daughters with me and followed you to the castle, just to see what mischief you had in yer head, for I knew yie would no' be going to Ayr castle just for vittals and the bonnie sea view." William tips his head forward, then he pours refreshing cool water through his hair; he then wipes his beard dry with his hand. He looks at Sean mòr and laughs, "Well I tell yie this Sean mòr, we really were in Ayr to collect vittals."

Sean mòr glares at William, his jet-black piercing eyes could not hide that they witnessed the worst machinations of man many times, and it shows in his dark and hawk like focus, for he has perpetrated many of the worst atrocities himself by his very nature and foreboding air of primeval authority, William is certain of that. "Vittals..." exclaims Sean mòr, he laughs out loud, "All o' that was just for vittals? Well Wallace, if that's how you Wolf and wildcat Gallóglaigh get your vittals, yie must be inviting me when yiez next go vittlin' for I have no' enjoyed myself se' much since I skinned a dozen English envoys, who came to make peace wie me and mine." William, now sitting on the warm grass stripped to the waist and basking in the sunlight, laughs at the bizarre circumstance of meeting the much feared and notorious Gallóglaigh chief, Sean mòr MacDhuibhsídhe. Suddenly William feels an enormous tug on his hair as his head is viciously jerked back, almost breaking his neck. He looks up into the dark, cold piercing eyes of Sean mòr; then he feels the stinging sensation of a sharp blade being pressed firmly against his throat, slightly cutting into his jugular. Hayde and the Wolf and wildcat Gallóglaigh are caught unexpectedly by this turn of events. They quickly raise their swords and ominously approach Sean mòr and his Dregern Gallóglaigh, encircling them, but Sean mòr has no interest, far less any fear as he presses the sharp blade deeper into William's throat. Sean mòr demands, "Where's my fuckin' siller (Silver) Wallace?" William grips Sean mòr's wrists, pulling frantically to stop the blade from cutting into his throat. He shouts out, "What fuckin' siller?" Sean mòr shakes William roughly and cuts ever deeper into his skin with the blade, "My fuckin siller Wallace, the siller you stole from the English at the castle... its fuckin' mine ah tell yie." William again pulls at Sean mòr's wrists, but he can't budge the tight grip.

He shouts again, "What fucking siller?" Sean mòr replies in anger and frustration, "My fuckin siller Wallace, I told yie, the siller that was in the barrels you lot stole from the castle... it's mine." Torrance swiftly brings a spartaxe up to Sean mòr's throat, but Sean mòr simply laughs, "And what are you going to be doing with that wee thing, will yie be thinkin' o' killin' me with it?" Torrance replies, "That's a given, the only reason I haven't yet is that I'm curious about the siller in those barrels too." Sean mòr replies, "You'll be dead before I hit the ground big man." Torrance laughs, "Dyie really think that I give a fuck Sean mòr? Wallace is my chief, where he goes, I go." Hayde says, "And me." O'Dale says, "Me too." Gormlaidh, standing beside Torrance, sighs, then he says, "Awe for fucks sake, me as well..." Sean mòr raises his head and laughs at the sky, but he doesn't release his vicious grip on William. He scowls at the Wolf and wildcat Gallóglaigh gathered round him, then he makes a short sharp whistle. A tense moment passes, then about a hundred or more of Sean mòr's Dregern Gallóglaigh and Gallóbhan step out from the shadows of the woodlands, archers are taught on the pull, others with ring spears, spartaxe and swords at the ready, Cur handlers with vicious looking wolf and deer hounds straining at the leash, are ready to rip the Wolf and wildcat Gallóglaigh apart. Sean mòr laughs again, then he says to Torrance, "Do you still hold to Wallace bein' your Chief, are yie still prepared to be going with him to the next life?"

Looking around at all the warriors, Torrance laughs out loud, "For fuck's sake Sean mòr, we'd heard you were a brave and fearsome warrior, we would never have taken yie for a theivin' back stabbin' murderin' bastard." Sean mòr replies, "Why big man, ah thank yie for the compliments." Torrance continues, "If you want to be parted from this life Sean mòr, and your siller too, then cut the throat o' Wallace, for going wie him will be better than stayin here wie the likes o' you. So ma answer to yer question is aye, ahm happy to be going with ma chief." Sean mòr grins, "I like the cut o' your men Wallace. Just give me ma share o' the siller then we can part the best o' friends."

At that moment, Alan O'Dale walks calmly towards Sean mòr and throws a sodden rag at him, hitting Sean mòr full in the face; it sticks to him like a lump of wet clay. Sean mòr angrily pulls it away... "What the fuck is this?" as a salty liquid runs onto his lips, he tastes it and immediately spits it out, exclaiming, "You just threw a rag o' piss in ma face yie scrawny wee bastard. Yie can be sure that when ah cut this cunt's head off, you're next." Torrance says, "You'll be goin' nowhere Sean mòr except straight to earth, the same as that big English fuck did in Ayr a wee while ago, but it'll be minus yer big stupit' fuckin' head." Alan O'Dale says, "Sean mòr, it's fiongeur ya fool, that's what's in those barrels, not bloody gold nor siller." Sean mòr wipes his lips, the bitter taste is still souring his mouth, he snarls "It is fuckin piss ah tell yie…"

"Ach for fucks sake," curses William, "Sean mòr… will yie cut ma throat or let me up ya big fuck, for you're tearing ma hair out and sawing through ma throat anyways, while yiez all chatter about the difference between piss and fiongeur." O'Dale reaches over to Sean mòr and snatches the sodden rag from his free hand and huffs; "Watch this…" O'Dale squats beside William, then he wipes the two long scars on his chest, caused by the yeoman's sharp bills the previous night. William jerks as the vinegar bites deep into his scars. O'Dale stands up and throws the rag back at Sean mòr, "There, do you think that I would wipe piss all over my chief's chest, moments before yie cut his throat?"

Sean mòr is greatly perplexed, then, much to everyone's great relief and surprise; Sean pulls his dirk away from William's throat and nonchalantly places it back in its sheath. He puts his hand down and pulls William to his feet, exclaiming, "Vinegar… fuckin' vinegar? Sixteen o' yiez, and you lot have just attacked an English military garrison and slaughtered a whole bunch o' them there fuckin' Sudrons, for what, a few wee barrels o' vinegar?"

"Aye," replies William as he angrily snatches the rag from Sean mòr's hand and dabs the fiongeur lightly upon the wounds on his chest, and other wounds that he is now only beginning to notice, including the new one round his throat. Scratching his head, Sean mòr is bemused… "Wallace, folk have said that I'm fuckin' mad, but at least me, I fight for gold, siller for joyous rewards and for ma people, or whatever cause takes me feckn fancy, but you lot… I don't understand yer limited wits man, you're out there fighting the English for feckn fiongeur? Ah'v never heard o' the likes afore." At that moment, Alan O'Dale arrives back with a barrel and drops it at the feet of Sean mòr, he says "If any o' yer folks are wounded Sean mòr, then get them to dip rags in this and bleach their wounds awhile, for it'll stop any bad maladies and the blood turnin' black. Sean mòr replies, "Ah'v just a few wee scratches and nicks here and there, but ma son here has lost three o' his fingers fightin' at the markets. Ah never named him when he was born, but now, now ma proud boy will forever be known as, *'Seven Fingers* MacDhuibhsídhe.'" Sean mòr becomes emotional and wipes his nose with the fiongeur rag. William is amused at the real pride Sean mòr is showing, while making this very personal and emotional gesture regarding one of his nameless sons. Even though his own throat is still stinging from the slight wound caused by the cutting blade of Sean mòr's dirk. Alan O'Dale begins to tend the fingerless stumps on the hand of *'Seven fingers'* as Sean mòr speaks with William.

"Sit wie me Wallace, for I would have words with yie, I like your grit boy and your men are surely loyal to yie too. Though ah could have ordered them all killed in the blink o' an eye." William grins, "Aye, ah suppose yie could, but it would o' been your last fuckin' blink in this world. If big Torrance hadn't got yie, my dirk was back-aimed straight up your arse, then Sean mòr, ah would o' happily been on ma journey to the next world, knowin' that for the rest of your miserable fuckin' life, every shit you ever had, would remind you o' me." Sean mòr laughs out loud, "Aye Wallace, you and yours will sure do me fine. I only questioned yie because I thought yiez were doing me out o' me fare share o' siller. Will yie take ma hand young Wallace, and I give yie ma word and ma bond too, so long as yie never change who yie are boy, ah'll stand and fight by your side if needs be, even if it's for feckn fiongeur." William grins triumphantly, "Yie just did." Sean mòr again laughs loudly, "Aye well, yie got me there Wallace, ah can die happy now knowin' ma life's work is complete." The two chiefs shake hands, then they pick at some cold vittals. Sean mòr enquires, "So, where do yie go from here Wallace, back to yer hole in the Wolf and wildcats?" William replies, "Naw, the fellas here are going back there with the fiongeur, for we have many men there who were badly wounded at the battle o' Dunbar, when they fought as the rearguard for King John. They've to be getting it back to our camp fast or many will die from bad blood if we don't. Me, well ahm going to go and find the last o' ma kinfolks up at Yardside, for there are English murder squads marauding Scotland with death lists, and the name o' Wallace is fairly high up on those lists."

Sean mòr says, "Ach son," "I will be welcoming you to the world of the wanted then young Wallace, for the name of MacDhuibhsídhe is even higher on those lists yie speak o'." William Exclaims, "Your clan is on the list too, I never saw your name on any of the lists?" Sean mòr replies, "Aye, ma cousin, Duncan MacDuff the Mormaer of Fife, did yie no' hear that he was murdered up at Pittillock near Falkland by English assassins. The murder was blamed publicly on our very own kinsmen, because they say Duncan was cruel and greedy beyond the average. The truth is, the English need our MacDuff blood wiped out, for they believe that our clan fosters the son of King Alexander, taken from Yolande at birth, to protect him from being murdered like his father, brothers and the maid. If Alexander's son appears later and makes a legitimate claim for the throne of Scotland, Longshanks is fucked. And we o' the MacDhuibhsídhe are also kin to the royal Llewellyn's of Cymru."

"Fuck," exclaims William, "Do your clan really have the son of Alexander?" Sean mòr replies, "Who knows anymore Wallace, how could it be proved? Everyone associated with that incident is now dead." Suddenly a guard shouts out a warning, "RIDERS APPROACH..." Everyone immediately grabs their weapons and moves aggressively in the direction the incoming riders. The sound of whistles and hunting horns shriek and bellow across the woodland, then just as suddenly, the combined Gallóglaigh force stand down, for the music of the woodland guard, intimates friendly riders approaching. Moments later, four riders come thundering into the glade and dismount. Two report with William, the other two reports to Sean mòr. After a few moments of discussion, Sean mòr approaches William and they both sit and talk awhile with great vigour and seriousness emanating from their body language, well perceived by the combined Gallóbhet gathering, in the glade of the Laglan wood. Sean mòr stands up and calls out...

"Comhairle nan Fianna..." (Council of the warrior)

Alan O'Dale approaches William and stands by his side, as all of the Gallóbhet gather shoulder to shoulder, forming a large circle round a hawthorn bush. "Gathering of the warriors." mutters Alan O'Dale. "I've heard of these Cruinnè gatherings Wallace, but never seen one before." William replies, "Aye Alan, the Cruinnè cearcall gealach (moon-Circle) it's a great thing when the ùghdar (Person of fact) speaks, for no one dare interrupt, after which, each in the circle may take their turn to talk. No one stands in the shadows and we're all equal, as each of us in the circle are close to one another, the very nature of the circle means from where we stand, we agree that we each see the same thing, but slightly different from the next, that's why you will never hear the Cruathnie faith or Gallóbhet argue nor dishonour one another." Alan O'Dale says, "Maybe we should go back to the old ways of the Cruinnè Cè Wallace?" William replies, "Maybe your no' so far wrong O'Dale, for it's the true way of the Céile Aicé and the divine Goddess for me, that's for sure." Alan O'Dale looks at William, he says, "If any man of creation poured from the womb, neglects the feminine face of God, then he does wrong his own soul and wrong the whole face of God." William turns to look at Alan O'Dale, completely surprised at what he has just said, then O'Dale says, "Aye, a Christian expression Wallace, but Cruinnè ceil Aicé I am." William laughs, then he says, "I've always wondered why I liked you, now ah know." Alan O'Dale laughs, "And I you Wallace." Then they hear Sean mòr declaring to all...

"Tighten up round the hawthorn mo chairde, for it will be servin' as our trystin' world." For a moment there is complete silence in natures very own little cathedral of the secretive Laglan glade. Both the men and women from the ancient race of Gael and Nordic peoples, stand as one, in that all of the Gallóglaigh and Gallóbhan may hear clearly and concisely the vital information brought to them from the hunter scouts, now to be shared amongst all. Such was the way of the Gallóbhet and Cruinnè cearcall gealach. Sean mòr again calls out from his place in the circle...

"Ùghdar, Liam Mac Alainn mòr... William, son of Alain Wallace, Guardian of the great Aicé, is the first speaker of fact." William clears his throat as he prepares to address the gathered Fianna. "As ùghdar, I speak these facts. I say to you ma kith and kin o' this ancient race of peoples who stand by my side this day. I now realise that I must make my stand with you and all others of our faith, and upon my oath, I will no longer cower in the sanctuary of my Wolf and wildcat home. I say to you all, that our ancient kingdom of Galloway, from Carrick to the Machars and Solway to the Cartlan, is now surrounded by Sudron's who wish to extinguish us as a race of people. They strive to end the faith of our Céile Aicé by the same Norman tyranny, as they have done so before in near every part of Ireland and Wales. Now this English king called Longshanks and his followers, they wish to bring an end of our people in the whole of Scotland. When the English attempt to conquer a territory, they try to eliminate the people and their faith, as did the Normans and Christians before them. They want to slay or enslave those of us who are Cruinne Céile Aicé, stating that we are lewd, wicked, barbarous, damned and that we must serve them as their slaves, or simply be killed. It's known to me that all families of the Céile Aicé will not be spared or taken into the usurper King's peace, we are to be killed with impunity and with the blessing of their church, then our land is to be given over to hoof and root. But my friends, as long as I draw breath and live, this will never happen, for I alone or with you, will ruthlessly drive this English pestilence far away from our land, or I will join our families, now gone to a better place than this in my endeavor."

The energy in the circle is electrifying upon hearing William's words. He knows he is finally accepting his mantle as a Chief among Chiefs. He feels relieved to no longer evade the duty that he has carried as a heavy burden all of his life. He continues, "The news from Yardside is that the English have put my kinfolk there to the sword, as they have done so at Auchencruive, Sundrum, Kilspindie, the Carse of Gowrie, Glen Afton and ach na Feàrna. I've also been informed that all my surviving kin and other Chieftains from the house of Wallace in the Wolf and wildcats, Kyle, Carrick and Galloway, Adam, Richard, Seoras, Bryan, Duncan, John and Simon, with Auchinleck of Gilbann, the Crauford's and the Halliday's of Corra, have already prepared in their own fastness and are gathering an army of Gallóbhet around the Torr Linn, there they will begin the fight for freedom against this foreign usurper. My Kin are raising arms to protect the lives, liberty and ancient Kingdom of Galloway, as the sovereign realm of our ancestors. So I state on oath to you as my brothers and sisters, pledging my blood and my life to protect all our families, kith and kin, as I stand by the side of Sean mòr MacDhuibhsídhe, the true and honourable Guardian of Devorguilla, mother of our rightfull king, the Lord John Baliol."

There is a murmur of common approval by all the Gallóbhet gathered in the glade. William concludes, "Ùghdar Sean mòr MacDhuibhsídhe, Sean of the great dark spirit..." Sean mòr speaks, "As ùghdar... I speak these facts. I am honoured by what young Wallace has pledged before us all this day, and ah humbly do state before yiez ma kith and kin, that I too pledge to him and to you all by return, swearin' ma oath by all the laws of the Céile Aicé, that I will do everything that is expected o' me as a man, a father, a Dregern Chief and commander of the Céile Aicé, that I do accept and will honour my station by my oath to you all, in that, I pledge to fight with the Wallace, my brother, to protect all that is his, all that is yours and all that is mine... including all o' the feckn gold and siller that I know the English are hidin' away in Ayr castle, it's all mine..."

An almighty roar of laughter and mirth fills the Laglan glade. *'Sean mòr is a wise chief,'* thinks William, for Sean honours the sanctity of the eternal oath and passions by which both has spoken. He also knows when the Cruathnie see a smile by its very essence, is a public display of inner peace and approval. William notes that every individual gathered here has been scrutinised by Sean mòr, as the eyes truly are windows to the soul. He is also aware that Sean mòr has the gift to see that truth in all who would give up their lives willingly, as the ultimate gift to give to others, for their nurture, happiness and love of life itself, is the pillar of the Gallóbhet and Cruathnie Céile Aicé beliefs. "Some lighter information ma friends," says Sean mòr, "That wee tussle we had earlier on in Ayr today, has been accounted to me by our scouts thus... Wallace, how many good men did you lose this day?" William replies, "None, a few cuts, slices, slashes and bruises, but we lost no men this day." Sean mòr says, "Isn't that good news me boys? Well, the Dregern Gallóglaigh lost none too, and like you fellas from the Wolf and wildcats, we've just got a few wee nicks here and there. Oh... and a few fingers missing from me now favourite son, Seven fingers over there..."

A relatively small dark Gallóglaigh with long thick black tousled hair, proudly holds up a hand wrapped in a bloody linen, minus three fingers. He waves his stump, honoured for all to see. Mirth and amusement ensue when he accompanies his stumpy wave with an enormous toothy grin. Sean mòr continues... "Well mo chairde, it's been brought to me attention, the Sudrons now mourn the loss of three dead knights, twenty-eight dead soldiers... and a grand unknown number of them who are still crawlin' about the markets in front of the castle, now looking desperately for body parts they be needin' to make themselves whole again."

Everyone laughs as Sean mòr continues, "But next time, we will send all o' them to a better place than this, and I do mean 'all.' So believe me this fact brothers and sisters, there will be a next time for sure." Another great roar of approval comes from the Gallóbhet as Sean mòr concludes, "For talkin' the fact, is there anyone here who would wish to speak?" Torrance says, "Aye, me. ùghdar... This is my fact. I know not of my birthin' ancestors, but ah say to Wallace here as ma Chief, that you have my bond and my life by your side. For the sake o' our children, we must have faith from our past to be providin' a way for their future." Torrance pauses and looks around into the face of each Gallóbhet, then he continues, "Ùghdar... I speak the fact by witness of the Céile Aicé, that all the Fianna here, do offer you our pledge, as you both have given your oath to us..."

Another great roar of approval rises high above the treetops in support of Torrance, from all of the Gallóbhet gathered in the little Laglan Cathedral. All others then speak of their facts, each of them making personal blood oaths and commitments, till the great circle is at an end. Sean mòr walks over to the trystin thorn and tears a bloody rag from his mantle, he then ties it to one of the branches. William follows the gifting, as does the next man and woman, till each Gallobhet has tied a piece of personal material to the trystyn' thorn and said a private prayer, concluding the ancient parliament of the Aicé Céile dé. Everyone disperses; eagerly discussing what they had heard, bolstered by a feeling of something greater than the individual is beginning to emerge.

"Sean mòr..." says William, "Ah'll thank yie for this day Sean mòr. For such a long time I've hidden away from doing ma duty, but now, standing here wie you, I know that unless we all stand together as one to protect our kith and kin, then we will all surely die. I had thought I could stay away from trouble, but it seems that the English have no ears to be hearing my plea for peace, nor the wit to think that I, as a freeman, will simply lay down for their pleasure." Sean mòr replies, "You're a good young man in the making for sure William Wallace, and my word is my bond. Just you put out the call and we of the black race will be by your side. One fella may start a battle, but all of us here standing together, will finish a war." Hayde and O'Dale approach with Warrior, while the other Wolf and wildcat Gallóglaigh are already mounting their horses and packers ready to depart. Hayde says, "We'd better be getting back Wallace, for the need is great to be returning with the fiongeur." William says, "Alan O'Dale, fetch to me another barrel of fiongeur." While he waits on O'Dale to return, William notices Just John and McGowan resting in their saddles. He says, "Your flights won the day for us." Just John and McGowan grin, honoured they are personally acknowledged by their Chief. William observes the rest of the tired Wolf and wildcat Gallóglaigh sitting patiently waiting to leave, he says to them all, "I am grateful to you ma family, I thank yie all." William sees Sean mòr grinning at him, "Sean mòr, I will no' be forgetting this day with you and your proud people." Sean mòr simply smiles.

Alan O'Dale soon returns with a barrel of fiongeur. William takes it and hands it to Sean mòr, "Take this second barrel Sean mòr, you may need it in time if you don't be needing it now. It's worth more than all the siller in Scotland, if it keeps the blood clean for one child o' your race." Sean mòr smiles, then he replies, "I was going to say keep it, but your thoughts for our children cannot be denied if it gives them an opportunity of life. You take care of yourself young Wallace. No doubt we'll be seeing each other in the very near future, my brother Brigand Chief."

William laughs, then he mounts Warrior, ready for his journey home, "You take care too Sean mòr." Pulling Warrior around, William walks on, followed by the Wolf and wildcat Gallóglaigh carrying their valuable cargo. Hayde, Torrance and O'Dale ride alongside William. Hayde says, "Well Wallace, what do we tell Marion now, for you were no' supposed to be getting into any trouble." William squirms at the thought, he replies, "Nuthin', just don't say nuthin'..." Hayde's eyebrows raise up in surprise, he exclaims, "What, nuthin'?"

"Aye, nuthin..." replies William "If anything, just tell her that we managed to get the fiongeur without any mishaps." Everyone laughs, then Hayde says, "Without any fuckin' mishaps? Fuck me Wallace, we've just wiped out near a third of an English garrison, that's hardly a wee mishap." Torrance comments, "Aye, thirty-odd English dead and at least three knights, then fuck knows how many are limbless Sudrons this night, and we're goin' home all cut up, battered and bruised, dyie no' think Marion might not just notice these wee signs?" William replies, "Naw, ah don't want to be worrying her." Hayde exclaims, "Are yie fuckin jestin' with us Wallace? Ahl wager half o' Scotland already knows what happened in Ayr this day. And with a few thousand folks chanting the name o' Wallace, as yie pulverised a fuckin' big English giant with yer fancy new mace... ah wouldn't think that you were bein' very discreet." Becoming flustered, William insists, "Naw, don't say nuthin' she doesn't need tae know."

"That's sure a pity," laughs Alan O'Dale, he says, "For I was going to write a ballad about it." Gormlaidh grins, "Ah wouldn't want tae be in your brogan when she finds out Wallace, and she will find out for sure, that's if she doesn't know already." William replies, "Well if she does find out, it'll be you lot that gets the blame for letting me go into Ayr in the first place." He raises his head and nudges Warrior onward, the Gallóglaigh follow on behind, continuing their wearisome journey towards the Wolf and wildcats.

Suddenly they hear a loud whistle coming from the road behind them. William turns to see Sean mòr riding fast towards them, waving frantically, with three riders following close behind. Torrance says, "That looks like our Stephen no' se' far behind Sean mòr... and there's two o' Bishop Wisharts dispatch riders wie' them too." The riders quickly catch up with William, pulling breathless panting horses to a halt beside him. William exclaims, "Stephen, what are you doing back here?" Stephen replies, "We were on our way to the Ayr marches to find yie when we ran into Sean mòr." William enquires, "So what's yer story?" Stephen says, "These two fellas are from that Bishop Wishart fella, he's sent yie an urgent message." William enquires, "What does Wishart want with me?" Stephen replies, "Dunnoe, they just say it's urgent? These fellas wouldn't tell us, they were looking for you and you alone, they said that they've an urgent message for your eyes only." The first dispatch rider passes William a sealed note, then he says, "This is for you from Bishop Wishart Wallace, you're to pick thirty o' your best men for whatever he wants yie to do. There to be yer best bowyers, crossbow and spartaxe fighters."

Opening the sealed note, William speedily reads the message. He exclaims, "Fuck..." Stephen enquires. "What is it? William shouts for McGowan and Just John to attend. Gormlaidh enquires, "What's in the message?" McGowan and Just John come riding over quickly. William issues them instructions to lead everyone back to the Wolf and wildcats. McGowan and Just John aknowledge their orders and bid farewell. Sean mòr enquires, "What is it Wallace, what does Wishart want that's se' urgent?"

William reads the message again, while everyone waits curiously to hear the contents. He says, "It's about young Andrew Moray, Wishart's askin' us to cut over to Invergarvane fast and meet with Rob MacGilchrist and John Blair, they'll be waitin' there for us, then we've to board three o' Morrison mòr's birlinns... It would appear that we're bound for some secretive mission down into England." Stephen enquires, "So what would a wee priesty boy be doin' comin' wit' us?" William, appearing slightly bemused, replies... "This is the strange part about this Stephen, wee Blair is coming with us in order to absolve us in the eyes of God?" Sean mòr enquires. "For doin' what?" William replies, "Anything that we may do that's contrary to ethical Christian beliefs?" Sean mòr looks at William with a wry smile, "We're no' Christians, so this means blood, English blood. Ahm no' gonnae be missin' this Wallace, ah can smell hot blood and fresh siller already. Ahm comin wit' yiez..." Stephen enquires, "Does it say anything else?" William replies, "Aye, we're to follow all o' big Rob's commands without question and do whatever is necessary to bring young Andrew Moray back home to Scotland..."

☦ To follow

The next trilogy in
Wallace: Legend of Braveheart series

Book Seven: Warlord

Book Eight: Guardian

Book Nine: Patriot

www.ingramcontent.com/pod-product-compliance
Lightning Source LLC
Chambersburg PA
CBHW021141080526
44588CB00008B/157